AF541259

AGRICULTURE AND CASH CROPS

AGRICULTURE
AND
CASH CROPS

By
H. Parameshwar Hegde
M.Sc., M.A.

DISCOVERY PUBLISHING HOUSE PVT. LTD.
NEW DELHI-110 002

Published by:
Tilak Wasan
DISCOVERY PUBLISHING HOUSE PVT. LTD.
4831/24, Ansari Road, Prahlad Street
Darya Ganj, New Delhi-110002 (India)
Phone: +91-11-23279245, 43764432
Fax: +91-11-23253475
E-mail: parul.wasan@gmail.com
discoverypublishinghouse@gmail.com
info@discoverypublishinggroup.com
web: www.discoverypublishinggroup.com

First Edition: 2011
ISBN: 978-81-8356-750-3

Agriculture and Cash Crops

Printed at:
Shree Balaji Art Press
Delhi

Preface

Agriculture refers to the production of food and goods through farming and forestry. Agriculture was the key development that led to the rise of civilization, with the husbandry of domesticated animals and plants (i.e. crops) creating food surpluses that enabled the development of more densely populated and stratified societies. The study of agriculture is known as agricultural science (the related practice of gardening is studied in horticulture).

Agriculture encompasses a wide variety of specialties. Cultivation of crops on arable land and the pastoral herding of livestock on rangeland remain at the foundation of agriculture. In the past century a distinction has been made between sustainable agriculture (e.g. permaculture or orgaic agriculture) and intensive farming (e.g. industrial agriculture).

In agriculture, a cash crop is a crop which is grown for money. The term is used to differentiate from subsistence crops, which are those fed to the producer's own livestock or grown as food for the producer's family. In earlier times cash crops were usually only a small (but vital) part of a farm's total yield, while today, especially in the developed countries, almost all crops are mainly grown for cash. In non-developed nations, cash crops are usually crops which attract demand in more developed nations, and hence have some export value.

In many tropical and subtropical areas, Arecanut, Betelnut, Cardamom, Pepper, coffee, cocoa, sugarcane, bananas, oranges and cotton are common cash crops. In cooler areas, grain crops, oil-yielding crops and some vegetables predominate an example of this, where corn, wheat, cannabis and soybeans are the predominant cash crops. Tobacco is also a cash crop.

Crop selection is largely a matter of preference and how you want to market your product. For example, some products can easily be sold only locally while other products can be sold nationally as well as locally. Herbs are examples of produce that can be sold both ways. You don't just plant one type of crop unless you have signed contracts to sell that crop, or have plenty of marketing experience. There are some exceptions to this rule: for example, specialized crops such as mushrooms and problems if something doesn't produce as well as expected, or if the market becomes saturated.

Using good mulching techniques will help to eliminate weeds and lessen the amount of labor you'll need to put into the garden. It will also keep the soil around your plants moist and produce stronger plants. Almost all successful small cash crop growers use the mulching method.

Author

Contents

Preface

1. **Agriculture** 1

Introduction; Etymology; Overview; History; Ancient Origins; Middle Ages; Modern Era; Crop Production Systems; Crop Statistics; Production Practices; Processing, Distribution, and Marketing; Crop Alteration and Biotechnology; Genetic Engineering; Herbicide-tolerant GMO Crops; Insect-Resistant GMO Crops; Costs and Benefits of GMOs; Food Safety and Labelling; Environmental Impact; Livestock Issues; Land Transformation and Degradation; Eutrophication; Pesticides; Climate Change; Distortions in Modern Global Agriculture; Agriculture and Petroleum; Mitigation of Effects of Petroleum Shortages; Agriculture Safety and Healt; United States

2. **Natural Resources** 28

Classification of Natural Forms; Renewable Resources; Non-renewable Resources; Natural Capital; Renewable or Non-renewable?

3. **Soil and Water** 35

Soil Forming Factors; Parent Material; Climate; Topography; Biological Factors; Time; Characteristics; Soil Horizons; Soil Classification; Soil

Orders; Organic Matter; Humus; Climate and Organics; Soil Solutions; In Nature; Uses; Degradation; Water; Types of Water; Water in the Universe; Water and Habitable Zone; Water on Earth; Water Cycle; Fresh Water Storage; Tides; Effects on Life; Aquatic Life Forms; Effects on Human Civilization; Health and Pollution; Agriculture; As a Scientific Standard; As a Dissolving Agent or Solvent; Extinguishing Fires; Recreation

4. **Cash Crop** 69

Small Fruits; Herbs; Vegetables; Speciality Crops; Landscaping Plants; Nut Crops; Bamboo; Seeds; Sprouts; Marketing Techniques; Getting Help

5. **Importance of Climate** 84

Climate Classification; Air Mass; Köppen; Thornthwaite; Paleoclimatology; Climate Change; Climate Models

6. **Areca Nut** 94

The Term "Betel Nut" and the Colonial Legacy; Tradition; Effects on Health; Chewing Betel Nut Alone has been linked to Oral Submucous Fibrosis; Vernacular Names; Modern Day Consumption; Arecanut Processing; Sources Attribute the Increase to the Spread of Areca Nut Cultivation to Non-traditional Areas; Areca Nut Curing; Method of Consumption and Curing in NE Region; Curing of Areca Nut in Meghalaya; Areca Nut Curing; Method of Consumption and Curing in NE Region; Curing of Areca nut in Meghalaya; The Method; Economics; Preservation of Fruits; Dried Ripe Nuts; Kalipak; Scented Supari; Uses of Arecanut Constituents and Byproducts

7. **Betel** 116

Vernacular Names; Cultivation; Compounds; Chewing; Medicinal Properties; Paan; Varieties; Effects on Health; Culture; Bangladesh; India; Philippines; Myanmar; Pakistan; Cambodia; Vietnam

8. **Cardamom** 129

Green Cardamom; Spice Description; Culinary Uses; Attributed Medicinal Properties; Plant Description and Cultivation; Other Names; Varieties; Uses; Black Cardamom; In Traditional Medicine; Names in Different Languages; Used Part; Etymology; Uses

9. **Black Pepper** 141

Ground Black Pepper and Pepper Shaker; History; Ancient Times; Postclassical Europe; China; As Medicine; Flavour; World Trade

10. **Vanilla** 153

Planting; Mulching; Harvesting and Curing; Quality Requirements; Traditional Curing Methods; Mexican Curing Methods; Bourbon Curing Method; Curing of Tahiti Vanilla; Yield; Market for Vanilla

11. **Banana** 172

Properties; Trade; Early Cultivation; Plantation Cultivation; Cultivation; Pests, Diseases, and Natural Disasters; Major Diseases; In Australia; In East Africa; Allergic Reactions; Fibre; Paper; Storage and Transport; Peels; Symbols; Blue Fluorescence, a Recent Discovery

12. **Sugarcane** 189

Cultivation and Uses; History of Sugarcane; Cultivation; Pests; Processing; Milling; Sugar

Crystals; Refining; Ribbon Cane Syrup; Cane Ethanol; Sugarcane as Food; Nitrogen Fixation

13. **Coffee** 200

Etymology; History; Biology; Cultivation; Production; Economics; Coffee as a Commodity; Roasting; Storage; Preparation; Presentation; Social Aspects; Health and Pharmacology; Caffeine Content

14. **Cocoa** 216

Harvesting; Processing; Chocolate; Health Benefits of Cocoa Consumption; Non-human Animal Consumption; Sustainable Cocoa; Roundtable for a Sustainable Cocoa Economy (RSCE); Child Labour in the Cocoa Production Industry; Organizations that Directly Support Sustainable Cocoa; Environmental Impact; Cocoa Trading

15. **Orange (Fruit)** 226

Fruit; Persian Orange; Navel Orange; Valencia Orange; Blood Orange; Acidity; Production; Etymology; Juice and other Products

16. **Cotton** 234

Tangüis Cotton; Cultivation; Genetically Modified Cotton; Organic Cotton; Pests and Weeds; Mechanized Harvesting; Competition from Synthetic Fibres; Uses; The International Cotton Trade; Leading Cotton-producing Countries; Fair Trade; Critical Temperatures

17. **Tobacco** 251

Etymology; Early Developments; Popularization; Contemporary; Nicotiana; Types; Impact; Demographic; Health; Economic; Production; Consumption

18. **Grape** 266

Description; Grapevines; Distribution and Production; Seedless Grapes; Raisins, Currants, and Sultanas; French Paradox; Resveratrol; Anthocyanins and Other Phenolics; Seed Constituents; Concord Grape Juice

19. **Coconut** 274

Origins; Natural Habitat; Cultivation; Pests and Diseases; Growing in the United States; Coconut Production in the Middle East; Production; Harvesting; Fruit; Husk; Roots; Inflorescence; Uses; Culinary; Non-culinary

20. **Tea** 289

Cultivation; Processing and Classification; Blending and Additives; Content; Origin and History; Origin Myths; Tea and the Tang Dynasty; China; Tea Spreads to the World; India; Potential Effects of Tea on Health; Economics of Tea; Production

21. **Flower** 300

Flower Specialization and Pollination; Morphology; Flowering Transition; Organ Development; Pollinatio; Attraction Methods; Pollination Mechanism; Flower-pollinator Relationships; Fertilization and Dispersal; Evolution; Symbolism; Usage; Floriculture

22. **Chili Pepper** 316

Intensity; Uses; Decoration; Superstition; Evolutionary Advantages; Spelling and Usage; Medicinal Use; Possible Health Benefits

Index *327*

1

Agriculture

Introduction

Agriculture refers to the production of food and goods through farming and forestry. Agriculture was the key development that led to the rise of civilization, with the husbandry of domesticated animals and plants (i.e. crops) creating food surpluses that enabled the development of more densely populated and stratified societies. The study of agriculture is known as agricultural science (the related practice of gardening is studied in horticulture).

Agriculture encompasses a wide variety of specialties. Cultivation of crops on arable land and the pastoral herding of livestock on rangeland remain at the foundation of agriculture. In the past century a distinction has been made between sustainable agriculture (e.g. permaculture or orgaic agriculture) and intensive farming (e.g. industrial agriculture).

Modern agronomy, plant breeding, pesticides and fertilizers, and technological improvements have sharply increased yields from cultivation, and at the same time have caused widespread ecological damage and negative human health effects. Selective breeding and modern practices in animal husbandry such as intensive pig farming (and similar practices applied to the chicken) have similarly increased the output of meat, but have raised concerns about animal cruelty and the health effects of the antibiotics, growth hormones, and other chemicals commonly used in industrial meat production.

The major agricultural products can be broadly grouped into foods, fibres, fuels, raw materials, pharmaceuticals and illegal drugs, and an assortment of ornamental or exotic products. In the 2000s, plants have been used to grow biofuels, biopharmaceuticals, bioplastics and pharmaceuticals Specific foods include cereals, vegetables, fruits, and kakaka. Fibers include cotton, wool, hemp, silk and flax. Raw materials include lumber and bamboo. Drugs include tobacco, alcohol, opium, cocaine,and digitalis. Other useful materials are produced by plants, such as resins. Biofuels include methane from biomass, ethanol, and biodiesel. Cut flowers, nursery plants, tropical fish and birds for the pet trade are some of the ornamental products.

In 2008 about one-third of the world's workers were employed in agriculture. However, the relative significance of farming has dropped steadily since the beginning of industrialization, and in 2003 – for the first time in history – the services sector overtook agriculture as the economic sector employing the most people worldwide Despite the fact that agriculture employs over one-third of the world's population, agricultural production accounts for less than five per cent of the gross world product (an aggregate of all gross domestic products).

Etymology

The word *agriculture* is the English adaptation of Latin *agricultura,* from *ager,* "a field" and *cultura,* "cultivation" in the strict sense of "tillage of the soil" Thus, a literal reading of the word yields "tillage of a field/of fields".

Overview

Agriculture has played a key role in the development of human civilization. Until the Industrial Revolution, the vast majority of the human population labored in agriculture. Development of agricultural techniques has steadily increased agricultural productivity, and the widespread diffusion of these techniques during a time period is often called an agricultural revolution. A remarkable shift in agricultural practices has occurred over the past century in response to new technologies. In particular, the Haber-Bosch method for synthesizing ammonium nitrate made the traditional practice of recycling nutrients with crop rotation and animal manure less necessary.

Fig.: 1.1

The per cent of the human population working in agriculture has decreased over time.

Synthetic nitrogen, along with mined rock phosphate, pesticides and mechanization, have greatly increased crop yields in the early 20th century. Increased supply of grains has led to cheaper livestock as well. Further, global yield increases were experienced later in the 20th century when high-yield varieties of common staple grains such as rice, wheat, and corn (maize) were introduced as a part of the Green Revolution. The Green Revolution exported the technologies (including pesticides and synthetic nitrogen) of the developed world out to the developing world. Thomas Malthus famously predicted that the Earth would not be able to support its growing population, but technologies such as the Green Revolution have allowed the world to produce a surplus of food.

Many governments have subsidized agriculture to ensure an adequate food supply. These agricultural subsidies are often linked to the production of certain commodities such as wheat, corn (maize), rice, soybeans, and milk. These subsidies, especially when done by developed countries have been noted as protectionist, inefficient, and environmentally damaging. In the past century agriculture has been characterized by enhanced productivity, the use of synthetic fertilizers and pesticides, selective breeding, mechanization, water contamination, and farm subsidies. Proponents of organic farming such as Sir Albert Howard argued in the early 1900s that the overuse of pesticides and synthetic fertilizers damages the long-term fertility of the soil. While this feeling lay dormant for decades, as environmental awareness has increased in the 2000s there has been a movement towards sustainable agriculture by some farmers, consumers, and policymakers. In recent years there has been a backlash against perceived external environmental effects of mainstream agriculture, particularly regarding water pollution resulting in the organic movement. One of the major forces behind this movement has been the European Union, which first certified organic food in 1991 and began reform of its Common Agricultural Policy (CAP) in 2005 to phase out commodity-linked farm subsidies also known as decoupling. The growth of organic farming has renewed research in alternative technologies such as integrated pest management and selective breeding. Recent mainstream technological developments include genetically modified food.

As of late 2007, several factors have pushed up the price of grain used to feed poultry and dairy cows and other cattle, causing higher prices of wheat (up 58%), soybean (up 32%), and maize (up 11%) over the year. Food riots have recently taken place in many countries across the world. An epidemic of stem rust on wheat caused by race Ug99 is currently spreading across Africa and into Asia and is causing major concern. Approximately 40% of the world's agricultural land is seriously degraded In Africa, if current trends of soil degradation continue, the continent might be able to feed just 25% of its population by 2025, according to UNU's Ghana-based Institute for Natural Resources in Africa.

History

Since its development roughly 10,000 years ago, agriculture has expanded vastly in geographical coverage and yields. Throughout this expansion, new technologies and new crops were integrated. Agricultural practices such as irrigation, crop rotation, fertilizers, and pesticides were developed long ago, but have made great strides in the past century. The history of agriculture has played a major role in human history, as agricultural progress has been a crucial factor in worldwide socio-economic change. Wealth-concentration and militaristic specializations rarely seen in hunter-gatherer cultures are commonplace in societies which practice agriculture. So, too, are arts such as epic literature and monumental architecture, as well as codified legal systems. When farmers became capable of producing food beyond the needs of their own families, others in their society were freed to devote themselves to projects other than food acquisition. Historians and anthropologists have long argued that the development of agriculture made civilization possible.

Ancient Origins

The Fertile Crescent of the Middle East, Egypt, and India were sites of the earliest planned sowing and harvesting of plants that had previously been gathered in the wild. Independent development of agriculture occurred in northern and southern China, Africa's Sahel, New Guinea and several regions of the Americas. The eight so-called Neolithic founder crops of agriculture appear: first emmer wheat and einkorn wheat, then hulled barley, peas, lentils, bitter vetch, chick peas and flax.By 7000 BC, small-scale agriculture reached Egypt. From at least 7000 BC the Indian subcontinent saw farming of wheat and barley, as attested by archaeological excavation at Mehrgarh in Balochistan. By 6000 BC, mid-scale farming was entrenched on the banks of the Nile. About this time, agriculture was developed independently in the Far East, with rice, rather than wheat, as the primary crop. Chinese and Indonesian farmers went on to domesticate taro and beans including mung, soy and azuki. To complement these new sources of carbohydrates, highly organized net fishing of rivers, lakes and ocean shores in these areas brought in great volumes of essential protein. Collectively, these new methods of farming and fishing inaugurated a human population boom dwarfing all previous expansions, and is one that continues today.

By 5000 BC, the Sumerians had developed core agricultural techniques including large scale intensive cultivation of land, mono-cropping, organized irrigation, and use of a specialized labour force, particularly along the waterway now known as the Shatt al-Arab, from its Persian Gulf delta to the confluence of the Tigris and Euphrates. Domestication of wild aurochs and mouflon into cattle and sheep, respectively, ushered in the large-scale use of animals for food/fibre and as beasts of burden. The shepherd joined the farmer as an essential provider for sedentary and semi-nomadic societies. Maize, manioc, and arrowroot were first domesticated in the Americas as far back as 5200 BC. The potato, tomato, pepper, squash, several varieties of bean, tobacco, and several other plants were also developed in the New World, as was extensive terracing of steep hillsides in much of Andean South America. The Greeks and Romans built on techniques pioneered by the Sumerians but made few fundamentally new advances. Southern Greeks struggled with very poor soils, yet managed to become a dominant society for years. The Romans were noted for an emphasis on the cultivation of crops for trade.

A water-raising machine invented by al-Jazari (1136-1206), an Arab inventor and engineer.

Middle Ages

During the Middle Ages, Muslim farmers in North Africa and the Near East developed and disseminated agricultural technologies including irrigation systems based on hydraulic and hydrostatic principles, the use of machines such as norias, and the use of water raising machines, dams, and reservoirs. They also wrote location-specific farming manuals, and were instrumental in the wider adoption of crops including sugar cane, rice, citrus fruit, apricots, cotton, artichokes, aubergines, and saffron. Muslims also brought lemons, oranges, cotton, almonds, figs and sub-tropical crops such as bananas to Spain. The invention of a three field system of crop rotation during the Middle Ages, and the importation of the Chinese-invented moldboard plow, vastly improved agricultural efficiency.

Modern Era

After 1492, a global exchange of previously local crops and livestock breeds occurred. Key crops involved in this exchange included the tomato, maize, potato, cocoa and tobacco going from the New World to the old, and several varieties of wheat, spices, coffee, and sugar cane going from the Old World to the New. The most important animal exportation from the Old World to the New were those of the horse and dog (dogs were already present in the pre-

Columbian Americas but not in the numbers and breeds suited to farm work). Although not usually food animals, the horse (including donkeys and ponies) and dog quickly filled essential production roles on western hemisphere farms.

By the early 1800s, agricultural techniques, implements, seed stocks and cultivated plants selected and given a unique name because of its decorative or useful characteristics had so improved that yield per land unit was many times that seen in the Middle Ages. With the rapid rise of mechanization in the late 19th and 20th centuries, particularly in the form of the tractor, farming tasks could be done with a speed and on a scale previously impossible. These advances have led to efficiencies enabling certain modern farms in the United States, Argentina, Israel, Germany, and a few other nations to output volumes of high quality produce per land unit at what may be the practical limit. The Haber-Bosch method for synthesizing ammonium nitrate represented a major breakthrough and allowed crop yields to overcome previous constraints. In the past century agriculture has been characterized by enhanced productivity, the substitution of labor for synthetic fertilizers and pesticides, selective breeding, mechanization, water pollution, and farm subsidies. In recent years there has been a backlash against the external environmental effects of conventional agriculture, resulting in the organic movement.

Agricultural exploration expeditions, since the late nineteenth century, have been mounted to find new species and new agricultural practices in different areas of the world. Two early examples of expeditions include Frank N. Meyer's fruit and nut collecting trip to China and Japan from 1916-1918 and the Dorsett-Morse Oriental Agricultural Exploration Expedition to China, Japan, and Korea from 1929-1931 to collect soybean germplasm to support the rise in soybean agriculture in the United States.

In 2005, the agricultural output of China was the largest in the world, accounting for almost one-sixth world share followed by the EU, India and the USA, according to the International Monetary Fund. Economists measure the total factor productivity of agriculture and by this measure agriculture in the United States is roughly 2.6 times more productive than it was in 1948.

Fig. 1.2

Crop Production Systems

Cropping systems vary from farms to farms depending on the available resources and constraints; geography and climate of the farm; government policy; economic, social and political pressures; and the philosophy and culture of the farmer Shifting cultivation (or slash and burn) is a system in which forests are burnt, releasing nutrients to support cultivation of annual and then perennial crops for a period of several years. Then the plot is left fallow to regrow forest, and the farmer moves to a new plot, returning after many more years (10-20). This fallow period is shortened if population density grows, requiring the input of nutrients (fertilizer or manure) and some manual pest control. Annual cultivation is the next phase of intensity in which there is no fallow period. This requires even greater nutrient and pest control inputs. Further industrialization lead to the use of monocultures, when one cultivar is planted on a large acreage. Due to the low biodiversity, nutrient use is uniform, and pests tend to build up, necessitating the greater use of pesticides and fertilizers Multiple cropping, in which several crops are grown sequentially in one year, and intercropping, when several crops are grown at the same time are other kinds of annual cropping systems known as polycultures.

In tropical environments, all of these cropping systems are practiced. In subtropical and arid environments, the timing and extent of agriculture may be limited by rainfall, either not allowing multiple annual crops in a year, or requiring irrigation. In all of these environments perennial crops are grown (coffee, chocolate) and systems are practiced such as agroforestry. In temperate environments, where ecosystems were predominantly grassland or prairie, highly productive annual cropping is the dominant farming system.

The last century has seen the intensification, concentration and specialization of agriculture, relying upon new technologies of agricultural chemicals (fertilizers and pesticides), mechanization, and plant breeding (hybrids and GMO's). In the past few decades, a move towards sustainability in agriculture has also developed, integrating ideas of socio-economic justice and conservation of resources and the environment within a farming system. This has led to the development of many responses to the conventional agriculture approach, including organic agriculture, urban agriculture, community supported agriculture, ecological or biological agriculture, integrated farming, and holistic management.

Crop Statistics

Important categories of crops include grains and pseudograins, pulses (legumes), forage, and fruits and vegetables. Specific crops are cultivated in distinct growing regions throughout the world. In millions of metric tons, based on FAO estimates.

Fig. 1.3

Ploughing rice paddies with water buffalo, in Indonesia. Animals, including horses, mules, oxen, camels, llamas, alpacas, and dogs, are often used to help cultivate fields, harvest crops, wrangle other animals, and transport farm products to buyers. Animal husbandry not only refers to the breeding and raising of animals for meat or to harvest animal products (like milk, eggs, or wool) on a continual basis, but also to the breeding and care of species for work and companionship. Livestock production systems can be defined based on feed source, as grassland-based, mixed, and landless. Grassland based livestock production relies upon plant material such as shrubland, rangeland, and pastures for feeding ruminant animals. Outside nutrient inputs may be used, however manure is returned directly to the grassland as a major nutrient source. This system is particularly important in areas where crop production is not feasible due to climate or soil, representing 30-40 million pastoralists

Mixed production systems use grassland, fodder crops and grain feed crops as feed for ruminant and monogastic (one stomach; mainly chickens and pigs) livestock. Manure is typically recycled in mixed systems as a fertilizer for crops. Approximately 68% of all agricultural land is permanent pastures used in the production of livestock Landless systems rely upon feed from outside the farm, representing the de-linking of crop and livestock production found more prevalently OECD member countries. In the U.S., 70% of the grain grown is fed to animals on feedlots. Synthetic fertilizers are more heavily relied upon for crop production and manure utilization becomes a challenge as well as a source for pollution.

Production Practices

Tillage is the practice of plowing soil to prepare for planting or for nutrient incorporation or for pest control. Tillage varies in intensity from conventional to no-till. It may improve productivity by warming the soil, incorporating fertilizer and controlling weeds, but also renders soil more prone to erosion, triggers the decomposition of organic matter releasing CO_2, and reduces the abundance and diversity of soil organisms.

Pest control includes the management of weeds, insects/mites, and diseases. Chemical (pesticides), biological (biocontrol), mechanical (tillage), and cultural practices are used. Cultural practices include crop rotation, culling, cover crops, intercropping, compost, avoidance, and resistance. Integrated pest management attempts to use all of these methods to keep pest populations below the number which would cause economic loss, and recommends pesticides as a last resort.

Nutrient management includes both the source of nutrient inputs for crop and livestock production, and the method of utilization of manure produced by livestock. Nutrient inputs can be chemical inorganic fertilizers, manure, green manure, compost and mined minerals Crop nutrient use may also be managed using cultural techniques such as crop rotation or a fallow period Manure is utilized either by holding livestock where the feed crop is growing such as in Managed intensive rotational grazing, or by spreading either dry or liquid formulations of manure on cropland or pastures.

Water management is where rainfall is insufficient or variable, which occurs to some degree in most regions of the world Some farmers use irrigation to supplement rainfall. In other areas such as the Great Plains in the U.S., farmers use a fallow year to conserve soil moisture to use for growing a crop in the following year Agriculture represents 70% of freshwater use worldwide.

Processing, Distribution, and Marketing

In the United States, food costs attributed to processing, distribution, and marketing have risen while the costs attributed to farming have declined. From 1960 to 1980 the farm share was around 40%, but by 1990 it had declined to 30% and by 1998, 22.2%. Market concentration has increased in the sector as well, with the top 20 food manufacturers accounting for half the food-processing value in 1995, over double that produced in 1954. As of 2000 the top 6 supermarkets had 50% of sales compared to 32% in 1992. Although the total effect of the increased market concentration is likely increased efficiency, the changes redistribute economic surplus from producers (farmers) and consumers, and may have negative implications for rural communities.

Crop Alteration and Biotechnology

Tractor and chaser bin. Crop alteration has been practiced by humankind for thousands of years, since the beginning of civilization. Altering crops through breeding practices changes the genetic make-up of a plant to develop crops with more beneficial characteristics for humans, for example, larger fruits or seeds, drought-tolerance, or resistance to pests. Significant advances in plant breeding ensued after the work of geneticist Gregor Mendel. His work on dominant and recessive alleles gave plant breeders a better understanding of genetics and brought great insights to the techniques utilized by plant breeders. Crop breeding includes techniques such as plant selection with desirable traits, self-pollination and cross-pollination, and molecular techniques that genetically modify the organism Domestication of plants has, over the centuries increased yield, improved disease resistance and drought tolerance, eased harvest and improved the taste and nutritional value of crop plants. Careful selection and breeding have had enormous effects on the characteristics of crop plants. Plant selection and breeding in the 1920s and 1930s improved pasture (grasses and clover) in New Zealand. Extensive X-ray an ultraviolet induced mutagenesis efforts (i.e. primitive genetic engineering) during the 1950s produced the modern commercial varieties of grains such as wheat, corn (maize) and barley.

The green revolution popularized the use of conventional hybridization to increase yield many folds by creating "high-yielding varieties". For example, average yields of corn (maize) in the USA have increased from around 2.5 tons per hectare (t/ha) (40 bushels per acre) in 1900 to about 9.4 t/ha (150 bushels per acre) in 2001. Similarly, worldwide average wheat yields have increased from less than 1 t/ha in 1900 to more than 2.5 t/ha in 1990. South American average wheat yields are around 2 t/ha, African under 1 t/ha, Egypt and Arabia up to 3.5 to 4 t/ha with irrigation. In contrast, the average wheat yield in countries such as France is over 8 t/ha. Variations in yields are due mainly to variation in climate, genetics, and the level of intensive farming techniques (use of fertilizers, chemical pest control, growth control to avoid lodging).

Genetic Engineering

Genetically Modified Organisms (GMO) are organisms whose genetic material has been altered by genetic engineering techniques generally known as recombinant DNA technology. Genetic engineering has expanded the genes available to breeders to utilize in creating desired germlines for new crops. After mechanical tomato-harvesters were developed in the early 1960s, agricultural scientists genetically modified tomatoes to be more resistant to mechanical handling. More recently, genetic engineering is being employed in various parts of the world, to create crops with other beneficial traits.

Herbicide-tolerant GMO Crops

Roundup-Ready seed has a herbicide resistance gene implanted into its genome that allows the plants to tolerate exposure to glyphosate. Roundup is a trade name for a glyphosate based product, which is a systemic, non-selective herbicide used to kill weeds. Roundup-Ready seeds allow the farmer to grow a crop that can be sprayed with glyphosate to controle weeds without harming the resistant crop. Herbicide-tolerant crops are used by farmers worldwide. Today, 92% of soybean acreage in the US is planted with genetically-modified herbicide-tolerant plants With the increasing use of herbicide-tolerant crops, comes an increase in the use of glyphosate based herbicide sprays. In some areas glyphosate resistant weeds have developed, causing farmers to switch to other herbicides Some studies also link widespread glyphosate usage to iron deficiencies in some crops, which is both a crop production and a nutritional quality concern, with potential economic and health implications.

Insect-Resistant GMO Crops

Other GMO crops utilized by growers include insect-resistant crops, which have a gene from the soil bacterium *Bacillus thuringiensis* (*Bt*) which produces a toxin specific to insects; insect-resistant crops protect plants from damage by insects, one such crop is Starlink. Another is *Bt* cotton, which accounts for 63% of US cotton acreage.

Some believe that similar or better pest-resistance traits can be acquired through traditional breeding practices, and resistance to various pests can be gained through hybridization or cross-pollination with wild species. In some cases, wild species are the primary source of resistance traits; some Tomato cultivars that have gained resistance to at least nineteen diseases, did so, through crossing with wild populations of tomatoes.

Costs and Benefits of GMOs

Genetic engineers may someday develop transgenic plants which would allow for irrigation, drainage, conservation, sanitary engineering, and maintaining or increasing yields while requiring fewer fossil fuel derived inputs than conventional crops. Such developments would be particularly important in areas which are normally arid and rely upon constant irrigation, and on large scale farms. However, genetic engineering of plants has proven to be controversial. Many issues surrounding food security and environmental impacts have risen regarding GMO practices. For example, GMOs are questioned by some ecologists and economists concerned with GMO practices such as terminator seeds, which is a genetic modification that creates sterile seeds. Terminator seeds are currently under strong international opposition and face continual efforts of global bans. Another controversial issue is the patent protection given to companies that develop new types of seed using genetic engineering. Since companies have intellectual ownership of their seeds, they have the power to dictate terms and conditions of their patented product. Currently, ten seed companies control over two-thirds of the global seed sales. Vandana Shiva argues that these companies are guilty of biopiracy by patenting life and exploiting organisms for profit Farmers using patented seed are restricted from saving seed for subsequent plantings, which forces farmers to buy new seed every year. Since seed saving is a traditional practice for many farmers in both developing and developed countries, GMO seeds legally bind farmers to change their seed saving practices to buying new seed every year.

Locally adapted seeds are an essential hertitage that has the potential to be lost with current hybridized crops and GMOs. Locally adapted seeds, also called land races or crop eco-types, are important because they have adapted over time to the specific microclimates, soils, other environmental conditions, field designs, and ethnic preference indigenous to the exact area of cultivation. Introducing GMOs and hybridized commercial seed to an area brings the risk of cross-pollination with local land races. Therefore, GMOs pose a threat to the sustainability of land races and the ethnic heritage of cultures. Once seed contains transgenic material, it becomes subject to the conditions of the seed company that owns the patent of the transgenic material.

There is also concern that GMOs will cross-pollinate with wild species and permanently alter native populations' genetic integrity; there are already identified populations of wild plants with transgenic genes. GMO gene flow to related weed species is a concern, as well as cross-pollination with non-transgenic crops. Since many GMO crops are harvested for their seed, such as rapeseed, seed spillage in is problematic for volunteer plants in rotated fields, as well as seed-spillage during transportation.

Food Safety and Labelling

Food security issues also coincide with food safety and food labelling concerns. Currently a global treaty, the BioSafety Protocol, regulates the trade of GMOs. The EU currently requires all GMO foods to be labelled, whereas the US does not require transparent labelling of GMO foods.

Since there are still questions regarding the safety and risks associated with GMO foods, some believe the public should have the freedom to choose and know what they are eating and require all GMO products to be labeled.

Environmental Impact

Agriculture imposes external costs upon society through pesticides, nutrient runoff, excessive water usage, and assorted other problems. A 2000 assessment of agriculture in the UK determined total external costs costs for 1996 of 2343 million British pounds or 208 pounds per hectare. A 2005 analysis of these costs in the USA concluded that cropland imposes approximately 5 to 16 billion dollars ($30 to $96 per hectare), while livestock production imposes 714 million dollars. Both studies concluded that more should be done to internalize external costs, and neither included subsidies in their analysis, but noted that subsidies also influence the cost of agriculture to society. Both focused on purely fiscal impacts. The 2000 review included reported pesticide poisonings but did not include speculative chronic effects of pesticides, and the 2004 review relied on a 1992 estimate of the total impact of pesticides.

Livestock Issues

A senior UN official and co-author of a UN report detailing this problem, Henning Steinfeld, said "Livestock are one of the most significant contributors to today's most serious environmental problems." Livestock production occupies 70% of all land used for agriculture, or 30% of the land surface of the planet It is one of the largest sources of greenhouse gases, responsible for 18% of the world's greenhouse gas emissions as measured in CO_2 equivalents. By comparison, all transportation emits 13.5% of the CO_2. It produces 65% of human-related nitrous oxide (which has 296 times the global warming potential of CO_2,) and 37% of all human-induced methane (which is 23 times as warming as CO_2). It also generates 64% of the ammonia, which contributes to acid rain and acidification of ecosystems. Livestock expansion is cited as a key factor driving deforestation, in the Amazon basin 70% of previously forested area is now occupied by pastures and the remainder used for feedcrops Through deforestation and land degradation, livestock is also driving reductions in biodiversity.

Land Transformation and Degradation

Land transformation, the use of land to yield goods and services, is the most substantial way humans alter the Earth's ecosystems, and is considered the driving force in the loss of biodiversity. Estimates of the amount of land transformed by humans vary from 39-50% Land degradation, the long-term decline in ecosystem function and productivity, is estimated to be occurring on 24% of land worldwide, with cropland overrepresented The UN-FAO report cites land management as the driving factor behind degradation and reports that 1.5 billion people rely upon the degrading land. Degradation can be deforestation, desertification, soil erosion, mineral depletion, or chemical degradation (acidification and salinization).

Eutrophication

Eutrophication, excessive nutrients in aquatic ecosystems resulting in algal blooms and anoxia, leads to fish kills, loss of biodiversity, and renders water unfit for drinking and other industrial uses. Excessive fertilization and manure application to cropland, as well as high livestock stocking densities cause nutrient (mainly nitrogen and phosphorus) runoff and leaching from agricultural land. These nutrients are major nonpoint pollutants contributing to eutrophication of aquatic ecosystems.

Pesticides

Pesticide use has increased since 1950 to 2.5 million tons annually worldwide, yet crop loss due to pests has remained relatively constant. The World Health Organization (WHO) estimated in 1992 that 3 million pesticide poisonings occur annually, causing 220,000 deaths. Pesticides select for pesticide resistance in the pest population, leading to a condition termed the 'pesticide treadmill' in which pest resistance warrants the development of a new pesticide. An alternative argument is that the way to 'save the environment' and prevent famine is by using pesticdes and intensive high yield farming. However critics argue that a tradeoff between the environment and a need for food is not inevitable and that pesticides simply replace good agronomic practices such as crop rotation.

Climate Change

Climate change has the potential to affect agriculture through changes in temperature and moisture regimes Agriculture can both mitigate or worsen global warming. Some of the increase in CO_2 in the atmosphere comes from the decomposition of organic matter in the soil, and much of the methane emitted into the atmosphere is due to the decomposition of organic matter in wet soils such as rice paddies. Further, wet or anaerobic soils also lose nitrogen through denitrification, releasing the greenhouse gas nitric oxide. Changes in management can reduce the release of these greenhouse gases, and soil can further be used to sequester some of the CO_2 in the atmosphere.

Distortions in Modern Global Agriculture

Differences in economic development, population density and culture mean that the farmers of the world operate under very different conditions.

A US cotton farmer may receive US$230 government subsidies per acre planted (as in 2003), farmers in Mali and other third world countries do without. When prices decline, the heavily subsidised US farmer is not forced to reduce his output, hence making it difficult for cotton prices to rebound, his Mali counterpart may go broke in the meantime.

A livestock farmer in South Korea can calculate with a (highly subsidized) salesprice of US$1300 for a calf produced. A South American Mercosur country rancher calculates with a calf's salesprice of US$120-200 (both 2008 figures) With the former, scarcety and high cost of land is compensated with public subsidies, the latter compensates absence of subsedies with economics of scale and low cost of land.

In PR China a rural household's productive asset may be one hectare of farmland. In Brazil, Paraguay and other countries where local legislature allows such purchases, international investors buy thousands of hectares of farmland or raw land at prices of a few hundred US$ per hectare.

Agriculture and Petroleum

Since the 1940s, agriculture has dramatically increased its productivity, due largely to the use of petrochemical derived pesticides, fertilizers, and increased mechanization (the so-called Green Revolution). Between 1950 and 1984, as the Green Revolution transformed agriculture around the globe, world grain production increased by 250% This has allowed world population to grow more than double over the last 50 years. However, every energy unit delivered in food grown using modern techniques requires over ten energy units to produce and deliver, although this statistic is contested by proponents of petroleum-based agriculture. The vast majority of this energy input comes from fossil fuel sources. Because of modern agriculture's current heavy reliance on petrochemicals and mechanization, there are warnings that the ever decreasing supply of oil (the dramatic nature of which is known as peak oil will inflict major damage on the modern industrial agriculture system, and could cause large food shortages.

Modern or industrialized agriculture is dependent on petroleum in two fundamental ways:

1. *Cultivation:* to get the crop from seed to harvest; and

2. *Transport:* to get the harvest from the farm to the consumer's refrigerator. It takes approximately 400 gallons of oil a year per citizen to fuel the tractors, combines and other equipment used on farms for cultivation or 17 per cent of the nation's total energy use Oil and natural gas are also the building blocks of the fertilizers, pesticides and herbicides used on farms. Petroleum is also providing the energy required to process food before it reaches the market. It takes the energy equivalent of a half-gallon of gasoline to produce a two-pound bag of breakfast cereal. And that still does not count the energy needed to transport that cereal to market; it is the transport of processed foods and crops that consumes the most oil. The kiwi from New Zealand, the asparagus from Argentina, the melons and broccoli from Guatemala, the organic lettuce from California-most food items on the consumer's plate travel average of 1,500 miles just to get there.

Oil shortages could interrupt this food supply. The consumer's growing awareness of this vulnerability is one of several factors fueling current interest in organic agriculture and other sustainable farming methods. Some farmers using modern organic-farming methods have reported yields as high as those available from conventional farming (but without the use of fossil-fuel-intensive artificial fertilizers or pesticides. However, the reconditioning of soil to restore nutrients lost during the use of monoculture agriculture techniques made possible by petroleum-based technology will take time.

The dependence on oil and vulnerability of the U.S. food supply has also led to the creation of a conscious consumption movement in which consumers count the "food miles" a food product has traveled. The Leopold Center for Sustainable Agriculture defines a food mile as:

> ". . . the distance food travels from where it is grown or raised to where it is ultimately purchased by the consumer or end-user."

In a comparison of locally-grown food and long-distance food, researchers at the Leopold Center found that local food traveled an average of 44.6 miles to reach its destination compared with 1,546 miles for conventionally-grown and shipped food.

Consumers in the new local food movement who count food miles call themselves "locavores" they advocate a return to a locally-based food system where food comes from as close as possible, whether or not it is organic. Locavores argue that an organically-grown lettuce from California that is shipped to New York is still an unsustainable food source because of dependence on fossil fuels to ship it. In addition to the "locavore" movement, concern over dependence on oil-based agriculture has also dramatically increased interest in home and community gardening.

Farmers have also begun raising crops such as corn (maize) for non-food use in an effort to help mitigate peak oil. This has contributed to a 60% rise in wheat prices recently, and has been indicated as a possible precursor to "serious social unrest in developing countries." Such situations would be exacerbated in the event of future rises in food and fuel costs, factors which have already impacted the ability of charitable donors to send food aid to starving populations.

One example of the chain reactions which could possibly be caused by peak oil issues involves the problems caused by farmers raising crops such as corn (maize) for non-food use in an effort to help mitigate peak oil. This has already lowered food production This food vs fuel issue will be exacerbated as demand for ethanol fuel rises. Rising food and fuel costs has already limited the abilities of some charitable donors to send food aid to starving populations In the UN, some warn that the recent 60% rise in wheat prices could cause "serious social unrest in developing countries. In 2007, higher incentives for farmers to grow non-food biofuel crops combined with other factors (such as over-development of former farm lands, rising transportation costs, climate change, growing consumer demand in China and India, and population growth) to cause food shortages in Asia, the Middle East, Africa, and Mexico, as well as rising food prices around the globe. As of December 2007, 37 countries faced food crises, and 20 had imposed some sort of food-price controls. Some of these shortages resulted in food riots and even deadly stampedes.

Another major petroleum issue in agriculture is the effect of petroleum supplies will have on fertilizer production. By far the biggest fossil fuel input to agriculture is the use of natural gas as a hydrogen source for the Haber-Bosch fertilizer-creation process. Natural gas is used because it is the cheapest currently available source of hydrogen When oil production becomes so scarce that natural gas is used as a partial stopgap replacement, and hydrogen use in transportation increases, natural gas will become much more expensive. If the Haber Process is unable to be commercialized using renewable energy (such as by electrolysis) or if other sources of hydrogen are not available to replace the Haber Process, in amounts sufficient to supply transportation and agricultural needs, this major source of fertilizer would either become extremely expensive or unavailable. This would either cause food shortages or dramatic rises in food prices.

Mitigation of Effects of Petroleum Shortages

One effect oil shortages could have on agriculture is a full return to organic agriculture. In light of peak oil concerns, organic methods are much more sustainable than contemporary practices because they use no petroleum-based pesticides, herbicides, or fertilizers. Some farmers using modern organic-farming methods have reported yields as high as those available from conventional farming Organic farming may however be more labor-intensive and would require a shift of work force from urban to rural areas.

It has been suggested that rural communities might obtain fuel from the biochar and synfuel process, which uses agricultural waste to provide charcoal fertilizer, some fuel and food, instead of the normal food vs fuel debate. As the synfuel would be used on site, the process would be more efficient and may just provide enough fuel for a new organic-agriculture fusion.

It has been suggested that some transgenic plants may some day bednal crops The possibility of success of these programs is questioned by ecologists and economists concerned with unsustainable GMO practices such as terminator seeds and a January 2008 report shows that GMO practices "fail to deliver environmental, social and economic benefits." While there has been some research on sustainability using GMO crops, at least one hyped and prominent multi-year attempt by Monsanto has been unsuccessful, though during the same period traditional breeding techniques yielded a more sustainable variety of the same crop Additionally, a survey by the bio-tech industry of subsistence farmers in Africa to discover what GMO research would most benefit sustainable agriculture only identified non-transgenic issues as areas needing to be addressed. Nonetheless, some governments in Africa continue to view investments in new transgenic technologies as an essential component of efforts to improve sustainability.

Agricultural policy focuses on the goals and methods of agricultural production. At the policy level, common goals of agriculture include:

- Conservation
- Economic stability
- Environmental impact
- *Food quality:* Ensuring that the food supply is of a consistent and known quality.
- *Food safety:* Ensuring that the food supply is free of contamination.

- *Food security:* Ensuring that the food supply meets the population's needs.
- Poverty Reduction.

Agriculture Safety and Health

Satellite image of circular crop fields characteristic of center pivot irrigation in Kansas. Healthy, growing crops are green; wheat fields are gold-coloured; and fallow fields are brown.

United States

Agriculture ranks among the most hazardous industries Farmers are at high risk for fatal and nonfatal injuries, work-related lung diseases, noise-induced hearing loss, skin diseases, and certain cancers associated with chemical use and prolonged sun exposure. Farming is one of the few industries in which the families (who often share the work and live on the premises) are also at risk for injuries, illness, and death. In an average year, 516 workers die doing farm work in the U.S. (1992-2005). Of these deaths, 101 are caused by tractor overturns. Every day, about 243 agricultural workers suffer lost-work-time injuries, and about 5% of these result in permanent impairment.

Agriculture is the most dangerous industry for young workers, accounting for 42% of all work-related fatalities of young workers in the U.S. between 1992 and 2000. Unlike other industries, half the young victims in agriculture were under age 15. For young agricultural workers aged 15-17, the risk of fatal injury is four times the risk for young workers in other workplaces Agricultural work exposes young workers to safety hazards such as machinery, confined spaces, work at elevations, and work around livestock.

An estimated 1.26 million children and adolescents under 20 years of age resided on farms in 2004, with about 699,000 of these youth performing work on the farms. In addition to the youth who live on farms, an additional 337,000 children and adolescents were hired to work on U.S. farms in 2004. On average, 103 children are killed annually on farms (1990-1996). Approximately 40 per cent of these deaths were work-related. In 2004, an estimated 27,600 children and adolescents were injured on farms; 8,100 of these injuries were due to farm work.

2

Natural Resources

Natural resources are naturally forming substances (such as land or raw materials) that are considered valuable in their relatively unmodified (natural) form. A natural resource's value rests in the amount and extractability of the material available and the demand for it. The latter is determined by its usefulness to production. A commodity is generally considered a natural resource when the primary activities associated with it are extraction and purification, as opposed to creation. Thus, mining, petroleum extraction, fishing, hunting, and forestry are generally considered natural-resource industries, while agriculture is not. Industries that are centered around the demand for visiting or living near attractive natural environments, (such as tourism, resorts, housing developments, etc.) are often also considered natural resource industries, and thus natural amenities such as panoramic vistas, lakes, waterfalls, and national parks are considered natural resources as well.

The term was introduced to a broad audience by E.F. Schumacher in his 1973 book *Small is Beautiful*. The term is defined by the United States Geological Survey as "The Nation's natural resources include its minerals, energy, land, water, and biota."

Classification of Natural Forms

Natural resources are mostly classified into renewable and non-renewable resources. Sometimes resources are classified as non-renewable even if they are technically renewable, just not easily renewed within a reasonable amount of time, such as fossil fuels.

Renewable Resources

Renewable resources are sometimes living resources, (trees and soil, for example), which can restock (renew) themselves if used sustainably and not over-harvested. There are also non-living resources that are renewable, such as hydroelectric power, solar power, biomass fuel, and wind power. If renewable resources are consumed at a rate above their natural rate of replacement, the standing stock will diminish and eventually run out. The rate of sustainable use of a renewable resource is determined by the replacement rate and amount of standing stock of that particular resource. Non-living renewable natural resources include dirt and water.

Flow renewable resources are very much like renewable resources, only they do not need regeneration, unlike renewable resources. Flow renewable resources include renewable energy sources such as the following renewable power sources: solar, geothermal, landfill gas, tides and wind.

Resources can also be classified on the basis of their origin as biotic and abiotic. Biotic resources are derived from living organisms. Abiotic resources are derived from the non-living world (e.g., land, water, and air). Mineral and power resources can be abiotic natural resources.

Non-renewable Resources

A non-renewable resource is a natural resource that exists in a fixed amount that cannot be re-made, re-grown or regenerated as fast as it is consumed and used up.

Some non-renewable resources can be renewable but take an extremely long time to renew. Fossil fuels, for example, take millions of years to form and so are not practically considered 'renewable'. Different non-renewable resources like oil, coal, natural gas etc. have different levels of demand from different sectors like transportation and residences with each resource specializing for each sector. Many environmentalists propose a tax on consumption of non renewable resources. Non-renewable resources cannot be replaced or can only be replaced over thousands or millions of years.

Natural Capital

Natural resources are natural capital converted to commodity inputs to infrastructural capital processes. They include soil, timber, oil, minerals, and other goods harvested from the Earth. Both extraction of the basic resource and refining it into a purer, directly usable form, (e.g., metals, refined oils) are generally considered natural-resource activities, even though the latter may not necessarily occur near the former. This process generates high profits due to the high demand for the natural resources and the energies that they are able to generate.

A nation's natural resources often determine its wealth in the world economic system and its diplomatic, military, and political influence. Developed nations are those which are less dependent on natural resources for wealth, due to their greater reliance on infrastructural capital for production. However, some see a resource curse whereby easily obtainable natural resources could actually hurt the prospects of a national economy by fostering political corruption.

Political corruption can negatively impact the national economy because time is spent giving bribes or other economically unproductive acts instead of the generation of generative economic activity. This has been seen over the years with legislation passed to appease companies who will benefit. There also tends to be concentrations of ownership over specific plots of land that have proven to yield natural resources.

The depletion of natural capital and attempts to move to sustainable development have been a major focus of development agencies. This is of particular concern in rainforest regions, which hold most of the Earth's natural biodiversity - irreplaceable genetic natural capital. Conservation of natural resources is the major focus of natural capitalism, environmentalism, the ecology movement, and green politics. Some view this depletion as a major source of social unrest and conflicts in developing nations.

Natural resources are materials or things that people use from the earth. There are two types of natural resources. The first are renewable natural resources. They are called renewable because they can grow again or never run out. The second are called non-renewable natural resources. These are things that can run out or be used up. They usually come from the ground. Let's look more closely at renewable natural resources. They are the ones that can grow again. Trees are a good example. If cut down, they can regrow from seeds and sprouts. Animals are another example. Baby animals are born and grow up. They replace older animals that die. Air and water are renewable natural resources too. They don't regrow like trees or have babies like animals. But, they are always being renewed. They move in cycles. They go from one place to another, and often back where they started, again and again. This is a good thing, because all living things need air and water to survive. There is one other type of renewable natural resource. It includes sources of power like sun and wind energy. These are never ending. Finally, remember this: renewable resources can regrow or be replaced within a person's lifespan.

Renewable or Non-renewable?

Now, let's look at non-renewable natural resources. They are found in the ground. There are fixed amounts of these resources. They are not living things, and they are sometimes hard to fi nd. They don't regrow and they are not replaced or renewed. They include the *fossil* fuels we burn for energy (natural gas, coal, and oil). Minerals, used for making metals, are also nonrenewable natural resources. Nonrenewable natural resources are things that take longer than a person's lifespan to be replaced. In fact, they can take millions of years to form. People use both types of natural resources to produce the things they need or want. Our homes, clothing, plastics, and foods are all made from natural resources. Let's look at each one of these to be sure. Your home is in a building. Buildings are made out of wood and minerals. Wood is from trees. Minerals are mined from the ground. Bricks, cement, and metals are made from minerals. How about your clothes? Most of your clothing is made from cotton, polyester, or nylon. Cotton comes from cotton plants. Polyester and nylon are made from oil. Plastics are made from oil too. How about your food? People eat grains, fruits, and other parts of plants. People may also enjoy dairy products and meat from animals. Everything we have or use is made from a natural resource. Which of those mentioned here are renewable? Which are nonrenewable?

Trees are one of the most useful renewable natural resources. We use trees to produce almost 8,000 diff erent things. Wood is used to make most of these products. Tree wood is in our homes, furniture, paper, and on and on. Tree chemicals are also used to produce things like rayon cloth, food, medicine, and rubber.

By-products are things made out of leftovers. For example, when a tree is cut down and sawn up for wood, the leftover sawdust can be used for fuel, making particle board, or animal bedding. These are by-products. Another by-product from harvesting trees is bark mulch for gardens.

All natural resources should be used wisely. We must *conserve* natural resources. Conserve means to not use up, spoil, or waste things. This is especially true for the non-renewable resources. However, even some renewable natural resources can run out if they are all killed or overused. We must also protect our natural resources from pollution. Pollution occurs when people put harmful chemicals and other things into nature. Oil spilled in water, toxic chemicals in the air, or garbage dumped on the side of the road are examples of this problem. So what can you do to take care of natural resources? You can reduce, reuse, and recycle! For example, turn off the lights when you are not in a room. This will reduce the use of fossil fuel used to make electricity. Ride your bicycle and walk more, to reduce the amount of gasoline used to transport you. You can reuse things. Things like plastic jugs, jars, paper, and bags can be reused. Each time you reuse something, you conserve the natural resources that would have been used to make new ones. Finally, you can recycle. Recycle means to reuse a natural resource or product to make something new. It also means to collect and send these things for reuse. Items that can be easily recycled include: glass, some plastics, paper, cardboard, aluminum, and steel. Some plastics and metals are hard to recycle. They are often made from mixtures of materials. Mixtures can be hard to separate. Try to buy and use things that you can recycle. Natural resources, both renewable and nonrenewable, are important to all of us. We must conserve and carefully use natural resources. Our future depends on them.

Where does your garbage go when you throw it away? One place it goes is to a landfill. A landfill is a place made for safely putting garbage. Garbage must stay closed in the landfi ll so it doesn't pollute the ground, air, or water. Another place that garbage can go is into an incinerator. An incinerator is a large oven that burns garbage down to ashes. The ashes are then put in a landfill. A third place that some types of garbage can go is into a compost pile. A compost pile is made from natural garbage such as food scraps, leaves, and grass clippings. Compost piles help this garbage rot. After it rots, it can be put back on the earth to fertilize plants. The movement of garbage from a home or community to one of these places, like a landfill, is called the waste stream.

Nutrients are chemicals that living things need. They are renewable natural resources. They move round and round in cycles and never run out. When an animal eats a plant, it takes in nutrients. The nutrients are used in the animal's body and then many come out as waste, which returns the nutrients to the soil. When the animal dies, nutrients will return to the soil as well. Plants take up the nutrients in the soil and continue the cycle.

3

Soil and Water

Soil is the naturally occurring, unconsolidated or loose covering on the Earth's surface. Soil is composed of particles of broken rock that have been altered by chemical and environmental processes including weathering and erosion. Soil is different from its parent rock(s) source(s), altered by interactions between the lithosphere, hydrosphere, atmosphere, and the biosphere It is a mixture of mineral and organic constituents that are in solid, gaseous and aqueous states Soil particles pack loosely, forming a soil structure filled with pore spaces. These pores contain sol solution (liquid) and air (gas) Accordingly, soils are often treated as a three state system. Most soils have a density between 1 and 2 g/ cm^3. Soil is also known as earth: it is the substance from which our planet takes its name. Little of the soil composition of the earth is older than Tertiary and most no older than Pleistocene.

Soil Forming Factors

Soil formation, or pedogenesis, is the combined effect of physical, chemical, biological, and anthropogenic processes on soil parent material. Soil genesis involves processes that develop layers or horizons in the soil profile. These processes involve additions, losses, transformations and translocations of material that compose the soil. Minerals derived from weathered rocks undergo changes that cause the formation of secondary minerals and other compounds that are variably soluble in water, these constitutes are moved (translocated) from one area of the soil to other areas by water and animal activity. The alteration and movement of materials within soil causes the formation of distinctive soil horizons. The weathering of bedrock produces the parent material that soils form from. An example of soil development from bare rock occurs on recent lava flows in warm regions under heavy and very frequent rainfall. In such climates plants become established very quickly on basaltic lava, even though there is very little organic material. The plants are supported by the porous rock becoming filled with nutrient bearing water, for example carrying dissolved bird droppings or guano. The developing plant roots themselves gradually break up the porous lava and organic matter soon accumulates. But even before it does, the predominantly porous broken lava in which the plant roots grow can be considered a soil. How the soil "life" cycle proceeds is influenced by at least five classic soil forming factors that are dyna-mically intert-wined in sha-ping the way soil is

Fig. 3.1

developed, they include: parent material, regional cli-mate, topography, biotic potential and the passage of time.

Parent Material

The material from which soils form is called parent material, they include: weathered primary bedrock, secondary material transported from other locations, e.g. colluvium and alluvium, deposits that are already present but mixed or altered in other ways - old soil formations, organic material including peat or alpine humus, anthropogenic materials - like landfill or mine waste. Few soils form directly from the underlying rocks they develop on. The soils that do form directly from the breakdown or weathering of rocks are often called "residual soils" and they have the same general chemistry as their parent rocks. Most soils are derived from materials that have been transported from other locations by the wind, water and gravity. Some of these materials may have moved many miles or only a few feet. Windblown material called loess is common in the Midwest of North America and in Central Asia and other locations. Glacial till is a component of many soils in the northern and southern latitudes and those formed near large mountains, and is the product of glacial ice moving over the ground, ice can break rock and larger stones into smaller pieces, it also can sort material into different sizes. As glacial ice melts, the melt water also moves and sorts material and deposits it varying distances from its origin. The deeper sections of the soil profile may have materials that are relatively unchanged from when they were deposited by water, ice, or wind.

Weather is the first stage in the transforming of parent material into soil material. In soils forming from bedrock, a thick layer of weathered material called saprolite may form. Saprolite is the result of weathering processes that include: hydrolysis (the replacement of a mineral's cations with hydrogen ions), chelation from organic compounds, hydration - the absorption of water by minerals, dissolution by solution - where minerals are dissolved by water, and physical processes that include freezing/thawing or wetting/drying. The mineralogical and chemical composition of the primary bedrock material, plus physical features, including grain size and degree of consolidation plus the rate and type of weathering transforms it into different soil materials.

Climate

Soil formation is greatly dependent on the climate, and soils from different climate zones show distinctive characteristics Temperature and moisture affect weathering and leaching. Wind moves sand and other particles from one location to another, especially in arid regions where there is no or little plant cover. The type and amount of precipitation influence soil formation by affecting the movement of ions and particles through the soil, aiding in the development of different soil profiles. Seasonal and daily temperature fluctuations affect the effectiveness of water in weathering parent rock material and affect soil dynamics, freezing and thawing is an affective mechanism to break up rocks and other consolidated materials. Temperature and precipitation rates affect biological activity, rates of chemical reactions, and types of vegetation cover.

Topography

Slope and surface orientation affect the moisture and temperature of soil and affect the rate of weathering of parent material. Steep slopes facing the sun are warmer. Steep land areas may erode faster than soil formation process or deposition rates add material, causing a net loss of topsoil. Low areas receive deposits from areas up slope, often producing deeper soils. Topography effects erosion and depositional rates; water moves materials from steep higher elevations to lower, flatter locations. Sediments along river banks, on flood plains and deltas have different textures, dependent on the rate and duration of water flow; fast moving water can move larger material along with fine material, while slow moving water moves finer material only Water in rivers and wind with strong enough currents leave gravel, rocks, and sand behind while removing smaller sized particles which are deposited when the currents slow down. Bodies of water like lakes, ponds and shallow seas leave fine textured material, which form fine textured sediments like clay and silt.

Fig. 3.2

Biological Factors

Plants, animals, fungi, bacteria and humans affect soil formation. Animals and micro-organisms mix soils and form burrows and pores allowing moisture and gases to seep into deeper layers. In the same way, plant roots open channels in the soils, especially plants with deep taproots which can penetrate many meters through the different soil layers bringing up nutrients from deeper in the soil. Plants with fibrous roots that spread out near the soil surface, have roots that are easily decomposed, adding organic matter. Micro-organisms, including fungi and bacteria affect chemical exchanges between roots and soil and act as a reserve of nutrients. Humans can impact soil formation by removing vegetation cover which promotes greater erosion and they can mix the different soil layers freely, restarting the soil formation process as less weathered material is mixed with and diluting the more developed upper layers.

Vegetation impacts soils in numerous ways; it can prevent erosion from rain or surface runoff, it shades soils - keeping them cooler and slows down the evaporation of soil moisture or can cause soils to dry out by transpiration. Plants can form new chemicals that break down or build up soil particles. Vegetation cover is dependent on climate, land form topography, and biological factors. Soil factors such as soil density, depth, chemistry, and Ph; plus temperature, and moisture levels greatly affect the type of plants that can grow in any given location. Dead plants and dropped leaves and stems of plants fall to the surface and decompose on the soil, where organisms feed on them and mix it with the upper soil layers; these organic compounds become part of the soil formation process, ultimately shaping the type of soil formed.

Time

Time is a factor in the interactions of all the above factors as they interplay to develop varying types of soils. Over time, soils evolve features dependent on the other forming factors, and soil formation is a time responsive process dependent on how the other factors interplay with each other, as such soils are always in a state of development or change. For instance, recently deposited material from a flood exhibits no soil development because there has not been enough time for soil forming activities. The underlining soil surface and horizons have become buried

Fig. 3.3

and the time clock resets for these soils. Soil is always changing. The long periods over which change occurs and the multiple influences of change mean that simple soils are rare, resulting in the formation of soil horizons. While soil can achieve relative stability in properties for extended periods of time, the soil life cycle ultimately ends in soil conditions that leave it vulnerable to erosion. Despite the inevitability of soils retrogression and degradation, most soil cycles are long and productive.

Soil forming factors continue to affect soils during their existence, even on "stable" landscapes that are long enduring, some for millions of years. Materials are deposited on top of them and materials are blown or washed away from the surface. With additions, removals, and alterations - soils are always subject to new conditions and whether these are slow or rapid changes, depending on climate, landscape position, and biological activity, soils are always in a dynamically dependent state of change.

Characteristics

Soil colour is often the first impression one has when viewing soil. Striking colors and contrasting patterns are especially memorable. The Red River (Mississippi watershed) carries sediment eroded from extensive reddish soils like Port Silt Loam in Oklahoma. The Yellow River in China carries yellow sediment from eroding loessal soils. Mollisols in the Great Plains are darkened and enriched by organic matter. Podsols in boreal forests have highly contrasting layers due to acidity and leaching. Soil color is primarily influenced by soil mineralogy. The extensive and various iron minerals in soils are responsible for many soil colors. The development and distribution of colour within a soil profile result from chemical weathering, especially redox reactions. As the primary minerals in soil parent material weather, the elements combine into new and colourful compounds. Iron forms secondary minerals with a yellow or red colour, organic matter decomposes into black and brown compounds, and manganese forms black mineral deposits. These pigments produce various colour patterns as a result of the affects by the environment during soil formation: aerobic conditions produce uniform or gradual colour changes, while reducing environments result in disrupted colour flow with complex, mottled patterns and points of colour concentration. Soil colour results from chemical and biological weathering. As the primary minerals in parent material weather, the elements combine into new and colourful compounds. Iron forms secondary minerals with a yellow or red colour; organic matter decomposes into brown compounds; and manganese, sulfur and nitrogen can form black mineral deposits.

Soil structure is the arrangement of soil particles into aggregates. These may have various shapes, sizes and degrees of development or expression Soil structure affects aeration, water movement, resistance to erosion, and plant root growth. Structure often gives clues to texture, organic matter content, biological activity, past soil evolution and human use, and chemical and mineralogical conditions under which the soil formed.

Soil texture refers to sand, silt and clay composition. Sand and silt are the product of physical weathering while soil is the product of chemical weathering. Soil content is influential on soil behavior, affecting the retention capacity for nutrients and water. Sand and silt are the products of physical weathering, while clay is the product of chemical weathering. Clay content is influential on soil behavior because it has retention capacity for nutrients and water. Clay soils resist wind and water erosion better than silty and sandy soils, because the particals are more tightly joined to each other. In medium textured soils, clay often is often translocated downward through the soil profile and accumulates in the subsoil.

The electrical resistivity of soil can affect the rate of galvanic corrosion of metallic structures in contact with it. Higher moister content or increased electrolyte concentration can lower the resistivity and thereby increase the rate of corrosion. Soil resistivity values typically range from about 2 to 1000 O·m, but more extreme values are not unusual.

Soil Horizons

The naming of soil horizons is based on the type of material the horizons are composed of; these materials reflect the duration of the specific processes used in soil formation. They are labeled using a short hand notation of letters and numbers They are described and classified by their color, size, texture, structure, consistency, root quantity, pH, voids, boundary characteristics, and if they have nodules or concretions Any one soil profile does not have all the major horizons covered below, soils may have few or many horizons.

The exposure of parent material to favorable conditions produces initial soils that are suitable for plant growth. Plant growth often results in the accumulation of organic residues, the accumulated organic layer is called the O horizon. Biological organisms colonize and break down organic materials, making available nutrients that other plants and animals can live on, and after sufficient time, a distinctive organic surface layer forms with humus which is called the A horizon.

Soil Classification

Soil is classified into different groups or categories so that relationships are better understood between different soils. The different groupings help determine the usefulness of any soil for any particular use. One of the first classification systems was developed by the Russian scientist Dokuchaev around 1880, it was modified a number of times by American and European researches and developed into the system commonly used until the 1960's. It was based on the idea that soils have a particular morphology based on the the materials and factors that form them. In the 1960's a different classification system began to emerge that stressed just soil morphology and relied less on soil parental materials and soil forming factors. Since then it has undergone further modifications.

Soil Orders

Orders are the highest category of soil classification, order types end in the letters sol. In the US classification system there are ten orders.

- *Entisol* - are recently formed soils, that lack well developed horizons. Commonly found on unconsolidated sediments like sand, some have an A horizon on top of bedrock.
- *Vertisol* - are inverted soils, they tend to swell when wet and shrink upon drying, often forming deep cracks that surface layers can fall into.
- *Inceptisol* - are young soils. They have subsurface horizon formation but show little eluviation and illuviation.
- *Aridisol* - are dry soils forming under desert conditions. They include nearly 20 per cent of soils worldwide. Soil formation is slow, and accumulated organic matter is scarce. May have a subsurface zones (calcic horizons) where calcium carbonates have accumulated from percolating water. Many have well developed Bt horizons showing clay movement from past periods of more moisture.
- *Mollisol* - are soft soils.
- *Spodosol* - are soils that are the product of podsolization. They are typical soils of coniferous and deciduous forests in cooler climates.

- *Alfisol* - soils with aluminum and iron. They have horizons of were clay accumulates and form where there is enough moisture and it is warm enough for at least three months of plants growth.
- *Ultisol* - are soils that are heavily leached.
- *Oxisol* - soil with heavy oxide content.
- *Histosol* - organic soils.

Other order schemes may include:

- *Andisols* - volcanic soils, tend to be high in glass content.
- *Gelisols* - permafrost soils.

Organic Matter

Most living things in soils, including plants, insects, bacteria and fungi, are dependent on organic matter for nutrients and energy. Soils often have varying degrees of organic compounds in different states of decomposition. Many soils, including desert and rocky-gravel soils, have no or little organic matter; while soils, such as peat (Histosols), that are all organic matter are infertile.

Humus

Humus refers to organic matter that has decomposed to a point where it is resistant to further breakdown or alteration. Humic acids and fulvic acids are important constituents of humus and typically form from plant residues such as foliage, stems and roots. After death, these plant residues begin to decay, starting the formation of humus. Humus formation involves changes within the soil and plant residue, there is a reduction of water soluble constituents including cellulose and hemicellulose; as the residues are deposited and break down, humin, lignin and lignin complexes accumulate within the soil; as microorganisms live and feed on the decaying plant matter, an increase in proteins occurs.

Lignin is resistant to breakdown and accumulates within the soil, it also chemically reacts with amino acids which add to its resistance to decomposition, including enzymatic decomposition by microbes. Fats and waxes from plant matter have some resistance to decomposition and persist in soils for a while. Proteins normally decompose readily but when bound to clay particles they become more resistant to decomposition, clay particles also absorb enzymes that would break down proteins, thus clay soils often have higher organic contents that persist longer than soils without clay. The addition of organic matter to clay soils, can render the organic matter and any added nutrients inaccessible to plants and microbes for many years, since they can bind strongly to the clay. High soil tannin (polyphenol) content from plants can cause nitrogen to be sequestered by proteins or cause nitrogen immobilization, also making nitrogen unavailable to plants.

Humus formation is a processes dependent on the amount of plant material added each year and the type of base soil; both are affected by climate and the type of microorganisms present. Soils with humus can vary in nitrogen content but have 3 to 6 per cent nitrogen typically; humus as a reserve of nitrogen and phosphorus, is a vital component effecting soil fertility Humus also adsorbs water, acting as a moisture reserve, that plants can utilize; it also expands and shrinks between dry and wet states, providing pore spaces. Humus is less stable than other soil constituents, because it is affected by microbial decomposition, and over time its concentration decreases without the addition of new organic matter.

Climate and Organics

The production and accumulation or degradation of organic matter and humus is greatly depended on climate conditions. Temperature and soil moisture are the major factors in the formation or degradation of organic matter, they along with topography, determine the formation of organic soils. Soils high in organic matter tend to form under wet conditions and/or were there is enough precipitation to sustain thick plant growth.

Soil Solutions

Different soils, under varying conditions, have diverse colloidal solutions. These solutions exchange gases with the soil atmosphere. These solutions can contain dissolved sugars, fulvic acids and other organic acids, plant micronutrients such as zinc, iron and copper, plus other metals, ammonium plus a host of others. Some soils have sodium solutions that great impact plant growth, calcium is common in forest soils. Soil pH effects the type and amount of anions and cations that soil solutions contain and exchange with the soil atmosphere and biological organisms.

In Nature

Biogeography is the study of special variations in biological communities. Soils are restricting factor as to what plants can grow in which environments. Soil scientists survey soils in the hope of understanding controls as to what vegetation can and will grow in a particular location.

Geologists also have a particular interest in the patterns of soil on the surface of the earth. Soil texture, color and chemistry often reflect the underlying geologic parent material and soil types often change at geologic unit boundaries. Buried paleosols mark previous land surfaces and record climatic conditions from previous eras. Geologists use this paleopedological record to understand the ecological relationships in past ecosystems. According to the theory of biorhexistasy, prolonged conditions conducive to forming deep, weathered soils result in increasing ocean salinity and the formation of limestone.

Geologists use soil profile features to establish the duration of surface stability in the context of geologic faults or slope stability. An offset subsoil horizon indicates rupture during soil formation and the degree of subsequent subsoil formation is relied upon to establish time since rupture.

Due to their thermal mass, rammed earth walls fit in with environmental sustainability aspirations.

A homeowner sifts soil made from his compost bin in background. Composting is an excellent way to recycle household and yard wastes.

Soil examined in shovel test pits is used by archaeologists for relative dating based on stratigraphy (as opposed to absolute dating). What is considered most typical is to use soil profile features to determine the maximum reasonable pit depth than needs to be examined for archaeological evidence in the interest of cultural resources management. Terra preta do Indio.

Uses

This section requires expansion with: examples of uses of soil as a material and uses involving soil as a natural resource. Soil is used in agriculture, where it serves as the primary nutrient base for the plants. The types of soil used in agriculture (among other things, such as the purported level of moisture in the soil) vary with respect to the species of plants that are cultivated.

Soil material is a critical component in the mining and construction industries. Soil serves as a foundation for most construction projects. Massive volumes of soil can be involved in surface mining, road building, and dam construction. Earth sheltering is the architectural practice of using soil for external thermal mass against building walls.

Soil resources are critical to the environment, as well as to food and fiber production. Soil provides minerals and water to plants. Soil absorbs rainwater and releases it later thus preventing floods and drought. Soil cleans the water as it percolates. Soil is the habitat for many organisms.

Waste management often has a soil component. Septic drain fields treat septic tank effluent using aerobic soil processes. Landfills use soil for daily cover.

Soils filter and purifying water and effect its chemistry. Rain water and pooled water from ponds, lakes and rivers percolated through the soil horizons and the upper rock strata, and thus becomes groundwater. Pollutants such as viruses, oils, metals, excess nutrients, and sediments are filtered out by the soil and soil organisms.

Degradation

Land degradation is a human induced or natural process which impairs the capacity of land to function. Soils are the critical component in land degradation when it involves acidification, contamination, desertification, erosion, or salination.

While soil acidification of alkaline soils is beneficial, it degrades land when soil acidity lowers crop productivity and increases soil vulnerability to contamination and erosion. Soils are often initially acid because their parent materials were acid and initially low in the basic cations (calcium, magnesium, potassium, and sodium). Acidification occurs when these elements are removed from the soil profile by normal rainfall or the harvesting of crops. Soil acidification is accelerated by the use of acid-forming nitrogenous fertilizers and by the effects of acid precipitation.

Soil contamination at low levels are often within soil capacity to treat and assimilate. Many waste treatment processes rely on this treatment capacity. Exceeding treatment capacity can damage soil biota and limit soil function. Derelict soils occur where industrial contamination or other development activity damages the soil to such a degree that the land cannot be used safely or productively. Remediation of derelict soil uses principles of geology, physics, chemistry, and biology to degrade, attenuate, isolate, or remove soil contaminants and to restore soil functions and values. Techniques include leaching, air sparging, chemical amendments, phytoremediation, bioremediation, and natural attenuation.

Desertification is an environmental process of ecosystem degradation in arid and semi-arid regions, or as a result of human activity. It is a common misconception that droughts cause desertification. Droughts are common in arid and semiarid lands. Well-managed lands can recover from drought when the rains return. Soil management tools include maintaining soil nutrient and organic matter levels, reduced tillage and increased cover. These help to control erosion and maintain productivity during periods when moisture is available. Continued land abuse during droughts, however, increases land degradation. Increased population and livestock pressure on marginal lands accelerates desertification.

Soil erosional loss is caused by wind, water, ice, movement in response to gravity. Although the processes may be simultaneous, erosion is distinguished from weathering. Erosion is an intrinsic natural process, but in many places it is increased by human land use. Poor land use practices include deforestation, overgrazing, and improper construction activity. Improved management can limit erosion using techniques like limiting disturbance during construction, avoiding construction during erosion prone periods, intercepting runoff, terrace-building, use of erosion suppressing cover materials and planting trees or other soil binding plants.

A serious and long-running water erosion problem is in China, on the middle reaches of the Yellow River and the upper reaches of the Yangtze River. From the Yellow River, over 1.6 billion tons of sediment flow each year into the ocean. The sediment originates primarily from water erosion (Gully erosion) in the Loess Plateau region of northwest China.

Soil piping is a particular form of soil erosion that occurs below the soil surface. It is associated with levee and dam failure as well as sink hole formation. Turbulent flow removes soil starting from the mouth of the seep flow and subsoil erosion advances upgradient The term sand boil is used to describe the appearance of the discharging end of an active soil pipe.

Soil salination is the accumulation of free salts to such an extent that it leads to degradation of soils and vegetation. Consequences include corrosion damage, reduced plant growth, erosion due to loss of plant cover and soil structure, and water quality problems due to sedimentation. Salination occurs due to a combination of natural and human caused processes. Aridic conditions favor salt accumulation. This is especially apparent when soil parent material is saline. Irrigation of arid lands is especially problematic. All irrigation water has some level of salinity. Irrigation, especially when it involves leakage from canals, often raise the underlying water table. Rapid salination occurs when the land surface is within the capillary fringe of saline groundwater. Salinity control involves flushing with higher levels of applied water in combination with tile drainage.

Water

Water in three states: liquid, solid (ice), and (invisible) vapor in air. Clouds are droplets of liquid, condensed from water vapour.

Water is a common chemical substance that is essential for the survival of all known forms of life. In typical usage, *water* refers only to its liquid form or state, but the substance also has a solid state, *ice*, and a gaseous state, *water vapour* or *steam*. Water covers 71% of the Earth's surface . On Earth, it is found mostly in oceans and other large water bodies, with 1.6% of water below ground in aquifers and 0.001% in the air as vapour, clouds (formed of solid and liquid water particles suspended in air), and precipitation Saltwater oceans hold 97% of surface water, glaciers and polar ice caps 2.4%, and other land surface water such as rivers, lakes and ponds 0.6%. A very small amount of the Earth's water is contained within biological bodies and manufactured products. Other water is trapped in ice caps, glaciers, aquifers, or in lakes, sometimes providing fresh water for life on land.

Fig. 3.4

Water moves continually through a cycle of evaporation or transpiration (evapotranspiration), precipitation, and runoff, usually reaching the sea. Winds carry water vapor over land at the same rate as runoff into the sea, about 36 Tt (1012kilograms) per year. Over land, evaporation and transpiration contribute another 71 Tt per year to the precipitation of 107 Tt per year over land.

Clean, fresh drinking water is essential to human and other life. Access to safe drinking water has improved steadily and substantially over the last decades in almost every part of the world However, some observers have estimated that by 2025 more than half of the world population will be facing water-based vulnerability a situation which has been called a water crisis by the United Nations. Water plays an important role in the world economy, as it functions as a solvent for a wide variety of chemical substances and facilitates industrial cooling and transportation. Approximately 70 per cent of freshwater is consumed by agriculture.

Types of Water

Water can appear in three states; it is one of the very few substances to be found naturally in all three states on earth. Water takes many different forms on Earth: water vapor and clouds in the sky; seawater and rarely icebergs in the ocean; glaciers and rivers in the mountains; and the liquid in aquifers in the ground.

Water can dissolve many different substances, giving it different tastes and odors. In fact, humans and other animals have developed senses which are, to a degree, able to evaluate the potability of water, avoiding water that is too salty or putrid. Humans also tend to prefer cold water to lukewarm; cold water is likely to contain fewer microbes. The taste advertised in spring water or mineral water derives from the minerals dissolved in it, as pure H_2O is tasteless. As such, purity in spring and mineral water refers to purity from toxins, pollutants, and microbes.

Water in the Universe

Much of the universe's water may be produced as a byproduct of star formation. When stars are born, their birth is accompanied by a strong outward wind of gas and dust. When this outflow of material eventually impacts the surrounding gas, the shock waves that are created compress and heat the gas. The water observed is quickly produced in this warm dense gas.

Water has been detected in interstellar clouds within our galaxy, the Milky Way. It is believed that water exists in abundance in other galaxies too, because its components, hydrogen and oxygen, are among the most abundant elements in the universe. Interstellar clouds eventually condense into solar nebulae and solar systems, such as ours.

Water vapour is present on:

- *Mercury* - 3.4% in the atmosphere, and large amounts of water in Mercury's exosphere.
- *Venus* - 0.002% in the atmosphere.
- *Earth* - trace in the atmosphere (varies with climate).
- *Mars* - 0.03% in the atmosphere.
- *Jupiter* - 0.0004% in the atmosphere.
- *Saturn* - in ices only.
- *Enceladus* (moon of Saturn) - 91% in the atmosphere exoplanets known as HD 189733 b and HD 209458 b.

Liquid water is present on:

- *Earth* - 71% of surface.
- *Moon* - small amounts of water have been found (in 2008) in the inside of volcanic pearls brought from Moon to Earth by the Apollo 15 crew in 1971. Strong evidence suggests that liquid water is present just under the surface of Saturn's moon Enceladus. There is probably some liquid water on Europa.

Water ice is present on:

- *Earth* - mainly on ice sheets
- polar ice caps on Mars
- Titan
- Europa
- Enceladus

Probability or possibility of distribution of water ice is at: lunar ice on the Moon, Ceres (dwarf planet), Tethys (moon). Ice is probably in internal structure of Uranus, Neptune, and Pluto and on comets.

Fig. 3.5

Water and Habitable Zone

The existence of liquid water, and to a lesser extent its gaseous and solid forms, on Earth is vital to the existence of life on Earth as we know it. The Earth is located in the habitable zone of the solar system; if it were slightly closer to or further from the Sun (about 5%, or about 8 million kilometres), the conditions which allow the three forms to be present simultaneously would be far less likely to exist.

Earth's mass allows gravity to hold an atmosphere. Water vapor and carbon dioxide in the atmosphere provide a greenhouse effect which helps maintain a relatively steady surface temperature. If Earth were smaller, a thinner atmosphere would cause temperature extremes preventing the accumulation of water except in polar ice caps (as on Mars).

It has been proposed that life itself may maintain the conditions that have allowed its continued existence. The surface temperature of Earth has been relatively constant through geologic time despite varying levels of incoming solar radiation (insolation), indicating that a dynamic process governs Earth's temperature via a combination of greenhouse gases and surface or atmospheric albedo. This proposal is known as the *Gaia hypothesis*.

The state of water also depends on a planet's gravity. If a planet is sufficiently massive, the water on it may be solid even at high temperatures, because of the high pressure caused by gravity.

There are various theories about origin of water on Earth.

Water on Earth

Water covers 71% of the Earth's surface; the oceans contain 97.2% of the Earth's water. The Antarctic ice sheet, which contains 90% of all fresh water on Earth, is visible at the bottom. Condensed atmospheric water can be seen as clouds, contributing to the Earth's albedo.

Hydrology is the study of the movement, distribution, and quality of water throughout the Earth. The study of the distribution of water is hydrography. The study of the distribution and movement of groundwater is hydrogeology, of glaciers is glaciology, of inland waters is limnology and distribution of oceans is oceanography. Ecological processes with hydrology are in focus of ecohydrology.

The collective mass of water found on, under, and over the surface of a planet is called the hydrosphere. Earth's approximate water volume (the total water supply of the world) is 1,360,000,000 km^3 (326 000 000 mi^3). Of this volume:

- 1,320,000,000 km^3 (316,900,000 mi^3 or 97.2%) is in the oceans.
- 25,000,000 km^3 (6,000,000 mi^3 or 1.8%) is in glaciers, ice caps and ice sheets.

- 13,000,000 km^3 (3,000,000 mi^3 or 0.9%) is groundwater.
- 250,000 km^3 (60,000 mi^3 or 0.02%) is fresh water in lakes, inland seas, and rivers.
- 13,000 km^3 (3,100 mi^3 or 0.001%) is atmospheric water vapour at any given time.

Groundwater and fresh water are useful or potentially useful to humans as water resources.

Liquid water is found in bodies of water, such as an ocean, sea, lake, river, stream, canal, pond, or puddle. The majority of water on Earth is sea water. Water is also present in the atmosphere in solid, liquid, and vapor states. It also exists as groundwater in aquifers.

The most important geological processes caused by water are: chemical weathering, water erosion, water sediment transport and sedimentation, mudflows, ice erosion and sedimentation by glacier.

Water Cycle

The water cycle (known scientifically as the hydrologic cycle) refers to the continuous exchange of water within the hydrosphere, between the atmosphere, soil water, surface water, groundwater, and plants.

Water moves perpetually through each of these regions in the *water cycle* consisting of following transfer processes:

- evaporation from oceans and other water bodies into the air and transpiration from land plants and animals into air.
- precipitation, from water vapor condensing from the air and falling to earth or ocean.

Most water vapour over the oceans returns to the oceans, but winds carry water vapor over land at the same rate as runoff into the sea, about 36 Tt per year. Over land, evaporation and transpiration contribute another 71 Tt per year. Precipitation, at a rate of 107 Tt per year over land, has several forms: most commonly rain, snow, and hail, with some contribution from fog and dew. Condensed water in the air may also refract sunlight to produce rainbows.

Water runoff often collects over watersheds flowing into rivers. A mathematical model used to simulate river or stream flow and calculate water quality parameters is hydrological transport model. Some of water is diverted to irrigation for agriculture. Rivers and seas offer opportunity for travel and commerce. Through erosion, runoff shapes the environment creating river valleys and deltas which provide rich soil and level ground for the establishment of population centers. A flood occurs when an area of land, usually low-lying, is covered with water. It is when a river overflows its banks or flood from the sea. A drought is an extended period of months or years when a region notes a deficiency in its water supply. This occurs when a region receives consistently below average precipitation.

Fresh Water Storage

Some runoff water is trapped for periods, for example in lakes. At high altitude, during winter, and in the far north and south, snow collects in ice caps, snow pack and glaciers. Water also infiltrates the ground and goes into aquifers. This groundwater later flows back to the surface in springs, or more spectacularly in hot springs and geysers. Groundwater is also extracted artificially in wells. This water storage is important, since clean, fresh water is essential to human and other land-based life. In many parts of the world, it is in short supply.

Tides

Tides are the cyclic rising and falling of Earth's ocean surface caused by the tidal forces of the Moon and the Sun acting on the oceans. Tides cause changes in the depth of the marine and estuarine water bodies and produce oscillating currents known as tidal streams. The changing tide produced at a given location is the result of the changing positions of the Moon and Sun relative to the Earth coupled with the effects of Earth rotation and the local bathymetry. The strip of seashore that is submerged at high tide and exposed at low tide, the intertidal zone, is an important ecological product of ocean tides.

Effects on Life

From a biological standpoint, water has many distinct properties that are critical for the proliferation of life that set it apart from other substances. It carries out this role by allowing organic compounds to react in ways that ultimately allow replication. All known forms of life depend on water. Water is vital both as a solvent in which many of the body's solutes dissolve and as an essential part of many metabolic processes within the body. Metabolism is the sum total of anabolism and catabolism. In anabolism, water is removed from molecules (through energy requiring enzymatic chemical reactions) in order to grow larger molecules (e.g. starches, triglycerides and proteins for storage of fuels and information). In catabolism, water is used to break bonds in order to generate smaller molecules (e.g. glucose, fatty acids and amino acids to be used for fuels for energy use or other purposes). Water is thus essential and central to these metabolic processes. Therefore, without water, these metabolic processes would cease to exist, leaving us to muse about what processes would be in its place, such as gas absorption, dust collection, etc.

Water is also central to photosynthesis and respiration. Photosynthetic cells use the sun's energy to split off water's hydrogen from oxygen. Hydrogen is combined with CO_2 (absorbed from air or water) to form glucose and release oxygen. All living cells use such fuels and oxidize the hydrogen and carbon to capture the sun's energy and reform water and CO_2 in the process (cellular respiration).

Water is also central to acid-base neutrality and enzyme function. An acid, a hydrogen ion (H^+, that is, a proton) donor, can be neutralized by a base, a proton acceptor such as hydroxide ion (OH^-) to form water. Water is considered to be neutral, with a pH (the negative log of the hydrogen ion concentration) of 7. Acids have pH values less than 7 while bases have values greater than 7. Stomach acid (HCl) is useful to digestion. However, its corrosive effect on the esophagus during reflux can temporarily be neutralized by ingestion of a base such as aluminum hydroxide to produce the neutral molecules water and the salt aluminum chloride. Human biochemistry that involves enzymes usually performs optimally around a biologically neutral pH of 7.4.

For example a cell of *Escherichia coli* contains 70% of water, a human body 60-70%, plant body up to 90% and the body of an adult jellyfish is made up of 94-98% water.

Aquatic Life Forms

Earth's waters are filled with life. The earliest life forms appeared in water; nearly all fish live exclusively in water, and there are many types of marine mammals, such as dolphins and whales that also live in the water. Some kinds of animals, such as amphibians, spend portions of their lives in water and portions on land. Plants such as kelp and algae grow in the water and are the basis for some underwater ecosystems. Plankton is generally the foundation of the ocean food chain.

Aquatic animals must obtain oxygen to survive, and they do so in various ways. Fish have gills instead of lungs, although some species of fish, such as the lungfish, have both. Marine mammals, such as dolphins, whales, otters, and seals need to surface periodically to breathe air. Smaller life forms are able to absorb oxygen through their skin.

Effects on Human Civilization

Civilization has historically flourished around rivers and major waterways; Mesopotamia, the so-called cradle of civilization, was situated between the major rivers Tigris and Euphrates; the ancient society of the Egyptians depended entirely upon the Nile. Large metropolises like Rotterdam, London, Montreal, Paris, New York City, Buenos Aires, Shanghai, Tokyo, Chicago, and Hong Kong owe their success in part to their easy accessibility via water and the resultant expansion of trade. Islands with safe water ports, like Singapore, have flourished for the same reason. In places such as North Africa and the Middle East, where water is more scarce, access to clean drinking water was and is a major factor in human development.

Health and Pollution

Water fit for human consumption is called drinking water or potable water. Water that is not potable can be made potable by filtration or distillation (heating it until it becomes water vapor, and then capturing the vapor without any of the impurities it leaves behind), or by other methods (chemical or heat treatment that kills bacteria). Sometimes the term safe water is applied to potable water of a lower quality threshold (i.e., it is used effectively for nutrition in humans that have weak access to water cleaning processes, and does more good than harm). Water that is not fit for drinking but is not harmful for humans when used for swimming or bathing is called by various names other than potable or drinking water, and is sometimes called safe water, or "safe for bathing". Chlorine is a skin and mucous membrane irritant that is used to make water safe for bathing or drinking. Its use is highly technical and is usually monitored by government regulations (typically 1 part per million (ppm) for drinking water, and 1-2 ppm of chlorine not yet reacted with impurities for bathing water).

This natural resource is becoming scarcer in certain places, and its availability is a major social and economic concern. Currently, about 1 billion people around the world routinely drink unhealthy water. Most countries accepted the goal of halving by 2015 the number of people worldwide who do not have access to safe water and sanitation during the 2003 G8 Evian summit. Even if this difficult goal is met, it will still leave more than an estimated half a billion people without access to safe drinking water and over 1 billion without access to adequate sanitation. Poor water quality and bad sanitation are deadly; some 5 million deaths a year are caused by polluted drinking water. The World Health Organization estimates that safe water could prevent 1.4 million child deaths from diarrhea each year. Water, however, is not a finite resource, but rather re-circulated as potable water in precipitation in quantities many degrees of magnitude higher than human consumption. Therefore, it is the relatively small quantity of water in reserve in the earth (about 1% of our drinking water supply, which is replenished in aquifers around every 1 to 10 years), that is a non-renewable resource, and it is, rather, the distribution of potable and irrigation water which is scarce, rather than the actual amount of it that exists on the earth. Water-poor countries use importation of goods as the primary method of importing water (to leave enough for local human consumption), since the manufacturing process uses around 10 to 100 times products' masses in water.

In the developing world, 90% of all wastewater still goes untreated into local rivers and streams. Some 50 countries, with roughly a third of the world's population, also suffer from medium or high water stress, and 17 of these extract more water annually than is recharged through their natural water cycles The strain not only affects surface freshwater bodies like rivers and lakes, but it also degrades groundwater resources.

Agriculture

The most important use of water in agriculture is for an irrigation and irrigation is key component to produce enough food. Irrigation takes up to 90% of water withdrawn in some developing countries.

As a Scientific Standard

On 7 April 1795, the gram was defined in France to be equal to "the absolute weight of a volume of pure water equal to a cube of one hundredth of a meter, and to the temperature of the melting ice. For practical purposes though, a metallic reference standard was required, one thousand times more massive, the kilogram. Work was therefore commissioned to determine precisely how massive one liter of water was. In spite of the fact that the decreed definition of the gram specified water at 0 °C—a highly stable *temperature* point—the scientists chose to redefine the standard and to perform their measurements at the most stable *density* point: the temperature at which water reaches maximum density, which was measured at the time as 4 °C.

The Kelvin temperature scale of the SI system is based on the triple point of water, defined as exactly 273.16 K or 0.01 °C. The scale is a more accurate development of the Celsius temperature scale, which is defined by the boiling point (100 °C) and melting point (0 °C) of water.

Natural water consists mainly of the isotopes hydrogen-1 and oxygen-16, but there is also small quantity of heavier isotopes such as hydrogen-2 (deuterium). The amount of deuterium oxides or heavy water is very small, but it still affects the properties of water. Water from rivers and lakes tends to contain less deuterium than seawater. Therefore, a standard water called Vienna Standard Mean Ocean Water is defined as the standard water.

The human body is anywhere from 55% to 78% water depending on body size. To function properly, the body requires between one and seven liters of water per day to avoid dehydration; the precise amount depends on the level of activity, temperature, humidity, and other factors. Most of this is ingested through foods or beverages other than drinking straight water. It is not clear how much water intake is needed by healthy people, though most advocates agree that 6-7 glasses of water (approximately 2 litres) daily is the minimum to maintain proper hydration Medical literature favors a lower consumption, typically 1 liter of water for an average male, excluding extra requirements due to fluid loss from exercise or warm weather. For those who have healthy kidneys, it is rather difficult to drink too much water, but (especially in warm humid weather and while exercising) it is dangerous to drink too little. People can drink far more water than necessary while exercising, however, putting them at risk of water intoxication (hyperhydration), which can be fatal. The "fact" that a person should consume eight glasses of water per day cannot be traced back to a scientific source. There are other myths such as the effect of water on weight loss and constipation that have been dispelled.

An original recommendation for water intake in 1945 by the Food and Nutrition Board of the National Research Council read: "An ordinary standard for diverse persons is 1 millilitre for each calorie of food. Most of this quantity is contained in prepared foods." The latest dietary reference intake report by the United States National Research Council in general recommended (including food sources): 2.7 liters of water total for women and 3.7 liters for men. Specifically, pregnant and breastfeeding women need additional fluids to stay hydrated. According to the Institute of Medicine—who recommend that, on average, women consume 2.2 litres and men 3.0 litres—this is recommended to be 2.4 litres (approx. 9 cups) for pregnant women and 3 litres (approx. 12.5 cups) for breastfeeding women since an especially large amount of fluid is lost during nursing Also noted is that normally, about 20 per cent of water intake comes from food, while the rest comes from drinking water and beverages (caffeinated included).

Water is excreted from the body in multiple forms; through urine and feces, through sweating, and by exhalation of water vapor in the breath. With physical exertion and heat exposure, water loss will increase and daily fluid needs may increase as well. Humans require water that does not contain too many impurities. Common impurities include metal salts and/or harmful bacteria, such as *Vibrio*. Some solutes are acceptable and even desirable for taste enhancement and to provide needed electrolytes.

The single largest freshwater resource suitable for drinking is Lake Baikal in Siberia, which has a very low salt and calcium content and is very clean.

As a Dissolving Agent or Solvent

Dissolving (or suspending) is used to wash everyday items such as the human body, clothes, floors, cars, food, and pets. Also, human wastes are carried by water in the sewage system. Its use as a cleaning solvent consumes most of water in industrialized countries. Water can facilitate the chemical processing of wastewater. An aqueous environment can be favourable to the breakdown of pollutants, due to the ability to gain an homogenous solution that is pumpable and flexible to treat.

Aerobic treatment can be used by applying oxygen or air to a solution reduce the reactivity of substances within it. Water also facilitates biological processing of waste that have been dissolved within it. Microorganisms that live within water can access dissolved wastes and can feed upon them breaking them down into less polluting substances.

Reedbeds and anaerobic digesters are both examples of biological systems that are particularly suited to the treatment of effluents. Typically from both chemical and biological treatment of wastes, there is often a solid residue or cake that is left over from the treatment process. Depending upon its constituent parts, this 'cake' may be dried and spread on land as a fertilizer if it has beneficial properties, or alternatively disposed of in landfill or incinerated. Water and steam are used as heat transfer fluids in diverse heat exchange systems, due to its availability and high heat capacity, both as a coolant and for heating. Cool water may even be naturally available from a lake or the sea. Condensing steam is a particularly efficient heating fluid because of the large heat of vaporization. A disadvantage is that water and steam are somewhat corrosive.

In almost all electric power plants, water is the coolant, which vaporizes and drives steam turbines to drive generators. In the nuclear industry, water can also be used as a neutron moderator. In a pressurized water reactor, water is both a coolant and a moderator. This provides a passive safety measure, as removing the water from the reactor also slows the nuclear reaction down.

Extinguishing Fires

Water has a high heat of vaporization and is relatively inert, which makes it a good fire extinguishing fluid. The evaporation of water carries heat away from the fire. However, water cannot be used to fight fires of electric equipment, because impure water is electrically conductive, or of oils and organic solvents, because they float on water and the explosive boiling of water tends to spread the burning liquid. Use of water in fire fighting should also take into account the hazards of a steam explosion, which may occur when water is used on very hot fires in confined spaces, and of a hydrogen explosion, when substances which react with water, such as certain metals or hot graphite, decompose the water, producing hydrogen gas. The power of such explosions was seen in the Chernobyl disaster, although the water involved did not come from fire-fighting at that time but the reactor's own water cooling system. A steam explosion occurred when the extreme over-heating of the core caused water to flash into steam. A hydrogen explosion may have occurred as a result of reaction between steam and hot zirconium.

Chemical Uses

Organic reactions are usually quenched with water or a water solution of a suitable acid, base or buffer. Water is generally effective in removing inorganic salts. In inorganic reactions, water is a common solvent. In organic reactions, it is usually not used as a reaction solvent, because it does not dissolve the reactants well and is amphoteric (acidic and basic) and nucleophilic. Nevertheless, these properties are sometimes desirable. Also, acceleration of Diels-Alder reactions by water has been observed. Supercritical water has recently been a topic of research. Oxygen-saturated supercritical water combusts organic pollutants efficiently.

Recreation

Humans use water for many recreational purposes, as well as for exercising and for sports. Some of these include swimming, waterskiing, boating, and diving. In addition, some sports, like ice hockey and ice skating, are played on ice. Lakesides, beaches and waterparks are popular places for people to go to relax and enjoy recreation. Many find the sound of flowing water to be calming, too. Some keep fish and other life in aquariums or ponds for show, fun, and companionship.

Humans also use water for snow sports i.e. skiing or snowboarding, which requires the water to be frozen. People may also use water for play fighting such as with snowballs, water guns or water balloons. They may also make fountains and use water in their public or private decorations. Water plays many critical roles within the field of food science. It is important for a food scientist to understand the roles that water plays within food processing to ensure the success of their products. Solutes such as salts and sugars found in water affect the physical properties of water. The boiling and freezing points of water is affected by solutes. One mole of sucrose (sugar) raises the boiling point of water by 0.52 °C, and one mole of salt raises the boiling point by 1.04 °C while lowering the freezing point of water in a similar way. Solutes in water also affect water activity which affects many chemical reactions and the growth of microbes in food Water activity can be described as a ratio of the vapor pressure of water in a solution to the vapor pressure of pure water Solutes in water lower water activity.

This is important to know because most bacterial growth ceases at low levels of water activity Not only does microbial growth affect the safety of food but also the preservation and shelf life of food. Water hardness is also a critical factor in food processing. It can dramatically affect the quality of a product as well as playing a role in sanitation. Water hardness is classified based on the amounts of removable calcium carbonate salt it contains per gallon. Water hardness is measured in grains; 0.064 g calcium carbonate is equivalent to one grain of hardness Water is classified as soft if it contains 1 to 4 grains, medium if it contains 5 to 10 grains and hard if it contains 11 to 20 grains. The hardness of water may be altered or treated by using a chemical ion exchange system.

The hardness of water also affects its pH balance which plays a critical role in food processing. For example, hard water prevents successful production of clear beverages. Water hardness also affects sanitation; with increasing hardness, there is a loss of effectiveness for its use as a sanitizer. Boiling, steaming, and simmering are popular cooking methods that often require immersing food in water or its gaseous state, steam. While cooking water is used for dishwashing too.

4

Cash Crop

In agriculture, a cash crop is a crop which is grown for money. The term is used to differentiate from subsistence crops, which are those fed to the producer's own livestock or grown as food for the producer's family. In earlier times cash crops were usually only a small (but vital) part of a farm's total yield, while today, especially in the developed countries, almost all crops are mainly grown for cash. In non-developed nations, cash crops are usually crops which attract demand in more developed nations, and hence have some export value.

In many tropical and subtropical areas, Arecanut, Betelnut, Cardamom, Pepper, coffee, cocoa, sugarcane, bananas, oranges and cotton are common cash crops. In cooler areas, grain crops, oil-yielding crops and some vegetables predominate an example of this is the United States, where corn, wheat, cannabis and soybeans are the predominant cash crops. In the 1600s, tobacco became a cash crop.

Prices for major cash crops are set in commodity markets with global scope, with some local variation (called basis) based on freight costs and local supply and demand balance. A consequence of this is that a nation, region, or individual producer relying on such a crop may suffer low prices should a bumper crop elsewhere lead to excess supply on the global markets. This system is criticized by traditional farmers. Coffee is a major part of this. Issues involving subsidies and trade barriers on such crops have become controversial in discussions of globalization. Many developing nations take the position that the current international trade system is unfair because it has caused tariffs to be lowered in industrial goods while allowing for high tariffs and agricultural subsidies for agricultural goods. This makes it difficult for a developing nation to export its goods overseas, and forces developing nations to compete with imported goods which are exported from developed nations at artificially low prices. The practice of exporting at artificially low prices is known as dumping, and is illegal in most nations. Controversy over this issue led to the collapse of the Cancún trade talks in 2003, when the Group of 22 refused to consider agenda items proposed by the European Union unless the issue of agricultural subsidies were addressed.

Agribusiness, with its high-capital-investment and industrial-scale agricultural practices, very often skews production towards cash crops and away from anything that is consumed locally or which cannot be preserved, shipped and sold abroad. When used in conjunction with practices which seek to maximize crop yield and which favor monoculture, increasing reliance on cash crops is seen by some to have adverse, long term environmental consequences. The prevalence of cash crops also makes ethical consumerism difficult, as production practices cannot easily be determined and removed.

How much land do you need to produce cash crops? In part, this will depend upon what you want to do. There are three different sizes of land that can be used:

1. less than 1 acre;
2. 1 to 2 acres; and
3. 6 to 20 acres.

The size of your garden determines what your best crops will be in order to produce the most cash. For example: if you have one acre or less, you won't want to try growing apple and peach trees. You need more space for fruit trees. Instead, focus on crops like asparagus, strawberries, raspberries, herbs and other similar crops that can produce large amounts in small spaces.

The other important factor is the type of soil in your area. Most crops require certain kinds of soil to produce the highest yield and the best quality. The good news is that you can improve your soil by using fertilizers. Most of customers will prefer "organically grown" produce. Since most "store bought" produce is usually laced with some kind of chemical, featuring organically grown crops can assure you of increased sales. There's always a market for health oriented produce.

A great way to improve your soil is by composting. Composting turns leaves, grass clippings, scrap food, and other organic material into a rich soil. There are both long and short procedures for producing compost. Here's how:

Pick a spot for a compost pile (4 × 4 or 6 × 6 feet) and begin by putting down a 4 to 5 inch layer of leaves or grass clippings.

Cover with an inch or so of dirt and a shovel-full or two of manure. Then start another layer of organic matter. Continue in this manner until the pile is 3 or 4 feet high. You can sprinkle each layer lightly with water. If you like, you can construct an enclosed wire "box" for this compost pile.

If you want to use the protracted method for composting, simply let the pile "cook" for about 9 months. If you want a "faster" compost wait 8 to 9 days then mix the pile. Then wait 3 or 4 days and mix again. Do this until the pile has turned into a rich soil-like mixture. This compost can then be worked into your oil.

The purpose of composting is to develop heat and moisture within the pile. This will cause the organic matter to decompose into components that are usable by the plants. It will produce a lot of nitrogen-rich material as well as material rich loaded with minerals. You may need to add a cup of lime or bone meal between the layers of the pile to make an even better compost. You should have your soil tested to determine its acid, nitrogen, and mineral condition, or content. You'll en be able to determine what to add to the soil to correct any deficiencies.

You'll also be able to determine what grows best in your type of soil. There are low cost soil testing kits available, or you can find local testing groups, such as your local county extension office or the agriculture department at most colleges.

Most of the small cash crop growers I've talked with use a rototiller for preparing the soil. If the soil has never been used for a garden, you should have it worked up good with a tractor the first year. After that, a rototiller can do the job. Of course, if you have more than a one acre garden you may still want to save a lot of work and hire someone with a tractor to plow your soil. You should find several full time and part time farmers advertising in the classified section of your local newspaper for their tilling services.

The better prepared your soil is, the better the results will be. So take the time to find out the soil's current condition, add plenty of fertilizing material and work the soil up in preparation forplanting. Crop selection is largely a matter of preference and how you want to market your product. For example, some products can easily be sold only locally while other products can be sold nationally as well as locally. Herbs are examples of produce that can be sold both ways.

You don't just plant one type of crop unless you have signed contracts to sell that crop, or have plenty of marketing experience. There are some exceptions to this rule: for example, specialized crops such as mushrooms and problems if something doesn't produce as well as expected, or if the market becomes saturated.

Using good mulching techniques will help to eliminate weeds and lessen the amount of labor you'll need to put into the garden. It will also keep the soil around your plants moist and produce stronger plants. Almost all successful small cash crop growers use the mulching method.

Small Fruits

There are tremendous opportunities for part time fruit growers. Every large metropolitan area could use more fruit producers. This section will focus on the basic small fruit crops, such as blueberries, raspberries and strawberries. These fruits generally produce an excellent return on your investment.

Much of the demand is for "U-Pick" fields near larger cities. Thus, a few acres of small fruits can produce a substantial income. Except for strawberries, most of the fruit plants can keep producing for as long as 10 years, or more. Also, small fruit crops produce a high return per acre — up to $15,000 gross income per acre.

Blueberries grow on small bushes and require an acid type soil. You can get about 1,000 bushes on an acre. Many farmers argue that blueberries are the best crop for "U-Pick" operations.

But blueberries take a little more care and careful adjustment of the soil acidity, and are a bit harder to grow than other berries. Yet once you have a good established stand of blueberries, they can produce an excellent income.

Grapes can be grown almost anywhere there is fertile, well drained soil. Grapevines will last decades (up to 80 years!) and therefore, can produce a permanent income. Grapes can be used in "U-Pick" operations, and also sold via retail stores. It's important to study the proper pruning methods for grapes. Further information can be gleaned from U.S. Government agriculture publications found in most libraries or from the U.S. Government Printing Office in Washington, DC.

Raspberries can produce quick results and will continue producing for many years. The plants are low cost to purchase and establish, have little disease problems, and usually produce large crops. Best of all, there simply aren't enough of these delicious berries available. Thus, the demand is high and they will bring a large price per quart. You can easily propagate new plants yourself, adding to your crop each year. Raspberries require lots of sun, fertile, well drained soil, and effective mulching.

Strawberries are also an extremely popular crop. You can easily sell all you grow either by the "U-Pick" arrangement or sell direct to the consumer. The cost to establish a strawberry patch is generally low. And yields range from 6,000 to 15,000 pounds per acre.

Here are a few tips for "U-Pick" operations:

1. Have adequate parking, signs, and portable restrooms available.
2. Send each picker into assigned rows.
3. Use reusable containers and sell by the container, instead of by the pound.
4. Have plenty of empty containers to use, and make your customers feel at home.

Some growers are also producing other types of lesser-known crops such as kiwi, guavas, and Chinese dates. But, for most people just starting in the "cash crop" business, the 4 small fruits recommended in this section are the most cost effective.

Flowers

There are several different ways to make profits from flowers: selling flower bulbs, cut flowers, and flower plants. These can be sold in a variety of wholesale and retail ways.

A sizable flower business can be built upon 1/2 acre or less. Thus, flowers are an excellent choice if you have very little space. Here are a few examples of the most popular types of flowers:

1. *Bulbs* - canna, crocus, daffodils, gladiolus, iris, lilies, tulips.
2. *Cut flowers* - carnations, chrysanthemums, roses, snapdragons.
3. *Live flowers* - roses, violets, wildflowers, and virtually all other types of flowers.

Recently, a USDA horticulturist stated that the production of flowers is the fastest growing agriculture business today. The emand far outstrips the supply.

A great way to start making money from flowers is by building a greenhouse. You can then grow plants for selling to the many retail outlets that sell flowers in the spring. A number of people have reported that they completely paid for a $7,000 - $10,000 greenhouse in just one season using this method.

Flowers are always popular and will remain so. If you want to get into this business, you must become knowledgeable. And, more importantly, you must have or develop a love for flowers.

Herbs

Herb crops can be divided into three primary groupings. There are some herbs that may fit into more than one of the following categories:

1. *Culinary herbs* - used for flavorings, or as food.

2. *Fragrant herbs* - used for scents, potpourris, and sachets.

3. *Medicinal* - herbs used for as herbal remedies.

Herbs are continually becoming more in demand. The demand outstrips the current domestic supply, thus there is plenty of opportunity for growing and selling herbs. It's a pleasant business that costs little to start, takes little space and can produce a substantial income. One of the best things about herbs is that you can produce a fair amount of income per acre. Some growers produce as much as $12,000 - $15,000 per acre.

Another important fact is that almost all areas of the United States are suitable for growing some type of herbs. Most herb crops can begin producing incomes in the same year they are planted. Therefore, you can plan a herb crop this winter and reap the profits next fall!

You can find sources for herb plants and seeds by looking through the various gardening and farming magazines. Publications like, The Mother Earth News, Fine Gardening, Harrowsmith and Organic Gardening contain many ads for herb suppliers. Look in both the classified and display ad sections.

Herbs can be sold in a wide variety of ways:

1. Direct to the customer as plants.
2. Direct to the customer as a finished product.
3. Wholesaling to retail stores.
4. Wholesaling to bulk herb buyers.
5. Wholesaling to arts and crafts people who use the herbs in other products.
6. Fresh herbs to restaurants.

If you wish to become involved in growing herbs for profit, the first thing to do is to educate yourself about the different herbs. You'll discover that some herbs take special growing conditions to flourish. Then devise a plan to detail what herbs you will grow and how you'll market them.

Here are a few examples of some popular herbs from the three classes listed earlier.

1. *Culinary herbs* - Basil, sage, chives, dill, parsley, ints, savory, rosemary, thyme.
2. *Fragrant herbs* - mints, tansy, clove, rue, thyme, rosemary, chamomile.
3. *Medicinal herbs* - borage, catnip, ginseng, gold seal, lobelia, pennyroyal, valerian.

Most successful herb growers plant a variety of herbs. They also use several different marketing techniques, such as: direct to the consumer, selling herb plants to other growers, and selling to restaurants. Dried herbs can also be sold by mail order. A few herb growers concentrate on one or to varieties for which there is a big demand. Examples include: peppermint and catnip. Usually, they already have contracts for selling the product to large wholesalers or companies that use the herbs in their products.

Vegetables

Fresh, home grown vegetables is a constant in-demand product. You can often beat the large supermarket chain on prices, and always on product quality. You can even become a supplier to small grocery stores. But most of your profits will come from direct retail sales to consumers who are looking for "farm fresh, chemical free" produce.

There are literally dozens of different vegetable crops you can grow. I recommend that you pick 8 or 10 of the most popular vegetables. Using intensive gardening techniques can greatlyincrease the amount produced per acre. Some growers have reported incomes of up to $20,000 per acre!

These are a few of the most popular vegetables:

- *Asparagus* - yields up to 2,000 pounds per acre at $2 per pound. Plants are started as roots and are ready to use in about 3 years. And will continue producing for up to 20 years.
- *Beans* - always one of the most popular crops, and come in many easy-to-grow varieties. Beans will produce several crops each growing season.
- *Brussels Sprouts* - relatively easy to grow and can produce late into the year, even after a frost.
- *Carrots* - requires lots of loose fertile soil. There is a strong demand for "baby carrots."
- *Corn* - one of the most popular fresh picked vegetables, although it does have a slightly lower profitability per acre.
- *Lettuce* - a quick and easy-to-grow vegetable. You should grow several different varieties, and it can be planted very early.
- *Peppers* - both the mild and hot varieties. Peppers need a long warm growing season and well drained soil. Other popular items include okra, onions, peas, radishes, spinach, squash, tomatoes, watermelon, and egg plant.

Vegetables can be marketed in a variety of ways. There are even many "U-Pick" vegetable operations. However, by far the bestway to sell vegetables is by operating a small roadside stand, or at an established farmer's market. Most communities have a farmer's market operating on weekends.

There's a booming market for organically grown vegetables. And that market will continue. Chemical free produce will always bring you premium prices. Organically grown vegetables take a little more soil preparation and effort, but they can be wellworth the extra effort.

Other ways to market vegetables are: directly to restaurants,local stores, and to food co-ops. The key to all of thesemarketing efforts is to have a high quality, chemical freeproducts.

Speciality Crops

This section will briefly cover other special cash crops. Some of these crops can only be grown in certain section of the countries. Also, some must have special growing conditions.

Landscaping Plants

Special plants for landscaping are always in demand. These plants include shrubs such as: rhododendron, azaleas and juniper, as well as some decorative trees. Landscaping plants can be sold directly to the consumer or to landscaping companies. If you begin supplying a landscape company or retail outlets with good stock, you'll soon have a steady source of income. A couple of important things to know about landscape plants are that they must be attractive and have a good survival rate. And you probably need to give some sort of guarantee that the plants are free from disease.

Nut Crops

Including almonds, chestnuts, filberts, pecans and walnuts. You can expect a wait of from 3 to 20 years for nut production. But some growers also produce and sell various aged nut trees for replanting. Nice two and three old trees will bring a premium price. Since nut tree crops require a long time to mature, some growers use a dual method ... they plant a raspberry crop between the nut trees. It takes about 8 to 10 years to get nut trees into nut production. But, after they have produced crops, they can also be used for valuable lumber production in 30 years or so. Nut trees could make an excellent retirement crop if you plant them while you're young. Some arrow-straight walnut trees, black walnut specifically, have brought as much as $10,000 each!

Bamboo

This crop is grown for its edible shoots, and can produce 3 to 10 tons per acre. Bamboo is also used for a wide variety of construction items, including furniture. Currently, U.S. growers cannot keep up with the demand, so bamboo is being imported from Asia.

Dried Plants - Are used for decoration and fragrance. Dried floral arrangements are especially popular. Many arts and craft shops, gift stores and specialty shops need a constant supply of dried flowers. There are two steps involved in producing these crops. First you must produce an attractive, quality plant. Next, you must usen the proper drying techniques to preserve the plants while maintaining its looks.

Mushrooms - Have become a very popular specialty food in fancy restaurants. The Shitake mushroom is specially adapted for production by small family farms. It can be harvested during the spring and fall. And it has both a meaty taste and medicinal properties. These mushrooms are usually grown outdoors on 6 to 8 foot logs. The logs are prepared and then inoculated with the mushroom spores. Then it's a 6 to 8 month wait for the first crop. A few growers have developed indoor growing techniqueswhich result in a shorter growing season.

Oyster Mushrooms - Is another variety that is fast becoming popular. These mushrooms are fast growing and produce high yields. They can be grown on easily available material, such as wheat straw. The largest market for specialty mushrooms are restaurants,food co-ops, grocers and health food stores. You can enjoy a year round booming market for dried Shitake mushrooms.

Seeds

Many small growers are supplying the large seed companies with special crop seed. These include flower seeds, wildflowers seeds and hard-to-find vegetables. Some small producers occasionally sell directly to the consumer.

Sprouts

Growing sprouts can be ideal for those who have very little space. Fresh sprouts can be supplied to major grocery stores as well as to restaurants and health food stores.

Marketing Techniques

There are a variety of selling techniques that can be used get cash from your crops. Some producers use several of the methods at the same time. Several things can help make your marketing efforts easier. The first is quality. You want to produce the best product possible. Your product's good, clean, healthy appearance will impress buyers. Sub-par products will be hard to sell.

The way to produce quality is by proper initial soil preparation, using good seeds and by adhering to accepted growing methods. There many plants that act as natural atnip, marigolds, nasturtiums, savory, garlic, horseradish, tansy, and thyme.

An important marketing consideration is timing. If you can get a crop ready when other producers aren't, sales will be easy. This can be done by using greenhouses, planting early, using hotbeds and, of course, good planning. Pricing is also important. Most sellers recommend that you price your products 10% to 20% below those in grocery stores. (But don't lock yourself into a price war by trying to undercut your competition from other small producers.) Products that are grown using organic methods will most often bring higher prices. Check will all the local retail stores and at farmers markets to get a feel for your local current selling rates.

One of the most common marketing techniques is selling your wares at roadside stands. Two of the most important factors to consider before setting up your stand are signs and ample parking space. Your signs should be no longer than 6 to 8 words, neat, legible and easy to understand. Signs need to be placed far enough ahead of your stand to give the customer time to pull into your parking area.

Next, you want your stand to be well organized and neat in appearance. Make it easy for the customer to see the product and prices. Neatness and cleanliness will pay off. Combined with quality products and good prices, you'll enjoy a lot of free advertising by "word of mouth."

A variation of the roadside stand is to sell from the back of your pickup truck or car. You'll need to locate a welltraveled road and a spot with parking that doesn't interfere with anyone. Of course, all of the previously mentioned factors apply.

Another common selling method is at farmer's markets and flea markets. These gatherings are held in most localities. If not, you'll want to get together with other producers and organize a farmer's market. All of these methods can also be aided by advertising in local newspapers, "penny saver" papers, radio stations, and by posting notices on bulletin boards.

Selling directly to retail grocery stores and restaurants isanother good procedure. If you can provide them with a steady supply of fresh produce, sales should be easy. When contactingthese stores be prepared to offer a 30% to 40% discount fromregular retail prices. This allows the retailer a good profit margin. If you are a reliable producer, you may be able to set upa weekly route to service several retail locations.

There are many food co-ops that are eager to buy largequantities of quality produce. You'll need to offer reasonablediscounts. Too, you'll want to scout out these local co-ops and contact them directly. For some products you may have to prepareneat individualized packages of produce. Example: 1 or 2 ounces of herbs in labeled, plastic bags.

U-Pick operations have been discussed previously. This marketing method will work for almost any product. However, it does present some special problems. Example: you cannot let very young kids into the picking areas as they may get hurt and/or damage some crops.

In order to operate a successful U-Pick operation, you'll need to get along well with people. You also need to be friendly, courteous and treat everyone as if they are individually important which, of course, they are.

Getting Help

There's a variety of ways to get help with gardening and marketing your products. Almost every state offers free agriculture help through universities and state agriculture offices. The U.S. Department of Agriculture also offers many free programs. Local bookstores, newsstands, and libraries also contain many informative sources. Study these diligently and become skillful in gardening. Finally, you'll be able to find many newsletters and growers associations advertised in the gardening magazines. These are often your best sources for plants, seeds, growing techniques, and marketing strategies.

5

Importance of Climate

Climate encompasses the temperatures, humidity, atmospheric pressure, winds, rainfall, atmospheric particle count and numerous other meteorological elements in a given region over long periods of time, as opposed to the term weather, which refers to current activity of these same elements. The climate of a location is affected by its latitude, terrain, altitude, persistent ice or snow cover, as well as nearby oceans and their currents. Climates can be classified using parameters such as temperature and rainfall to define specific climate types. The most commonly used classification scheme is the one originally developed by Wladimir Köppen. The Thornthwaite system in use since 1948, incorporates evapotranspiration in addition to temperature and precipitation information and is used in studying animal species diversity and potential impacts of climate changes. The Bergeron and Spatial Synoptic Classification systems focus on the origin of air masses defining the climate for certain areas.

Paleoclimatology is the study and description of ancient climates using information from both non-biotic factors such as sediments found in lake beds and ice cores, and biotic factors such as tree rings and coral, and can be used to extend back the temperature or rainfall information for particular locations to a time before various weather instruments were used to monitor weather conditions. Climate models are mathematical models of past, present and future climates and can be used to describe the likely patterns of future changes.

Climate (from Ancient Greek klima, meaning inclination) is commonly defined as the weather averaged over a long period of time. The standard averaging period is 30 years, but other periods may be used depending on the purpose. Climate also includes statistics other than the average, such as the magnitudes of day-to-day or year-to-year variations. The Intergovernmental Panel on Climate Change (IPCC) glossary definition is:

> Climate in a narrow sense is usually defined as the "average weather", or more rigorously, as the statistical description in terms of the mean and variability of relevant quantities over a period of time ranging from months to thousands or millions of years. The classical period is 30 years, as defined by the World Meteorological Organization (WMO). These quantities are most often surface variables such as temperature, precipitation, and wind. Climate in a wider sense is the state, including a statistical description, of the climate system.

The difference between climate and weather is usefully summarized by the popular phrase "Climate is what you expect, weather is what you get. Over historical time spans there are a number of static variables that determine climate, including latitude, altitude, proportion of land to water, and proximity to oceans and mountains. Other climate determinants are more dynamic: for example, the thermohaline circulation of the ocean leads to a 5 °C (9 °F) warming of the northern Atlantic ocean compared to other ocean basins Other ocean currents redistribute heat between land and water on a more regional scale. The density and type of vegetation coverage affects solar heat absorption water retention, and rainfall on a regional level. Alterations in the quantity of atmospheric greenhouse gases determines the amount of solar energy retained by the planet, leading to global warming or global cooling. The variables which determine climate are numerous and the interactions complex, but there is general agreement that the broad outlines are understood, at least insofar as the determinants of historical climate change are concerned.

Fig. 5.1

Climate Classification

There are several ways to classify climates into similar regimes. Originally, climes were defined in Ancient Greece to describe the weather depending upon a location's latitude. Modern climate classification methods can be broadly divided into genetic methods, which focus on the causes of climate, and empiric methods, which focus on the effects of climate. Examples of genetic classification include methods based on the relative frequency of different air mass types or locations within synoptic weather disturbances. Examples of empiric classifications include climate zones defined by plant hardiness, evapotranspiration, air mass origin, or more generally the Köppen climate classification which was originally designed to identify the climates associated with certain biomes. A common shortcoming of these classification schemes is that they produce distinct boundaries between the zones they define, rather than the gradual transition of climate properties more common in nature.

Air Mass

The most generic classification is that involving the concept of air masses. The Bergeron classification is the most widely accepted form of air mass classification. Air mass classification involves three letters. The first letter describes its moisture properties, with c used for continental air masses (dry) and m for maritime air masses (moist). The second letter describes the thermal characteristic of its source region: T for tropical, P for polar, A for Arctic or Antarctic, M for monsoon, E for equatorial, and S for superior air (dry air formed by significant downward motion in the atmosphere). The third letter is used to designate the stability of the atmosphere. If the air mass is colder than the ground below it, it is labeled k. If the air mass is warmer than the ground below it, it is labeled w. While air mass identification was originally used in weather forecasting during the 1950s, climatologists began to establish synoptic climatologies based on this idea in 1973.

Based upon the Bergeron classification scheme is the Spatial Synoptic Classification system (SSC). There are six categories within the SSC scheme: Dry Polar (similar to continental polar), Dry Moderate (similar to maritime superior), Dry Tropical (similar to continental tropical), Moist Polar (similar to maritime polar), Moist Moderate (a hybrid between maritime polar and maritime tropical), and Moist Tropical (similar to maritime tropical, maritime monsoon, or maritime equatorial).

Köppen

Monthly average surface temperatures from 1961-1990. This is an example of how climate varies with location and seasonMain article: Köppen climate classification.

The Köppen classification includes climate regimes such as rain forest, monsoon, tropical savanna, humid subtropical, humid continental, oceanic climate, Mediterranean climate, steppe, subarctic climate, tundra, polar ice cap, and desert.

Rain forests are characterized by high rainfall, with definitions setting minimum normal annual rainfall between 1,750 millimetres (69 in) and 2,000 millimetres (79 in). Mean monthly temperatures exceed 18 °C (64 °F) during all months of the year. A monsoon is a seasonal prevailing wind which lasts for several months, ushering in a region's rainy season. Regions such as within North America, South America.

Sub-Saharan Africa, Australia and East Asia to qualify as monsoon regimes. A tropical Savanna is a grassland biome located in semi-arid to semi-humid climate regions of subtropical and tropical latitudes, with average temperatures remain at or above 18 °C (64 °F) year round and rainfall between 750 millimetres (30 in) and 1,270 millimetres (50 in) a year. They are widespread on Africa, and are also found in India, the northern parts of South America, Malaysia, and Australia. The humid subtropical climate zone where winter rainfall (and sometimes snowfall) is associated with large storms that the westerlies steer from west to east. Most summer rainfall occurs during thunderstorms and from occasional tropical cyclones.

Humid subtropical climates lie on the east side continents, roughly between latitudes 20° and 40° degrees away from the equator. Humid continental climate worldwideA humid continental climate is marked by variable weather patterns and a large seasonal temperature variance. Places with a hottest monthly temperature above 10 °C (50 °F) and a coldest month temperature below -3 °C (26.6 °F) and which do not meet the criteria for an arid climate, are classified as continental.

An oceanic climate is typically found along the west coasts at the middle latitudes of all the world's continents, and in southeastern Australia, and is accompanied by plentiful precipitation year round. The Mediterranean climate regime resembles the climate of the lands in the Mediterranean Basin, parts of western North America, parts of Western and South Australia, in southwestern South Africa and in parts of central Chile.

The climate is characterized by hot, dry summers and cool, wet winters. A steppe is a dry grassland with an annual temperature range in the summer of up to 40 °C (104 °F) and during the winter down to -40 °C (-40.0 °F).

A subarctic climate has little precipitation and monthly temperatures which are above 10 °C (50 °F) for one to three months of the year, with continuous permafrost due to the very cold winters. Winters within subarctic climates include up to six months of temperatures averaging below 0 °C (32 °F). Tundra occurs in the far Northern Hemisphere, north of the taiga belt, including vast areas of northern Russia and Canada.

A polar ice cap, or polar ice sheet, is a high-latitude region of a planet or moon that is covered in ice. Ice caps form because high-latitude regions receive less energy in the form of solar radiation from the sun than equatorial regions, resulting in lower surface temperatures. A desert is a landscape form or region that receives very little precipitation. Deserts usually have a large diurnal and seasonal temperature range, with high daytime temperatures (in summer up to 45 °C or 113 °F), and low night-time temperatures (in winter down to 0 °C; 32 °F) due to extremely low humidity. Many deserts are formed by rain shadows, as mountains block the path of moisture and precipitation to the desert.

Thornthwaite

This climate classification method monitors the soil water budget using the concept of evapotranspiration. It monitors the portion of total precipitation used to nourish vegetation over a certain area It uses indices such as a humidity index and an aridity index to determine an area's moisture regime based upon its average temperature, average rainfall, and average vegetation type.

The lower the value of the index is any given area, the drier the area is. The moisture classification includes climatic classes with descriptors such as hyperhumid, humid, subhumid, subarid, semi-arid (values of -20 to -40), and arid (values below -40) Humid regions experience more precipitation than evaporation each year, while arid regions experience greater evaporation than precipitation on an annual basis. A total of 33 per cent of the earth's landmass is considered either arid of semi-arid, including southwest North America, southwest South America, most of northern and a small part of southern Africa, southwest and portions of eastern Asia, as well as much of Australia Studies suggest that precipitation effectiveness (PE) within the Thornthwaite moisture index is overestimated in the summer and underestimated in the winter.

This index can be effectively used to determine the number of herbivore and mammal species numbers within a given area The index is also used in studies of climate change. Thermal classifications within the Thornthwaite scheme include microthermal, mesothermal, and megathermal regimes. A mircothermal climate is one of low annual mean temperatures, generally between 0 °C (32 °F) and 14 °C (57 °F) which experiences short summers and has a potential evaporation between 14 centimetres (5.5 in) and 43 centimetres (17 in). A mesothermal climate lacks persistent heat or persistent cold, with potential evaporation between 57 centimetres (22 in) and 114 centimetres (45 in). A megathermal climate is one with persistent high temperatures and abundant rainfall, with potential evaporation in excess of 114 centimetres (45 in).

Details of the modern climate record are known through the taking of measurements from such weather instruments as thermometers, barometers, and anemometers during the past few centuries. The instruments used to study weather conditions over the modern time scale, their known error, their immediate environment, and their exposure have changed over the years, which must be considered when studying the climate of centuries past.

Paleoclimatology

Paleoclimatology is the study of past climate over a great period of the Earth's history. It uses evidence from ice sheets, tree rings, sediments, coral, and rocks to determine the past state of the climate. It demonstrates periods of stability and periods of change and can indicate whether changes follow patterns such as regular cycles.

Climate Change

Climate change refers to the variation in the Earth's global climate or in regional climates over time. It describes changes in the variability or average state of the atmosphere over time scales ranging from decades to millions of years. These changes can be caused by processes internal to the Earth, external forces (e.g. variations in sunlight intensity) or, more recently, human activities.

In recent usage, especially in the context of environmental policy, the term "climate change" often refers only to changes in modern climate, including the rise in average surface temperature known as global warming. In some cases, the term is also used with a presumption of human causation, as in the United Nations Framework Convention on Climate Change (UNFCCC). The UNFCCC uses "climate variability" for non-human caused variations.

Earth has undergone periodic climate shifts in the past, including four major ice ages. These consisting of glacial periods where conditions are colder than normal, separated by interglacial periods. The accumulation of snow and ice during a glacial period increases the surface albedo, reflecting more of the Sun's energy into space and maintaining a lower atmospheric temperature. Increases in greenhouse gases, such as by volcanic activity, can increase the global temperature and produce an interglacial. Suggested causes of ice age periods include the positions of the continents, variations in the Earth's orbit, changes in the solar output, and vulcanism.

Climate Models

Climate models use quantitative methods to simulate the interactions of the atmosphere, oceans, land surface and ice. They are used for a variety of purposes from study of the dynamics of the weather and climate system to projections of future climate. All climate models balance, or very nearly balance, incoming energy as short wave (including visible) electromagnetic radiation to the earth with outgoing energy as long wave (infrared) electromagnetic radiation from the earth. Any imbalance results in a change in the average temperature of the earth.

The most talked-about models of recent years have been those relating temperature to the build-up of greenhouse gases in the atmosphere, primarily carbon dioxide. These models predict an upward trend in the global mean surface temperature, with the most rapid increase in temperature being projected for the higher latitudes of the Northern Hemisphere.Models can range from relatively simple to quite complex.

A simple radiant heat transfer model that treats the earth as a single point and averages outgoing energy this can be expanded vertically (radiative-convective models), or horizontally finally, (coupled) atmosphere–ocean–sea ice global climate models discretise and solve the full equations for mass and energy transfer and radiant exchange.

6

Areca Nut

The areca nut is not a true nut but rather a drupe. It is commercially available in dried, cured and fresh forms. While fresh, the husk is green and the nut inside is so soft that it can easily be cut with an average knife. In the ripe fruit the husk becomes yellow or orange and, as it dries, the fruit inside hardens to a wood-like consistency. At that stage the areca nut can only be sliced using a special scissor-like cutter.

Usually a few slices of the nut are wrapped in a Betel leaf along with lime and may include clove, cardamom, catechu (kattha), etc. for extra flavouring. Betel leaf has a fresh, peppery taste, but it can be bitter depending on the variety. This is called *tamboolam* in Sanskrit.

Areca nuts are chewed with betel leaf for their effects as a mild stimulant, causing a mild hot sensation in the body and slightly heightened alertness, although the effects vary from person to person. The effect of chewing betel nut is relatively mild and could be compared to drinking a cup of coffee. The areca nut contains tannin, gallic acid, a fixed oil gum, a little terpineol, lignin, various saline substances and three main alkaloids: Arecoline, Arecain and Guracine which have vasoconstricting properties. The betel leaf chewed along with it contains eugenol, also a vasoconstrictor. Many chewers also add small pieces of tobacco leaf to the mixture, thereby adding the effect of the nicotine, which causes greater addiction than the drugs contained in the nut and the betel.

Fig. 6.1

In China, East and North-East India areca nuts are not only chewed along with betel leaf but are also used in the preparation of Ayurvedic and Traditional Chinese medicines. Powdered areca nut is used as a constituent in some tooth powders. Other medicinal uses include the removal of tapeworms and other intestinal parasites by swallowing a few teaspoons of powdered areca nut, drunk as a decoction, or by taking tablets containing the extracted alkaloids.

The Term "Betel Nut" and the Colonial Legacy

In English, the areca nut is also widely known as Betel nut (or "Betelnut"), because it is mostly chewed along with Betel, the leaf of a vine belonging to the Piperaceae family. The term "Betel nut" is technically incorrect, for the betel vine produces no nuts, and this inaccurate term creates quite a bit of confusion regarding the discernment between the nut and the leaf. Generally, "paan" is used to refer to the betel leaf. However, the common use of the word "paan" refers mostly to the chewing mixture, including areca nut, wrapped in the leaves.

The muddling between the areca nut and the betel leaf, by calling the nut "betel nut", is restricted to the languages of the colonizing powers, like English, French, Dutch, Portuguese and German. This lack of accuracy is likely a legacy of the colonial era in which chewing the mixture was restricted to "the natives". In the languages of the places where the Areca nut is traditionally chewed there is a clear and separate term for the areca nut and another for the betel leaf. This clear distinction is important in societies where both the areca nut and the betel leaf have a ceremonial and even sacred value. Furthermore, there is commonly a specific verb for the activity of chewing both of them together.

Fig. 6.2

There was a certain amount of prejudice among the European colonial powers against the tradition of chewing of Areca nut and betel. Unlike the quick adoption of tobacco by Europeans in the American colonies, chewing areca nut and betel was an addictive habit not adopted by the colonizers of South and Southeast Asia. Officers freshly posted in the East India or Indochina colonies, whether British, French or Dutch, regarded the red-stained mouths of pan-chewers with dread, as something too foreign and weird for them. This abhorrence is not only evident in the writings of authors of the Victorian era, but in more recent writers like George Orwell, Somerset Maugham and V.S. Naipaul. Often this spirit expresses itself in mockery and ridicule, like in the Broadway musical tune "Bloody Mary" (from Rodgers and Hammerstein's *South Pacific*) with the line *"Bloody Mary's chewing betel nuts ... and she don't use Pepsodent."*

Tradition

Chewing the mixture of areca nut and betel leaf is a tradition, custom or ritual which dates back thousands of years from South Asia to the Pacific. It constitutes an important and popular cultural activity in many Asian and Oceanic countries, including Taiwan, Myanmar, Cambodia, the Solomon Islands, Thailand, Laos, and Vietnam. It is not known how and when the areca nut and the betel leaf were combined together into one psychoactive drug. Archaeological evidence from Thailand, Indonesia and the Philippines suggests that they have been used in tandem for four thousand years or more.

In Vietnam the areca nut and the betel leaf are such important symbols of love and marriage that in Vietnamese the phrase "matters of betel and areca" is synonymous with marriage. Areca nut chewing starts the talk between the groom's parents and the bride's parents about the young couple's marriage. Therefore the leaves and juices are used ceremonially in Vietnamese weddings. The folk tale explaining the origin of this Vietnamese tradition is a good illustration of the fact that the combination of areca nut and the betel leaf is ideal to the point that they are practically inseparable, like an idealized married couple.

Fig. 6.3

Malay culture and tradition hold betel nut and leaves in high esteem. Traditionally, guests who visits a malay house are given a tray of betel nuts and betel leaves, the same way as one offering drinks to a guests now. There's even a malay proverb about the betel nut, *"bagaikan pinang dibelah dua"*, loosely translated, like a betelnut divided in half. It usually refers to newlyweds, who are compatible to each other, just like a betel nut when divided in half. The Proverb is closely analogous to the contemporary "two peas in a pod".

Fig. 6.4

In the Indian Sub-continent the chewing of betel and areca nut dates back to the pre-Vedic period Harappan empire. Formerly in India and Sri Lanka it was a custom of the royalty to chew Areca nut and betel leaf. Kings had special attendants carrying a box with the ingredients for a good chewing session. There was also a custom to chew Areca nut and betel leaf among lovers because of its breath-freshening and relaxant properties. Hence there was a sexual symbolism attached to the chewing of the nut and the leaf. The areca nut represented the male and the betel leaf the female principle. Considered an auspicious ingredient in Hinduism, the Areca nut is still used along with betel leaf in religious ceremonies and also while honoring individuals in most of Southern Asia.

In Assam it is a tradition to offer *Pan-tamul* (Betel leaves and raw areca nut) to guests after tea or meals in a brass plate with stands called a *Bota*. Among the Assamese the areca nut also has a variety of uses during religious and marriage ceremonies, where it has the role of a fertility symbol. A tradition from Upper Assam is to invite guests to wedding receptions by offering a few areca nuts with betel leaves. During Bihu, the *husori* players are offered areca nuts and betel leaves by each household while their blessings are solicited.

Spanish mariner Álvaro de Mendaña reported how the Solomon Islanders were chewing the nut and the leaf with caustic lime that stained their mouths red. He noticed that friendly and genial chief Malope in Santa Isabel Island was offering him the stuff as a token of friendship every time they met.

The adding of tobacco leaf to the chewing mixture is a relatively recent introduction, for tobacco was introduced from the American continent in colonial times.

Effects on Health

The International Agency for Research on Cancer (IARC) regards the chewing of betel and and areca nut to be a known human carcinogen Certain studies have sought to prove that regular chewers of betel leaf and and areca nut have a higher risk of damaging their gums and acquiring cancer of the mouth, pharynx, oesophagus and stomach. Studies have found tobacco and caustic lime increase the risk of cancer from betel nut preparations.

Studies exist of the use of a "pure" *paan* preparation: areca nut, betel leaf, and lime. A single recent study claimed that unprocessed areca nuts, at high doses, displayed a very weak carcinogenicity. In contrast, since 1971 many studies have found betel nut extracts to cause cancer in rodents In 2003 the International Agency for Research on Cancer (IARC) reached the conclusion that there is sufficient evidence that the habit of chewing betel quid with or without tobacco is carcinogenic to humans Support is provided by a recent study which found that paan without tobacco is a risk factor for oral cancer. They found paan with and without tobacco increased oral cancer risk by 9.9 and 8.4 times respectively. The paan and extract studies suggest betel nut alone is extremely carcinogenic.

Fig. 6.5

Chewing Betel Nut alone has been linked to Oral Submucous Fibrosis

According to Medline Plus, "Long-term use has been associated with oral submucous fibrosis (OSF), pre-cancerous oral lesions and squamous cell carcinoma. Acute effects of betel chewing include asthma exacerbation, hypertension, and tachycardia. There may be a higher risk of cancers of the liver, mouth, esophagus, stomach, prostate, cervix, and lung with regular betel use. Other effects can include a possible effect on blood sugar levels, possibly increasing the risk of type two diabetes.

Regular betel chewing causes the teeth and gums to be stained orange/red, a color that was formerly considered attractive in certain cultures. In Telugu poetry the slightly red-stained lips of a young woman chewing areca nut and betel are considered a mark of beauty. It is believed that regular chewing reduces the incidence of cavities, and toothpastes were once produced containing betel extracts. However, the increase in mouth ulcers and gum deterioration caused by areca nut and betel chewing may outweigh any positive effects.

According to traditional Ayurvedic medicine chewing areca nut and betel leaf is a good remedy against bad breath (halitosis). MedlinePlus indicates "poor-quality research" showing a possible beneficial effect for sufferers of anaemia during pregnancy. However, it counsels against areca nut chewing due to a possible risk of spontaneous abortions. It also indicates "poor-quality studies" showing a possible beneficial effect on schizophrenia and for stroke recovery. Some people claim that chewing Areca nuts with betel increases the capacity to work.

Vernacular Names

Sanskrit: *Puga* or *Pugaphala*, Bengali: *Shupari*, Hindi, Marathi: *Supari*

Modern Day Consumption

In India (the largest consumer of areca nut) and Pakistan the ld in ready-to-chew pouches called "Pan Masala" or supari, as a mixture of many flavors whose primary base is areca nut crushed into small pieces. Pan Masala with a small quantity of tobacco is called gutka. The easily-discarded small plastic supari or gutka pouches are an ubiquitous pollutant of the South Asian environment. Some of the liquid in the mouth is usually disposed of by spitting, producing bright red spots which are highly vis and Sri Lanka are a sure indication of the popularity of betel chewing in an area. The Shimoga District in Karnataka is presently the largest producer of betelnut in India.

In the Maldives areca nut chewing is very popular, but spitting is frowned upon and regarded as an unrefined, gross way of chewing. Usually people prefer to chew thin slices of the dry nut, which is sometimes roasted. "Kili", a mixture of areca nut, betel, cloves, cardamom and sugar is sold in small home-made paper pouches. Old people who have lost their teeth keep "chewing" by pounding the mixture of areca nut and betel with a small mortar and pestle.

In Papua New Guinea and the Solomon Islands, fresh areca nut, betel leaf or 'fruit leaf' ("daka" in PNG) and lime are sold on street corners. In these countries, dried or flavoured areca nut is not popular. Areca nut chewing has recently been introduced into Vanuatu where it is growing in popularity, especially in the northern islands of the country. In Guam, betel and areca nut chewing is a social pastime as a means to extend friendship, and can be found in many, if not most, large gatherings as part of the food display.

Betel nut beauty" on the road between Taipei and Hsinchu

In Taiwan, bags of 20 to 40 areca nuts are purchased fresh daily by a large number of consumers. To meet the steady year-round demand, there exist two kinds of betelnut shops, each of which sells cigarettes and drinks including beer in addition to their primary purpose of supplying betel and nuts. On one hand, there are small mom and pop shops that are often poorly maintained and often do not stand out from other stores nearby. On the other hand, the second provides a sight unique to Taiwan. Such a shop often consists of nothing more than a single free-standing room, or booth, elevated one meter above the street that measures less than 3 meters by 2 meters. Large picture windows comprise two or more of the walls, allowing those who pass by a complete view of the interior. The interior is often painted brightly. Within such a shop, a sexily dressed young woman can be seen preparing betel and areca nuts (see "Betel nut beauty"). Shops are often identified by multicolored (commonly green) fluorescent tubes or neon lights that frame the windows or that are arranged radially above a store. Customers stop on the side of the road and wait for the girls to bring their betel and areca nut to their vehicles.

In Thailand the consumption of areca nut has declined gradually in the last decades. The younger generation rarely chews the substance, especially in the cities. Most of the present-day consumption is confined to older generations, that is mostly people above fifty. Even so, small trays of betel leves and sliced tender arecanut are sold in markets and used as offerings in Buddhist shrines.

In the Philippines, chewing the areca nut and betel leaf was a very important tradition in the past. Nowadays this tradition is almost dead among the urban people in the cities and big towns who consider that it is against the general trend of being westernized. Except in some small towns, chewing betel has largely been replaced by chewing gum and cigarettes.

In the United States, areca nut is not a controlled or specially taxed substance and may be found in some Asian grocery stores. However, importation of areca nut in a form other than whole or carved kernels of nuts *can* be stopped at the discretion of US Customs officers on the grounds of food, agricultural, or medicinal drug violations. Such actions by Customs are very rare. In the United Kingdom areca nut is readily available in Asian grocery stores and even in shredded forms from the World Food aisles of larger Tesco supermarkets.

Arecanut Processing

Arecanut palm (*Areca catechu L.*) is cultivated for its kernel, which is chewed in its tender, ripe or processed form. The north-eastern region of India is a major producer of arecanut in India, producing 21% of the total national production. Most of the production is exported to outside the region.

The major processing clusters are in northeast India with large (5-7 tonnes of processed arecanut produced weekly) and medium sized (2-3 tonne of processed arecanut produced weekly) units located in Rupahi and Howly, in the state of Assam. Apart from these clusters, thousands of cottage-level processing units are also found in Cachar, Karimganj, Darrang, Dhubri and Kokrajhar districts of Assam.

There are two varieties of processed arecanut processed in the state of Assam and other states in India: Boiled, dried nuts (red in colour, called chikni) and non-boiled, sun dried nuts (called supari). Tender green arecanut are dehusked, boiled and dried to obtain the chikni. Boiling is done in batches in fl at, open, iron pans (4-5 feet diameter) where chopped nut pieces are mixed with colour and boiled at 70–80°C, to cook and absorb the colour.

The first batch of boiling in a day takes 50 minutes and subsequent batches take 30 minutes. Though the nuts should be boiled for 20 minutes to get restrict the boiling time to save the scarce fuelwood. The drying (slow heating) is done in brick-cement/brick-mud frame sheds (7 feet height and 7.5 feet width) with vertical partitions. Thick bamboo mats are used to spread the chopped nuts out for drying and wood is fi red in each partition on the ground, well below the bamboo mats. In the large and medium sized units, fire curing is initially done for 12 hours at a temperature of 70-75°C and then the dried product is further sun dried for 2-3 days to remove any residual moisture.

On average 100 to 150 kg fuelwood arecanut, of which 60% is used for boiling and the rest for drying. The average wood-burning rate for boiling is 115 kg per hour, with SFC (specific fuel consumption) of 0.70 kg wood per kg boiled nut. Detailed water boiling tests carried out on the vessel-bhatti combination currently used, revealed that the useful power requirement is 30-35 kWth. TERI has successfully developed an integrated gasifier-based system for boiling, as well as drying, and has successfully demonstrated the application in the Rupahi cluster. The gasifier with a wood consumption rate of about 20 kg/hr capacity, was used for boiling arecanut in the existing boiling pan and also utilized the hot flue gases for drying. The gasifier could also be operated successfully using waste arecanut husk (a by-product during de-husking operation) that makes the gasifier option even more attractive Area under areca nut and production of arecanut in the country have increased considerably in 11 years till 2004-05, according to a database on arecanut and spices published by the Directorate of Arecanut and Spices Development, Kozhikode, under the Union Ministry of Agriculture, in 2007.

In response, sources in Mangalore Agriculturists' Sahakari Sangha (MASS) and Central Arecanut and Cocoa Marketing and Processing Cooperative Limited (CAMPCO) told The Hindu that this is not a healthy trend in the interest of a recanut growers, especially in traditional areas, as it will affect the market.

As per the database, imports of arecanut had also gone up in the last five years from 14,788 tonnes in 2001-02 to

53,275 tonnes in 2005-06. This meant that crises in the domestic market would also increase, they said.

The database said that the statistics from 1994-95 to 2004-05 were sourced from the Directorate of Economics and Statistics, Delhi. Area under arecanut went up from 2.43 lakh hectares in 1994-95 to 3.74 lakh hectares in 2004-05. Production went up from 2.89 lakh tonnes to 4.56 lakh tonnes, respectively, it said.

Sources Attribute the Increase to the Spread of Areca Nut Cultivation to Non-traditional Areas

For example, as per the database, area under Hassan district (non-traditional area) went up from 1,922 hectares in 2001-02 to 3,193 hectares in 2003-04, it was 645 hectares from 400 hectares in Mysore and 1,998 hectares from 514 hectares in Bangalore Rural. A solution could be to find out new consumers for the produce through value addition. But that could take a long time. As per the database, Karnataka had 40 per cent of the 3.74 lakh hectares under arecanut in the country in 2004-05. The State's production constituted 45 per cent the of 4.56 lakh tonnes that the country produced during this year.

Areca Nut Curing

Areca nut (Areca catechu) is popularly known in India as Supari and Shrivardhani. In Meghalaya it is named as Kwai. It thrives in the area owing to heavy rainfall and good drainage. The areca nut is a shade loving plant. The climatic conditions of Meghalaya suit the trees due to the high rainfall (3000 mm). Steep slopes allow continual drainage and clouds provide enough shade for the luxuriant growth of the plant. There is around 6200 hectare area under nut cultivation, which yield around 4200 to 5900 tonnes of the produce every year in the state. Areca nut is considered to be a native of Malaya. This is extensively grown in North Eastern part as well as peninsular Indian region. The palm is tall and slender with a smooth whitish stem reaching a height of 12 to 18m. The stem surmounted by a crown of pinnate leaves. 1-2 m long among which the pinnate is confluent. The fruit is ovoid which is approximately 2.25 cm across and 3.79-6.00 cm long. The fully ripe fruits look bright orange. The pericarp (60%) is hard and fibrous and the kernel (seed 40%) is called areca nut. The nut is about 2.25-3.25 cm in diameter, 2.00-3.00 cm long, varying in shape from conical to spherical and brown in colour with the white tints.

Method of Consumption and Curing in NE Region

The fruit (nut) is consumed in different manners. The crudest way is to get the ripe fresh fruit, shell it with a knife and then cut it into four pieces. One such piece is consumed (chewed) with lime and betel leaf. Ripe fruits are generally harvested for a large scale sale. The nut is also consumed after curing in water. The fresh fruits with husk (little less ripe) are cured in flowing water for some period. The process helps in loosening the husk. This way husk can come out from the nut by hand. About 22% of husk still remains over which is removed with the help of knife. The nut is consumed along with lime and betel leaf and relished by the local Khasis. The curing is mainly for taste, improvement in colour and easy removal of husk. These practices are common in Meghalaya.

Assam and Tripura also grow areca nut extensively. In Tripura state the dry nut is consumed in small pieces with betel leaf and lime. No special type of curing is practiced in the state. Nuts are cured in Upper Assam by keeping the fruits in the pits. A circular pit is dug in the open area around the houses. The size of the pits varies from 2 to 3 m in diameter and 3 to 4 m in depth as required. The pit is plastered with leaves and cowdung at the bottom and inside on the wall. The freshly harvested fruits are charged normally in April and early May for curing. The upper half-meter layer is again filled with leaves, cowdung up to the ground level. Then the pits are opened in December to

January for sale and consumption of the cured produce. Another popular method of processing of nuts in Assam consists of boiling of the immature fruit for about 2 hours after the removal of husk and drying in the sun. The produce is known as *Chikani*. Such fruits are relished by local Assamese people. The modern methods of nut- producing consists of reducing the nut into slices, wafers or grits, followed by drying, flavouring, scenting, colouring and softening. Such processed nut is chewed with betel leaf and eaten sometimes directly.

Curing of Areca Nut in Meghalaya

People of Meghalaya are fond of taking fresh fruit instead of processed one. But fresh fruits are not available round the year as the harvesting periods in the areas are November to December and March to April. Some of the produce is disposed off in the market, whereas slightly immature fruits are cured to improve their quality. The Khasi cure the areca nut in the flowing water. The technique might have been developed by the trial and error method. In olden day a tribal family used to store the areca nuts in earthen pots of water for maintaining their moisture and freshness.

Areca Nut Curing

Areca nut (Areca catechu) is popularly known in India as Supari and Shrivardhani. In Meghalaya it is named as Kwai. It thrives in the area owing to heavy rainfall and good drainage. The areca nut is a shade loving plant. The climatic conditions of Meghalaya suit the trees due to the high rainfall (3000 mm). Steep slopes allow continual drainage and clouds provide enough shade for the luxuriant growth of the plant. There is around 6200 hectare area under nut cultivation, which yield around 4200 to 5900 tonnes of the produce every year in the state. Areca nut is considered to be a native of Malaya. This is extensively grown in North Eastern part as well as peninsular Indian region. The palm is tall and slender with a smooth whitish stem reaching a height of 12 to 18m. The stem surmounted by a crown of pinnate leaves. 1-2 m long among which the pinnate is confluent. The fruit is ovoid which is approximately 2.25 cm across and 3.79-6.00 cm long. The fully ripe fruits look bright orange. The pericarp (60%) is hard and fibrous and the kernel (seed 40%) is called areca nut. The nut is about 2.25-3.25 cm in diameter, 2.00-3.00 cm long, varying in shape from conical to spherical and brown in colour with the white tints.

Method of Consumption and Curing in NE Region

The fruit (nut) is consumed in different manners. The crudest way is to get the ripe fresh fruit, shell it with a knife and then cut it into four pieces. One such piece is consumed (chewed) with lime and betel leaf. Ripe fruits are generally harvested for a large scale sale. The nut is also consumed after curing in water. The fresh fruits with husk (little less ripe) are cured in flowing water for some period. The process helps in loosening the husk. This way husk can come out from the nut by hand. About 22% of husk still remains over which is removed with the help of knife. The nut is consumed along with lime and betel leaf and relished by the local khasis. The curing is mainly for taste, improvement in colour and easy removal of husk. These practices are common in Meghalaya.

Assam and Tripura also grow areca nut extensively. In Tripura state the dry nut is consumed in small pieces with betel leaf and lime. No special type of curing is practiced in the state. Nuts are cured in Upper Assam by keeping the fruits in the pits. A circular pit is dug in the open area around the houses. The size of the pits varies from 2 to 3 m in diameter and 3 to 4 m in depth as required. The pit is plastered with leaves and cowdung at the bottom and inside on the wall. The freshly harvested fruits are charged normally in April and early May for curing. The upper half-meter layer is again filled with leaves, cowdung up to the ground level. Then the pits are opened in December to

January for sale and consumption of the cured produce. Another popular method of processing of nuts in Assam consists of boiling of the immature fruit for about 2 hours after the removal of husk and drying in the sun. The produce is known as Chikani. Such fruits are relished by local Assamese people. The modern methods of nut-producing consists of reducing the nut into slices, wafers or grits, followed by drying, flavouring, scenting, colouring and softening. Such processed nut is chewed with betel leaf and eaten sometimes directly.

Curing of Areca nut in Meghalaya

People of Meghalaya are fond of taking fresh fruit instead of proessed one. But fresh fruits are not available round the year as th harvesting periods in the areas are November to December and March to April. Some of the produce is disposed off in the market, whereas slightly immature fruits are cured to improve thei quality. The Khasi cure the areca nut in the flowing water. The technique might have been developed by the trial and error method. In olden day a tribal family used to store the areca nut in earthen pots of water for maintaining their moisture and freshness.

The water used to be changed every week. Now the areca nuts are cured collectively as a community project in the Ri-War area of Meghalaya. A typical curing of Areca nut consists of the following components:

- **Curing pond:** A pond for the curing of Areca nut is contructed of stones and masonry. It is normally in the size of 15m length, 10m width and 2.5m depth. Such a pond can take 150 baskets of nuts. The size and shape of a pond may vary as per requirement and the land scape of the area; however the depth remains the same.
- **Water flowing Channel:** The perennial stream is the main reuisite for the location of a pond. In the typical arrangement, water flow is diverted from the upstream of the nearby pond at one end and outlet is kept

diagonally opposite of the inlet. The water level maintained 2.35 m from the bottom with the continuous flow.

- **Holding basket:** The holding baskets are locally (Nongpriang village) prepared of bamboo by matting of the size of 1m diameter a top and 2.65 m height with the square bottom of 0.65m. The matting is done with 1 cm bamboo strips by keeping the 3 cm perforation. Each basket has a capacity to hold 1200 kg of areca nut which is equivalent to 12 gunny bags of areca nut.
- **Raising basket:** A small bamboo basket is used for raising the cured fruit from the pond. This basket is matted in the size of 36 cm diameter a top, 30 cm high with the square base of 16 cm.

The Method

The pond is at first fragmented into the square of 90 cm 90 cm each at the top with frames made of the strong bamboo. Thus the holding baskets of 1 m diameter when inserted into these squares could be reduced to that size. The bamboo frames hold the individual baskets and keep them vertical. These baskets are filled with the freshly harvested areca nut. Fruits normally float on the water. The baskets are therefore covered with jute clothes and stone weights are kept over them in order to ensure the proper curing. Once the areca nuts are charged into the holding baskets, then they are not disturbed till the curing is completed. No special care is required except the maintenance of the water level of the pond and water flow. The minimum water flow is assured (361it/min) to prevent the fruits from being spoiled. Excess water flow is considered good for keeping the fruit fresh.

The criteria for adequate curing are:

(i) Yellow colour turns prominently bright yellow; and

(ii) the husk gets freed from kernels.

The normal curing time is around 4 to 5 months. The fruits are then taken out from the pond. The fruits are sometimes cured for one and half months and disposed as and when demand for them arises. Once the fruits are raised from one holding basket then that basket should be completely raised out otherwise the rest of the fruits will be spoiled. The loss in curing is generally 15-30% of the total weight. The loss can be minimized by keeping the same lot in one basket. The units of fresh fruits and nuts in one kg amount to 42 and 75 in number respectively. The dry nuts in one kg however amount to 135 in number. Curing improves colour, taste and freshness of the nut. Cured kernels are less astringent and are better to chew and taste.

Economics

These ponds are constructed by local masons. The cost of the construction of the pond approximates Rs. 20,000 not including the channel-outlet for water. The owner charges Rs. 50 per basket (1200 kg) from the growers. Thus one pond owner earns minimum Rs. 7,000 per 150 baskets capacity pond for one curing. Such curing is done twice a year, and thus utilizing its full capacity.

Preservation of Fruits

Fully ripe arecanuts after preserving are used throughout the year. These are quite very popular in Kerala and Assam. In Assam, fresh fruits are preserved in thick layers of mud. This product is known as Bura Tamul. In Kerala, fresh fruits are stored by steeping in water, resulting in discolouration of outer husk and foul smell due to bacterial attack but the inner core is well preserved. This product is known as Neettadakka. Use of a solution containing sodium benzoate (0.1 %) and potassium metabisulphate (0.2%) acidified to a pH of 3.5-4.0 with hydrochloric acid for steeping ripe nuts after initial heat blanching is suggested to eliminate the foul smell and improve the quality of nuts.

Dried Ripe Nuts

The most popular trade form of arecanut is dried whole nut known as Chali or Kottapak. Ripe nuts are dried in the sun for 35-40 days, dehusked and marketed as whole nuts. The optimum moisture content is around 12%. Inadequate drying results in fungal infection and in a poor quality product. Depending on size, different grades of decrease order are *Moti, Srivardhan, Jamnagar* and *Jini.* The main producing states of Chali are Kerala, Karnataka, Assam and Maharashtra. To facilitate drying and dehusking, the fruits are cut longitudinally into 2 halves and sun-dried for 10 days. The kernels are scooped out and given a final drying. This product, known as Pareha, is popular in Kerala and Karnataka. Mechanical driers are also used to make Chali. Drying takes 60-70 hours over a period of 7-8 days at 45° - 75° C. The dehusking can be done using a manually-operated arecanut dehusker developed by CPCRI, Kasaragod. About 40 kg *chali* can be made within a period of 8 hours.

Kalipak

It is another important processed product of arecanut. Kerala and Karnataka are main producers of Kalipak. Tender nuts of 6-7 months are dehusked, cut into pieces, boiled with water or a diluted extract from previous boiling, coated with *kali* and dried. *Kali* coating can be repeated 3-4 times to get a glossy appearance. *Kali* is the concentrated extract obtained after 3-4 batches of boiling. The *kalipak* is known by different names depending on number, shape and size of the cuts. *Api* or *unde* (without any cuts), *batlu* (transverse cut into halves), *choor* (several longitudinal cuts), *podi* (both longitudinal and transverse cuts) and *erazel* (transverse thin slices). *Iylon* is another variety made from green nuts which are cut transversely into 5-6 discs and without *kali* coating. During preparation of kalipak, the tannin content is reduced substantially. A well-dried product with a dark brown colour, glossy appearance, crisp chewing feel, well-toned astringency and absence of over-mature nuts are rated superior.

Scented Supari

It is made both from chali and kalipak. Chali supari is more popular. The dried nuts are broken into bits, blended with spices and flavour mixture and packed in butter paper. Instead of raw spices, essential oils are used for easy blending, with coconut gratings to avoid microbial growth. Saccharin is occasionally used for sweetening. Rose essence and menthol are commonly used for flavouring.

Uses of Arecanut Constituents and Byproducts

- *Tannins:* Polyphenols or tannins from the major constituent of the nut. Tender nut contains tannins 30-37%, while ripe nuts have only 16-22%. The areca tannins obtained as byproduct from tender nut processing can be utilized for drying clothes, leather, rope, for making black writing ink along with ferrous sulphate, as an adhesive in plywood manufacture and even as food colour.
- *Fat:* The nuts contain 8-12% fat, which is extractable with organic solvents like hexane or chloroform. The fat is rich in myristic acid and can be a good source of myristic acid and its derivatives. Refining of fat with alkai makes it edible. It can be mixed with cocoa fat for confectionery products and as an extender to cocoa butter for various products. It can be a substitute for vanaspati in preparations of sweets and biscuits.
- *Alkaloids:* Arecanut has 1.5% of alkaloids such as arecoline, arecoline, arecaidine guvacine, idoguvacine and guvacolidine. Of them, arecoline alone accounts for 0.24 %. They possess anthelmintic property and are effective against tapeworms and rounworms. It is also used as a CNS depressant drug. It has got anti-bacterial property and inhibits the growth of Escherichia coli, Staphylococcus typhi and Staphylococcus aureus. The blood sugar lowering effect of arecoline is mentioned in Ayurveda.

- *Areca husk:* The husk of arecanut constitutes 60-80% of the total weight of fresh nut. Several processes have been developed for utilization of areca husk for making hard boards, plastic boards and brown wrapping paper. The husk fibre extracted by soaking in water for 3 weeks and beating with a mallet can be used for thick boards, fluffy cushions and non-woven fabrics. It can be a good source of furfural and xylose for industrial applications.
- *Areca stem and leaf sheath:* Arecanut stem is a useful building material. Its timber can be used for making a variety of elegant utility articles like rulers, shelves and waste-paper baskets, due to its hardness. Hollow stem can be used as drainage and irrigation pipes. A process has been developed at CPCRI, Kasaragod, for making plyboards from leaf sheath for tea chest, sint case and file board manufacture. The CFTRI, Mysore, has developed a machine for making cups and throw-away plates which can substitute the paper plates.

7

Betel

The Betel (*Piper betle*) is the leaf of a vine belonging to the Piperaceae family, which includes pepper and Kava. It is valued both as a mild stimulant and for its medicinal properties. The betel plant is an evergreen and perennial creeper, with glossy heart-shaped leaves and white catkin. The Betel plant originated from South (India and Sri Lanka) and South East Asia.

Fig. 7.1

Vernacular Names

The betel leaf is known as *paan* in Urdu/Hindi, and *Taambuul* and *Nagavalli* in Sanskrit. Some of the names in the regions in which it is consumed are: *Vetrilai* (Tamil), *Tamalapaku* (Telugu), *idyache pan* (Marathi), *veeleya/vilya* (Kannada).

Cultivation

The betel leaf is cultivated in most of South and Southeast Asia. Since it is a creeper, it needs a compatible tree or a long pole for suppport.

Paan cultivation is a special type of agriculture. High land and special fertile soil are best for betel. Waterlogged, saline and alkali soils are unsuitable for its cultivation. Farmers who are called barui prepare garden for this. Paan garden is called barouj. Barouj is fenced with bamboo sticks and coconut leaves and on top it is also covered by paddy leaves. The land is dug well and laid out into furrows of 10-15 m length, 75 cm width and 75 cm depth. Oil cakes, cow dung, rotten farmyard manure and leaves are thoroughly incorporated with the topsoil of the furrows and wood ash. The creeper cuttings are planted after proper dressing in the months of May and June, at the beginning of the monsoon season. The plants are neatly arranged in parallel rows about two feet apart, and the saplings are twined around upright sticks of split bamboo and reeds.

Proper shade and irrigation are essential for the successful cultivation of this crop. The plants are regularly watered in the hot months. The leaves of the plant become ready for plucking after one year of planting and the production of the barouj lasts for several years from the date of planting. Betel needs constantly moist soil, but there should not be excessive moisture. Hence, frequent light irrigations are given. The quantity of irrigation water should be such that the standing water should not remain for more than half an hour in the bed. If water logging by heavy rains or excess irrigation occurs, drainage should be arranged immediately. The best time for irrigation is morning or evening.

Dried leaves and wood ash are applied to the furrows at fortnightly intervals and cow dung slurry is sprinkled. Application of different kinds of leaves at monthly intervals is found advantageous for the growth of the betel.

Fig. 7.2

Betel leaf and Areca nut consumption in the world.

In about 3-6 months time, vines grow to a height 150-180 cm. At this stage branching is noticed in the vines. Leaves are removed along with the petiole with the right thumb. Once harvesting is commenced, it is continued almost every day or week. The interval of harvesting varies from 15 days to about a month till the next lowering of vines. After each harvest, manuring has to be done.

There are various types of leaves, the most popular being: Calcutta, Banarasi, Magahi, etc. In South Asia Dinajpur, Rangpur, Chittagong, Faridpur, Jessore, Narayanganj, Barisal and Sylhet are the areas producing most betel. The harvested leaves are used both for domestic consumption and for export to Middle East, to European countries, USA, UK, Pakistan, and Myanmar. Paan is one of the major economic sources of rural Bangladesh. The best Betel leaf is the "Magadhi" variety (literally from the Magadha region) grown near Patna in Bihar, India. In Kerala, the famous variety of betel leaf is from Venmony near Chengannur and it is called "Venmony

Vettila". Betel leaf cultivated in Tirur, Kerala is also of fine quality. Betel leaves exported from Tirur are famous in Pakistan as "Tirur Pan".

Compounds

The active ingredients of betel oil, which is obtained from the leaves, are primarily a class of allylbenzene compounds. Though particular emphasis has been placed on chavibetol (betel-phenol; 3-hydroxy-4-methoxyallylbenzene), it also contains chavicol (p-allyl-phenol; 4-allyl-phenol), estragole (p-allyl-anisole; 4-methoxy-allylbenzene), eugenol (allylguaiacol; 4-hydroxy-3-methoxy-allylbenzene; 2-methoxy-4-allyl-phenol), methyl eugenol (eugenol methyl ether; 3,4-dimethoxy-allylbenzene), and hydroxycatechol (2,4-dihydroxy-allylbenzene).

Several terpenes and terpenoids are present in the betel oil as well. There are two monoterpenes, p-cymene and terpinene, and two monoterpenoids, eucalyptol and carvacrol. Additionally, there are two sesquiterpenes, cadinene and caryophyllene.

Chewing

Fig. 7.3

Chewing display of the items usually included in a chewing session. The leaves are folded in different ways according to the country and have mostly some Calcium hydroxide daubed inside. Slices of the dry areca nut are on the upper left hand and slices of the tender areca nut on the upper right. The pouch on the lower right contains tobacco, a relatively recent introduction.

There is archaeological evidence that the betel leaves are chewed along with the areca nut since very ancient times. It is not known, however, when these two different stimulants substances were put together for the first time. In most countries the mixture of both has a ceremonial and highly symbolical value.

In India, Burma, Nepal, Sri Lanka and other parts of South Asia, as well as Southeast Asia, the leaves are chewed together in a wrapped package along with the areca nut (which, by association, is often inaccurately called the "betel nut") and mineral slaked lime (calcium hydroxide). Catechu, called "Kattha" in Hindi, and ther lavoring substances and spices might be added. The lime acts to keep the active ingredient in its freebase or alkaline form, thus enabling it to enter the bloodstream via sublingual absorption. The areca nut contains the alkaloid arecoline, which promotes salivation (the saliva is stained red), and is itself a stimulant. This combination, known as a "betel quid", has been used for several thousand years. Tobacco is sometimes added.

Betel leaves are used as a stimulant, an antiseptic and a breath-freshener Paan. In India, the betel and areca play an important role in Indian culture, especially among Hindus. Many traditional ceremonies governing the lives of Hindus use betel and areca. For example to pay money to the priest, they keep money in the betel leaves and place it beside the priest.

The betel and areca also play an important role in Vietnamese culture. In Vietnamese there is a saying that "the betel begins the conversation", referring to the practice of people chewing betel in formal occasions or "to break the ice" in awkward situational conversations. The betel leaves and areca nuts are used ceremonially in traditional Vietnamese weddings. Based on a folk tale about the origins of these plants, the groom traditionally offer the bride's parents betel leaves and areca nuts (among other things) in exchange for the bride. The betel and areca nut are praised as an ideal combination to the point that have become important symbols of the ideal married couple bound together in love. Therefore in Vietnamese the phrase "matters of betel and areca") is synonymous with marriage.

The high rate of oral cancer in India is thought to be due to the chewing of betel preparations, though it is unclear whether this can be attributed to the betel leaf, the areca nut, or to the tobacco which is added to some betel preparations. There is an association between the chewing of betel preparations and oral and esophageal squamous cell carcinoma. It is also unclear whether similar health risks exist with traditional recipes as those that are associated with modern betel mixtures. The addition of tobacco leaf (the most harmful and addictive component) to the chewing mixture is a relatively recent one, introduced during colonial times a mere few centuries ago.

The muddling between the betel leaf and the areca nut, by calling the nut "betel nut", is restricted to the colonial languages, like English, French, Dutch and German. This lack of accuracy is likely a legacy of the colonial era in which chewing the mixture was restricted to "the natives". In the languages of the places where the Areca nut is traditionally chewed there is a clear and separate term for the areca nut and another for the betel leaf. This clear distinction is important in societies where both the areca nut and the betel leaf have a ceremonial and even sacred value. Furthermore, there is commonly a specific verb for the activity of chewing both of them together.

There was a certain amount of prejudice among the European colonial powers against the tradition of chewing of Areca nut and betel. Unlike the quick adoption of tobacco by Europeans in the American colonies, chewing areca nut and betel was an addictive habit not adopted by the colonizers of South and Southeast Asia. Officers freshly posted in the East India or Indochina colonies, whether British, French or Dutch, regarded the red-stained mouths of pan-chewers with dread, as something too foreign for them. This abhorrence is not only evident in the writings of authors of the Victorian era, but also in the works of more recent writers like George Orwell, Somerset Maugham and V.S. Naipaul. Often this spirit expresses itself in mockery and ridicule, like in the Broadway musical South Pacific tune "There Is Nothing Like a Dame," with the line *"Bloody Mary's chewing betel nuts ... and she don't use Pepsodent."*

Medicinal Properties

In India, betel is used to cast out (cure) worms. And according to traditional Ayurvedic medicine, chewing areca nut and betel leaf is a good remedy against bad breath (halitosis). They are also said to have aphrodisiac properties.

In Malaysia they are used to treat headaches, arthritis and joint pain. In the Philippines, Thailand, Indonesia and China they are used to relieve toothache. In the Philippines, they are used specifically as a stimulant. In Indonesia they are drunk as an infusion and used as an antibiotic. They are also used in an infusion to cure indigestion, as a topical cure for constipation, as a decongestant and as an aid to lactation.

A related plant *P. sarmentosum,* which is used in cooking, is sometimes called "wild betel leaf".

Paan

Paan, from the word *pan* in Urdu and Hindi is a South and South East Asian tradition which consists of chewing Betel leaf (*Piper betle*) combined with the areca nut. There are many regional variations.

Paan is chewed as a palate cleanser and a breath freshener. It is also commonly offered to guests and visitors as a sign of hospitality and as "ice breaker" to start conversation. It also has a symbolic value at ceremonies and cultural events in South and Southeast Asia. Paan makers may use mukhwas or tobacco as an ingredient in their paan fillings. Although most types of paan contain areca nuts as a filling, some do not. Other types include what is called sweet paan, where sugar, candied fruit and fennel seeds are used.

"Arcea Nut" is often mistakenly translated in the English language as "*Betel nut*", a misnomer, for the betel vine has no nuts. This name originated with the fact that the betel leaf is chewed along with the areca nut, the seed of the tropical palm *Areca catechu*. *Supari* or *adakka* is the term for the nut in many Indic languages.

Although "paan" is generally used to refer to the leaves of the betel vine, the common use of this word refers mostly to the chewing mixture wrapped in the leaves.

Varieties

Paan is available in many different forms and flavours. The most commonly found include:

- *Tobacco (tambaku paan):* Betel leaf filled with powdered tobacco with spices.
- *Betel nut (paan supari, paan masala or sada paan):* Betel leaf filled with a mixture consisting of a coarsely ground or chopped betel nuts and other spices.
- *"Sweet" (meetha paan)*: Betel leaf with neither tobacco nor areca nuts. The filling is made up primarily of coconut, fruit preserves, and various spices. It is also often served with a maraschino cherry.
- *"Trento" (olarno paan)*: It is said that it tastes like betel but has a minty after taste. Eaten along with fresh potatoes, it is served in most Indian restaurants.

There are a variety of betel leaves grown in different parts of India and Bangladesh; the method of preparation also differs from region to region. The delicately flavoured paan from Bengal is known as *Desi Mahoba*. *Maghai* and *Jagannath* are the main paans of Benaras. Paan prepared from small and fragile leaves from south India is known as *Chigrlayele*. The thicker black paan leaves, the *ambadi* and *Kariyele*, are more popular and are chewed with tobacco.

Effects on Health

The International Agency for Research on Cancer (IARC) regards the chewing of betel-quid and areca nut to be a known human carcinogen The main carcinogenic factor is believed to be betel nut. A recent study found that betel-nut paan with and without tobacco increased oral cancer risk by 9.9 and 8.4 times respectively.

Culture

Chewing the mixture of areca nut and betel leaf is a tradition, custom or ritual which dates back thousands of years from South Asia to the Pacific. Ibn Battuta describes this practice as follows: "The betel is a tree which is cultivated in the same manner as the grape-vine; ... The betel has no fruit and is grown only for the sake of its leaves ... The manner of its use is that before eating it one takes areca nut; this is like a nutmeg but is broken up until it is reduced to small pellets, and one places these in his mouth and chews them. Then he takes the leaves of betel, puts a little chalk on them, and masticates them along with the betel."

It constitutes an important and popular cultural activity in many Asian and Oceanic countries, including Myanmar, Cambodia, the Solomon Islands, Thailand, Philippines, Laos, and Vietnam. It is not known how and when the areca nut and the betel leaf were married together as one drug. Archaeological evidence from Thailand, Indonesia and the Philippines suggests that they have been used in tandem for four thousand years or more

Paan is a ubiquitous sight in many parts of South and Southeast Asia, It is known as *beeda* (in Tamil), *sireh* (in Bahasa Melayu) and *Pan Dan* (in Urdu). In urban areas, chewing paan is generally considered a nuisance because some chewers spit the paan out in public areas. The red stain generated by the combination of ingredients when chewed are known to make a colorful stain on the ground. This is becoming an unwanted eyesore in Indian cities like Mumbai, although most see it as an integral part to Indian culture. This is also common in some of the Persian Gulf countries like the UAE and Qatar, where many Asians live. Recently, the Dubai government has banned the import and sale of Paan and the like.

According to traditional Ayurvedic medicine, chewing areca nut and betel leaf is a good remedy against bad breath (halitosis) However, as mentioned previously in this article, chewing this mixture can possibly lead to oral cancer.

Bangladesh

In Bangladesh paan is chewed all over the country by all classe of people. Paan is offered to the guests and festivals irrespective of all religion. A mixture called Dhakai pan khili is famous in Bangladesh and the subcontinent. The sweet pan of the Khasia tribe is famous for its special quality. Paan is also used in Hindu puja and wedding festival and to visit relatives. It has become a rituals and tradition and culture of Bangladesh society. Adult women gathered with pandani along with friends and relatives in leisure time.

India

In he Indian Subcontinent the chewing of betel and areca nut datesback to the pre-Vedic Harappan empire Formerly in India and Sri Lanka it was a custom of the royalty to chew Arecanut and betel leaf. Kings had special attendants carrying a box wit the ingredients for a good chewing session. There was also acustom to chew Areca nut and betel leaf among lovers because of its breath-freshening and relaxant properties. Hence there was a sexual symbolism attached to the chewing of the nut and the leaf. The areca nut represented the male and the betel leaf the female principle. Considered an auspicious ingredient in Hinduism, the Areca nut is still used along with betel leaf in religious ceremonies and also while honoring individuals in most of Southern Asia.

The skilled paan maker is known in North India as a paanwala. Many people believe that their paanwala is the best, considering it an art that takes practice and expert touch.

Paan eating was taken to its zenith of cultural refinement in the pre-partition era in North India, mainly Lucknow, where paan eating became an elaborate cultural custom, and was seen as a ritual of the utmost sophistication. The traditional way of paan making, storing and serving is interesting. The leaves are stored wrapped in a moist, red colored cloth called 'shaal-baaf', inside a metal casket called 'PaanDaani'. The PaanDaani has several lidded compartments, each for storing a different filling or spice. To serve, a leaf is removed from the wrapping cloth, de-veined, and kattha and lime paste is generously applied on its surface. This is topped with tiny pieces of betel nuts, cardamom saffron, (un)/roasted coconut pieces/powder, cloves, tobacco etc, according to the eater's personal preferences. The leaf is then folded in a special manner into a triangle, called 'Gilouree' and is ready to be eaten. On special occasions, the gilouree is wrapped in delicate silver leaf (vark). To serve, a silver pin is inserted to prevent the gilouree from unfolding, and placed inside a domed casket called 'Khaas-daan'. Alternatively, the gilouree is sometimes held together by a paper or foil folded into a funnel with the gilouree's pointed end inserted inside it. Voracious paan eaters do not swallow; instead, they chew it, enjoying its flavours, and then spit it into a spittoon

It is interesting to note that paan made it into Bollywood in the 1970s. In the Bollywood movie "Don" starring Amitabh Bachchan there is a song about paan.

Philippines

Paan has been part of the culture in the Philippines. Known mainl as *tempak sirih* in Bahasa Melayu, it is also commonly and simply referred to as *nga-nga* in the Tagalog dialect. *Nga-nga* literally means "to chew/gnaw". Nowadays, it is mostly popular with the older populations.

Myanmar

Kun-ya is the word for paan in Myanmar, formerly Burma, and has very long tradition. Both men and women loved it and everyhousehold, right up to the 1960s, used to have a special lacqurware box for paan called *kun-it* which would be offered to an visitor together with cheroots to smoke and green tea to drink.The leaves are kept inside the bottom of the box which looks rather like a small hat box but with a top tray for small tins,silver in well-to-do homes, of various other ingredients such as th betel nuts, slaked lime, cutch, aniseed and a nut cutter. The seet form (*acho*) is popular with the young but grownups tend toprefer it with cardamom, cloves and tobacco. Spittoons threfore are still ubiquitous, and signs saying "No paan-spitting" are comonplace as it makes a messy red splodge on floors and walls; many people display betel-stained teeth from the habit. Paan stalls and kiosks used to be run mainly by people of Indianorigin in towns and cities. Smokers who want to kick the habit would also use betel nut to wean themselves off tobacco.

Taugoo in Lower Burma is where the best areca palms are grown indicated by the popular expression "like a betel lover taken to Taungoo". Other parts of the country contribute to the best paan according to another saying "Tada-U for the leaves, Ngamyagyi for the tobacco, Taungoo for the nuts, Sagaing for the slaked lime, Pyay for the cutch". *Kun, hsay, lahpet* (paan, tobacco and pickled tea) are deemed essential items to offer monks and elders particularly in the old days. Young maidens traditionally carry ornamental betel boxes on a stand called *kundaung* and gilded flowers (*pandaung*) in a shinbyu (novitiation) procession. Burmese history also mentions an ancient custom of a condemned enemy asking for 'a paan and a drink of water' before being executed.

Pakistan

The consumption of paan has been a very popular cultural tradition throughout Pakistan since the start, especially in Sindhi households. Pakistan grows a large variety of betel leaf (specifically in the coastal areas of Sindh) although paan is imported in large numbers from countries like Bangladesh, India, Sri Lanka and recently, Thailand. The paan business is famously handled and run by Memon traders, who migrated from western India when Pakistan was created in 1947. To explain the popularity level that the paan is sold at, rough estimates show that an average Pakistani can consume up to 7-8 paans a day.

Cambodia

The chewing of the paan is part of the Khmer culture. Cultivation of Areca nut palm and betel leaves is common in rural areas of Cambodia. In the present times many young people have given up the habit in the urban areas. But most old people still keep it up. In Cambodia everyone has two to four old aunts/fathers and/or mother who chew(s).

Vietnam

In Vietnam the areca nut and the betel leaf are such important symbols of love and marriage that in Vietnamese the phrase "matters of betel and areca" is synonymous with marriage. Areca nut chewing starts the talk between the groom's parents and the bride's parents about the young couple's marriage. Therefore the leaves and juices are used ceremonially in Vietnamese weddings. The folk tale explaining the origin of this Vietnamese tradition is a good illustration of the fact that the combination of areca nut and the betel leaf is ideal to the point that they are practically inseparable, like an idealized married couple.

8

Cardamom

GREEN CARDAMOM

Fig. 8.1

Cardamom is one of the world's very ancient spices and also known as the queen of all spices. It is native to the East originating in the forests of the western ghats in southern India, where it grows wild. Cardamom is grown in Kerala, Tamil Nadu and Karnataka. It is the dried fruit of a herbaceous perennial plant. Warm humid climate, loamy soil rich in organic matter, distributed rainfall and special cultivation and processing methods all combine to make Indian cardamom truly unique-in aroma, flavour, size and it has parrot green colour. It has well established culinary values, and it is used in a wide range of sweets and confectionery. It is an important ingredient of *gram masala,* a combination spice for many vegetarian and non-vegetarian dishes. Cardamom acts as a mouth-freshener after metals. Tea and coffee made with cardamom are pleasantly aromatic and refreshing.

There are three grades in which Indian cardamom is well known in the International market, 'Aleppey green Extra Bold' (AGEB), 'Alleppey Green Bold' (AGB) and 'Alleppey Green Superior' (AGS). Cardamom oil is an essential factor in food items and in preparation of certain medicines. Indian cardamom is known world wide for its quality and is exported to various countries. Today it also grows in Sri Lanka, Guatemala, Indo China and Tanzania. The ancient Egyptians chewed cardamom seeds as a tooth cleaner; the Greeks and Romans used it as a perfume. Vikings came upon cardamom about one thousand years ago, in Constantinople, and introduced it into Scandinavia, where it remains popular to this day.

Cardamom is an expensive spice, second only to saffron. It is often adulterated and there are many inferior substitutes from cardamom-related plants, such as Siam cardamom, Nepal cardamom, winged Java cardamom, and bastard cardamom. However, it is only Elettaria cardamomum which is the true cardamom. Indian cardamom is known in two main varieties: Malabar cardamom and Mysore cardamom. The Mysore variety contains higher levels of cineol and limonene and hence is more aromatic.

Spice Description

Cardamom comes from the seeds of a ginger-like plant. The small, brown-black sticky seeds are contained in a pod in three double rows with about six seeds in each row. The pods are between 5-20 mm (1/4"-3/4") long, the larger variety known as 'black', being brown and the smaller being green. White-bleached pods are also available. The pods are roughly triangular in cross section and oval or oblate. Their dried surface is rough and furrowed, the large 'blacks' having deep wrinkles. The texture of the pod is that of tough paper. Pods are available whole or split and the seeds are sold loose or ground. It is best to buy the whole pods as ground cardamom quickly loses flavour.

Bouquet: Pungent, warm and aromatic.

Flavour: Warm and eucalyptine with camphorous and lemony undertones. Black cardamom is blunter, the eucalyptus and camphor suggestions very pronounced.

Culinary Uses

The pods can be used whole or split when cooked in Indian substantial meals — such as pulses. Otherwise, the seeds can be bruised and fried before adding main ingredients to the pan, or pounded with other spices as required. Keep the pods whole until use. The pod itself is neutral in flavour and not generally used, imparting an unpleasant bitter flavour when left in dishes.

Cardamom is used mainly in the Near and Far East. Its commonest Western manifestation is in Dutch 'windmill' biscuits and Scandinavian-style cakes and pastries, and in akvavit. It features in curries, is essential in pilaus (rice dishes) and gives character to pulse dishes. Cardamom is often included in Indian sweet dishes and drinks. At least partially because of its high price, it is seen as a 'festive' spice. Other uses are; in pickles, especially pickled herring; in punches and mulled wines; occasionally with meat, poultry and shellfish. It flavours custards, and some Russian liqueurs. Cardamom is also chewed habitually (like nuts) where freely available, as in the East Indies, and in the Indian masticory, betel pan. It is a flavouring for Arab and Turkish coffee which is served with an elaborate ritual.

Attributed Medicinal Properties

A stimulant and carminative, cardamom is not used in Western medicine for it own properties, but forms a flavouring and basis for medicinal preparations for indigestion and flatulence using other substances, entering into a synergetic relationship with them. The Arabs attributed aphrodisiac qualities to it (it features regularly in the Arabian Nights) and the ancient Indians regarded it as a cure for obesity. It has been used as a digestive since ancient times. A medicinal (perhaps aphrodisiac) cordial can be made by macerating seeds in hot water.

Plant Description and Cultivation

A perennial bush of the ginger family, with sheathed stems reaching 2-5m (6-16 feet) in height. It has a large tuberous rhizome and long, dark green leaves 30-60 cm (1-2 ft) long, 5-15 cm (2-6") wide. It grows in the tropics, wild and in plantations. Trailing leafy stalks grow from the plant base at ground level. These bear the seed pods. The flowers are green with a white purple-veined tip.

Cardamoms are traditionally grown in partially cleared tropical rain forests, leaving some shade. Similarly, in plantation cultivation, forest undergrowth is cleared and trees thinned to give just enough shade and the rhizome or seeds planted at 3m (10 ft) intervals. The plants are gathered in October-December, before they ripen, to avoid the capsules splitting during drying. They are dried in the sun or bleached with sulphur fumes.

Other Names

Cardamon, Lesser Cardamom

French: cardamome

German: Kardamom

Italian: cardamomo, cardamone

Spanish: cardamomo

Burmese: phalazee

Chinese: ts'ao-k'ou

Indian: chhoti elachi, e(e)lachie, ela(i)chi, illaichi

Indonesian: kapulaga

Malay: buah pelaga

Sinhalese: enasal

Tamil: elam

Thai: grawahn, kravan

The name cardamom is used for herbs within two genera of the ginger family Zingiberaceae, namely *Elettaria* and *Amomum*. Both varieties take the form of a small seedpod, triangular in cross-section and spindle-shaped, with a thin papery outer shell and small black seeds. Elettaria pods are light green in color, while Amomum pods are larger and dark brown.

The two main *genera* of the ginger family that are named as forms of cardamom are distributed as follows:

- *Elettaria* (commonly called cardamom, green cardamom, or true cardamom) is distributed from India to Malaysia.
- *Amomum* (commonly known as black cardamom, brown cardamom, Kravan, Java cardamom, Bengal cardamom, Siamese cardamom, white or red cardamom) is distributed mainly in Asia and Australia.

The Sanskrit name for cardamom is "ela". In Urdu/ Hindi/Gujarati and some Southern Indian languages. It is called "elaichi" or "elchi."

Varieties

There were initially three natural varieties of cardamom plants.

1. *Malabar (Nadan/Native)* - As the name suggests, this is the native variety of Kerala. These plants have pannicles which grow horizontally along the ground.
2. *Mysore* - As the name suggests, this is a native veriety of Karnataka. These plants have pannicles which grow vertically upwards.
3. *Vazhuka* - This is a naturally occouring hybrid between Malabar and Mysore varieties, and the pannicles dont grow vertically nor horizontally, but in between both.

A few planters isolated high yielding plants and started multiplying them on a large scale.

Fig. 8.2

The most popular high yielding variety is Njallani. Njallani, also known as "rup-ree-t" is a unique high-yielding cardamom variety developed by an Indian farmer Sebastian Joseph at Kattappana in the South Indian state of Kerala. Sebastian Joseph and his son Regimon let bees cross-pollinate the cardamom plants and came up with a new high-yielding variety that he named *Njallani,* after his ancestral home. This variety yields 1500 kg/hectare as compared to the conventional 200 kg/ha. The increased yield revolutionised cardamom cultivation in the state of Kerala.

Uses

Both forms of cardamom are used as flavorings in both food and drink, as cooking spices and as a medicine. *Elettaria*

Fig. 8.3

cardamomum (the usual type of cardamom) is used as a spice, a masticatory, and in medicine; it is also smoked sometimes; it is used as a food plant by the larva of the moth *Endoclita hosei*. Cardamom has a strong, unique taste, with an intensely aromatic fragrance. Black cardamom has a distinctly more astringent aroma, though not bitter, with a coolness similar to mint, though with a different aroma. It is a common ingredient in Indian cooking, and is often used in baking in Nordic countries, such as in the Finnish sweet-bread pulla. It is one of the most expensive spices by weight and little is needed to impart the flavor. Cardamom is best stored in pod form because once the seeds are exposed or ground they quickly lose their flavor. However, high-quality ground cardamom is often more readily (and cheaply) available and is an acceptable substitute. For recipes requiring whole cardamom pods, a generally accepted equivalent is 10 pods equals 1½ teaspoons of ground cardamom. In the Middle East, green cardamom powder is used as a spice for sweet dishes as well as traditional flavouring in coffee and tea.

Cardamom pods are ground together with coffee beans to produce a powdered mixture of the two, which is boiled with water to make coffee. Cardamom is also used in some extent in savoury dishes. In Arabic, cardamom is called *al-Hayl.* In Persian, it is called *hel.* In Hebrew, it is also called *hel.* In Gujurati (a derivative of Hindi), it is "E-li-che". In some Middle Eastern countries, coffee and cardamom are often ground in a wooden mortar and cooked together in a mihbaz, an oven using wood or gas, to produce a mixtures that are as much as forty per cent cardamom.

In South Asia, green cardamom is often used in traditional Indian sweets and in *Masala chai (spiced tea).*

Black Cardamom

Black cardamom is usually used in *garam masala* for curries. It is occasionally used as a garnish in basmati rice and other dishes. It is often referred to as fat cardamom due its size ('Moti Elaichi'). Individual seeds are sometimes chewed, in much the same way as chewing-gum. In Northern Europe, cardamom is commonly used in sweet foods, pastries or cakes. It has also been known to be used for gin making.

In Traditional Medicine

Green cardamom in South Asia is broadly used to treat infections in teeth and gums, to prevent and treat throat troubles, congestion of the lungs and pulmonary tuberculosis, inflammation of eyelids and also digestive disorders. It is also reportedly used as an antidote for both snake and scorpion venom bite. *Amomum* is used as a spice and as an ingredient in traditional medicine in systems of the traditional Chinese medicine in China, in Ayurveda in India, Japan, Korea and Vietnam.

Species in the genus *Amomum* are also used in traditional Indian medicine. Among other species, varieties and cultivars, *Amomum villosum* cultivated in China, Laos and Vietnam is used in traditional Chinese medicine to treat stomach-aches, constipation, dysentery, and other digestion problems. "Tsaoko" cardamom *Amomum tsao-ko* is cultivated in Yunnan, China and northwest Vietnam, both for medicinal purposes and as a spice. Increased demand since the 1980s, principally from China, for both *Amomum villosum* and *Amomum tsao-ko* has provided a key source of income for poor farmers living at higher altitudes in localized areas of China, Laos and Vietnam, people typically isolated from many other markets. Until recently, Nepal has been the world's largest producer of large cardamom.Guatemala has become the world's largest producer and exporter of cardamom, with a staggering export total of US$137.2 million for 2007.

Names in Different Languages

In Hindi, Urdu, and Gujarati cardamom is called *elaichi,* and "yelakki" in Kannada and other South Indian languages. It is called Elakka in Malayalam, which is the language of Kerala an Indian province that accounts for 70% of Indian cardamom. In South Asia green cardamom, called "Elaichi" in Marathi, Hindi and Urdu. It is called "Yalakulu in Telugu, "elam" in Tamil. In Hebrew, it is known as Hel . In Persian it is also known as Hel . In Arabic, it is called Hayl.

Cardamom is native to South India and Sri Lanka. Although these countries are the largest producers of cardamom, only a small part of production is exported because of large domestic demand. The main exporting country today is Guatemala, where cardamom cultivation was introduced less than a century ago and the crop is grown entirely for export.

Used Part

Seeds: Because the seeds lose fragrance rather quickly, the fruits (pods) are normally sold and often used whole, or chopped with the seeds.

Family: Zingiberaceae (ginger family).

Effect: Sweet and aromatic, usually described as very pleasant.

Etymology

The spice has similar names in almost all European languages, e.g. *cardamom* (German, English), *kardemomme* (Norwegian, Danish), *cardamomo* (Italian, Portuguese, Spanish) and *kardamon* (Polish, Croatian, Bulgarian and Russian).

The Greek name *kardamomon* is recorded for a spice of Persian origin, but this was probably a cress, whereas in Modern Greek the name *kardamo* can stand for both cardamom and cress. Roman sources tell of the similar spices *amọmum* and *cardamomum*, both of Eastern origin and probably different varieties of cardamom.

In the New Testament the name *amomon* appears in reference to an aromatic plant and may derive from the adjective *amomos* "without reproach". The genus name *elettaria* is derived from the name in Indian languages, e.g. Hindi *elaichi* and Punjabi *ilaichi*. The common source is Sanskrit, where cardamom is called *ela* or *ellka*. From the corresponding Dravidian root *el*, many modern names of cardamom are directly derived, e.g. Tamil *elakkai*.

Uses

Cardamom is often called "the third most expensive spice in the world" (after saffron and vanilla) and the high price reflects the reputation of this most pleasantly scented spice. Despite numerous applications in the cooking styles of Sri Lanka, India and Iran, 60% of world production is exported to Arab countries where it is used to prepare coffee. Cardamom-flavoured coffee *qahwa al-arabiya* is a symbol of Arab hospitality, prepared by adding freshly ground seeds to coffee powder or by steeping a few pods in hot coffee.

Cardamom is also used for cookery in the spicy mixture *baharat* from the Arabic peninsular and in the fiery chilli paste *zhoug* from Yemen. It is often employed for rice-and-meat dishes, e.g. Arabic *kabsah* and *machboos*. To prepare these, meats (sometimes vegetables) are braised in a thick, aromatic sauce and uncooked rice is added and cooked slowly so that it absorbs the sauce and all its flavour.

Fig. 8.4

Indian *biryani* is made by placing layers of cooked rice and aromatic meat or vegetable stews in a large pot. After addition of dried fruits and nuts, the pot is sealed and heated in the oven so that the different flavours mingle. Cardamom is also popular in North and East Africa, where the population is predominantly Arabic. It appears in the Moroccan mixture *ras el hanout* and in the Ethiopian spice mix *berbere*.

In European cuisines, cardamom is less well-known but appears in biscuit recipes (e.g. German *lebkuchen*). European use is low, except in Scandinavian countries, where cardamom is popular not only for biscuits and sweet breads but also for pastries and sausages.

In the Mogul cuisine, cardamom is found in several mild meat dishes in which the pods are fried together with onion, Indian bay leaves and other sweet spices to intensify their fragrance. In Sri Lanka, the pods are added to fiery beef or chicken curries, together with cinnamon. Indian cardamom is slightly smaller than Sri Lankan cardamom, but is generally considered to be more aromatic.

Cardamom-flavoured sweets are found across India, e.g. *gajar halva,* a creamy dessert made from milk, grated carrots, palm sugar and ground cardamom. Sometimes *curry powder* contains small amounts of cardamom and it is also frequently added to the North Indian *garam masala,* especially in Kashmir where Mogul influence is particularly strong. Kashmiri people like sweet green tea flavoured with cardamom pods.

Cardamom seeds lose their flavour quickly when ground. Even if left whole, the seeds show a loss of about 40% of the essential oil per year. Therefore, only whole cardamom pods should be bought and the pods crushed prior to use. Green pods are significantly superior in fragrance to the yellow or white bleached ones. Black (or brown) cardamom is a collective name for several cardamom-related plants growing in mountains from Central Africa to Vietnam. Nepalese cardamom is most often traded in the West. The taste of this spice differs significantly from that of green cardamom and neither can act as a substitute for the other.

9

Black Pepper

Black pepper (*Piper nigrum*) is a flowering vine in the family Piperaceae, cultivated for its fruit, which is usually dried and used as a spice and seasoning. The fruit, known as a peppercorn when dried, is a small drupe five millimetres in diameter, dark red when fully mature, containing a single seed. Peppercorns, and the powdered pepper derived from grinding them, may be described as black pepper, white pepper, red/pink pepper, green pepper, and very often simply pepper. The terms *pink peppercorns, red pepper,* and *green pepper* are also used to describe the fruits of other, unrelated plants.

Fig. 9.1

Black pepper is native to South India (Tamil:milagu, Kannada: meNasu, Malayalam:kurumulaku, Telugu:miriyam, ; Konkani:miriya konu;) and is extensively cultivated there and elsewhere in tropical regions. Black pepper is also cultivated in the Coorg area of Karnataka.

Dried ground pepper is one of the most common spices in European cuisine and its descendants, having been known and prized since antiquity for both its flavour and its use as a medicine. The spiciness of black pepper is due to the chemical piperine. It may be found on nearly every dinner table in some parts of the world, often alongside table salt.

The word "pepper" is ultimately derived from the Sanskrit *pippali*, the word for long pepper via the Latin *piper* which was used by the Romans to refer both to pepper and long pepper, as the Romans erroneously believed that both of these spices were derived from the same plant The English word for pepper is derived from the Old English *pipor*. The Latin word is also the source of German *Pfeffer*, French *poivre*, Dutch *peper*, and other similar forms. In the 16th century, *pepper* started referring to the unrelated New World chile peppers as well. "Pepper" was used in a figurative sense to mean "spirit" or "energy" at least as far back as the 1840s; in the early 20th century, this was shortened to *pep*.

Black pepper is produced from the still-green unripe berries of the pepper plant. The berries are cooked briefly in hot water, both to clean them and to prepare them for drying. The heat ruptures cell walls in the fruit, speeding the work of browning enzymes during drying. The berries are dried in the sun or by machine for several days, during which the fruit around the seed shrinks and darkens into a thin, wrinkled black layer. Once dried, the fruits are called black peppercorns.

White pepper consists of the seed only, with the skin of the fruit removed. This is usually accomplished by process known as retting, where fully ripe berries are soaked in water for about a week, during which the flesh of the fruit softens and decomposes. Rubbing then removes what remains of the fruit, and the naked seed is dried. Alternative processes are used for removing the outer fruit from the seed, including decortication, the removal of the outer layer from black pepper from berries through mechanical, chemical or biological methods

In the U.S., white pepper is often used in dishes like light-colored sauces or mashed potatoes, where ground black pepper would visibly stand out. There is disagreement regarding which is generally spicier. They have differing flavors due to the presence of certain compounds in the outer fruit layer of the berry that are not found in the seed.

Ground Black Pepper and Pepper Shaker

Green pepper, like black, is made from the unripe berries. Dried green peppercorns are treated in a manner that retains the green colour, such as treatment with sulfur dioxide or freeze-drying. Pickled peppercorns, also green, are unripe berries preserved in brine or vinegar. Fresh, unpreserved green pepper berries, largely unknown in the West, are used in some Asian cuisines, particularly Thai cuisine. Their flavor has been described as piquant and fresh, with a bright aroma They decay quickly if not dried or preserved.

A product called orange pepper or red pepper consists of ripe red pepper berries preserved in brine and vinegar. Ripe red peppercorns can also be dried using the same colour-preserving techniques used to produce green pepper Pink pepper from *Piper nigrum* is distinct from the more-common dried "pink peppercorns", which are the fruits of a plant from a different family, the Peruvian pepper tree, *Schinus molle*, and its relative the Brazilian pepper tree, *Schinus terebinthifolius*. In years past there was debate as to the health safety of pink peppercorns, which is mostly no longer an issue Sichuan peppercorn is another "pepper" that is botanically unrelated to black pepper.

Peppercorns are often categorised under a label describing their region or port of origin. Two well-known types come from India's Malabar Coast: Malabar pepper and Tellicherry pepper. Tellicherry is a higher-grade pepper, made from the largest, ripest 10% of berries from Malabar plants grown on Mount Tellicherry Sarawak pepper is produced in the Malaysian portion of Borneo, and Lampong pepper on Indonesia's island of Sumatra. White Muntok pepper is another Indonesian product, from Bangka Island.

The pepper plant is a perennial woody vine growing to four metres in height on supporting trees, poles, or trellises. It is a spreading vine, rooting readily where trailing stems touch the ground. The leaves are alternate, entire, five to ten centimetres long and three to six centimetres broad. The flowers are small, produced on pendulous spikes four to eight centimetres long at the leaf nodes, the spikes lengthening to seven to 15 centimeters as the fruit matures. Black pepper is grown in soil that is neither too dry nor susceptible to flooding, moist, well-drained and rich in organic matter. The plants are propagated by cuttings about 40 to 50 centimetres long, tied up to neighbouring trees or climbing frames at distances of about two metres apart; trees with rough bark are favoured over those with smooth bark, as the pepper plants climb rough bark more readily. Competing plants are cleared away, leaving only sufficient trees to provide shade and permit free ventilation. The roots are covered in leaf mulch and manure, and the shoots are trimmed twice a year. On dry soils the young plants require watering every other day during the dry season for the first three years. The plants bear fruit from the fourth or fifth year, and typically continue to bear fruit for seven years. The cuttings are usually cultivars, selected both for yield and quality of fruit. A single stem will bear 20 to 30 fruiting spikes. The harvest begins as soon as one or two berries at the base of the spikes begin to turn red, and before the fruit is mature, but when full grown and still hard; if allowed to ripen, the berries lose pungency, and ultimately fall off and are lost. The spikes are collected and spread out to dry in the sun, then the peppercorns are stripped off the spikes.

Black pepper is native to India. Within the genus *Piper*, it is most closely related to other Asian species such as *Piper caninum*.

History

Pepper has been used as a spice in India since prehistoric times. Pepper is native to India and has been known to Indian cooking since at least 2000 BC J. Innes Miller notes that while pepper was grown in southern Thailand and in Malaysia, its most important source was India, particularly the Malabar Coast, in what is now the state of Kerala. Peppercorns were a much prized trade good, often referred to as "black gold" and used as a form of commodity money. The term "peppercorn rent" still exists today.

The ancient history of black pepper is often interlinked with (and confused with) that of long pepper, the dried fruit of closely related *Piper longum*. The Romans knew of both and often referred to either as just "piper". In fact, it was not until the discovery of the New World and of chile peppers that the popularity of long pepper entirely declined. Chile peppers, some of which when dried are similar in shape and taste to long pepper, were easier to grow in a variety of locations more convenient to Europe.

Until well after the Middle Ages, virtually all of the black pepper found in Europe, the Middle East, and North Africa traveled there from India's Malabar region. By the 16th century, pepper was also being grown in Java, Sunda, Sumatra, Madagascar, Malaysia, and elsewhere in Southeast Asia, but these areas traded mainly with China, or used the pepper locally. Ports in the Malabar area also served as a stop-off point for much of the trade in other spices from farther east in the Indian Ocean.

Black pepper, along with other spices from India and lands farther east, changed the course of world history. It was in some part the preciousness of these spices that led to the European efforts to find a sea route to India and consequently to the European colonial occupation of that country, as well as the European discovery and colonization of the Americas.

Ancient Times

Black peppercorns were found stuffed in the nostrils of Ramesses II, placed there as part of the mummification rituals shortly after his death in 1213 BC Little else is known about the use of pepper in ancient Egypt, nor how it reached the Nile from India.

Pepper (both long and black) was known in Greece at least as early as the 4th century BC, though it was probably an uncommon and expensive item that only the very rich could afford. Trade routes of the time were by land, or in ships which hugged the coastlines of the Arabian Sea. Long pepper, growing in the north-western part of India, was more accessible than the black pepper from further south; this trade advantage, plus long pepper's greater spiciness, probably made black pepper less popular at the time.

By the time of the early Roman Empire, especially after Rome's conquest of Egypt in 30 BC, open-ocean crossing of the Arabian Sea directly to southern India's Malabar Coast was near routine. Details of this trading across the Indian Ocean have been passed down in the *Periplus of the Erythraean Sea*. According to the Roman geographer Strabo, the early Empire sent a fleet of around 120 ships on an annual one-year trip to India and back. The fleet timed its travel across the Arabian Sea to take advantage of the predictable monsoon winds. Returning from India, the ships travelled up the Red Sea, from where the cargo was carried overland or via the Nile Canal to the Nile River, barged to Alexandria, and shipped from there to Italy and Rome. The rough geographical outlines of this same trade route would dominate the pepper trade into Europe for a millennium and a half to come.

With ships sailing directly to the Malabar coast, black pepper was now travelling a shorter trade route than long pepper, and the prices reflected it. Pliny the Elder's *Natural History* tells us the prices in Rome around 77 CE: "Long pepper . . . is fifteen denarii per pound, while that of white pepper is seven, and of black, four." Pliny also complains "there is no year in which India does not drain the Roman Empire of fifty million sesterces," and further moralises on pepper:

> Black pepper was a well-known and widespread, if expensive, seasoning in the Roman Empire. Apicius' De re coquinaria, a 3rd-century cookbook probably based at least partly on one from the 1st century CE, includes pepper in a majority of its recipes. Edward Gibbon wrote, in *The History of the Decline and Fall of the Roman Empire*, that pepper was "a favourite ingredient of the most expensive Roman cookery".

Postclassical Europe

Pepper was so valuable that it was often used as collateral or even currency. The taste for pepper (or the appreciation of its monetary value) was passed on to those who would see Rome fall. It is said that Alaric the Visigoth and Attila the Hun each demanded from Rome a ransom of more than a ton of pepper when they besieged the city in 5th century. After the fall of Rome, others took over the middle legs of the spice trade, first the Persians and then the Arabs; Innes Miller cites the account of Cosmas Indicopleustes, who travelled east to India, as proof that "pepper was still being exported from India in the sixth century". By the end of the Dark Ages, the central portions of the spice trade were firmly under Islamic control. Once into the Mediterranean, the trade was largely monopolised by Italian powers, especially Venice and Genoa. The rise of these city-states was funded in large part by the spice trade.

It is commonly believed that during the Middle Ages, pepper was used to conceal the taste of partially rotten meat. There is no evidence to support this claim, and historians view it as highly unlikely: in the Middle Ages, pepper was a luxury item, affordable only to the wealthy, who certainly had unspoiled meat available as well In addition, people of the time certainly knew that eating spoiled food would make them sick. Similarly, the belief that pepper was widely used as a preservative is questionable: it is true that piperine, the compound that gives pepper its spiciness, has some antimicrobial properties, but at the concentrations present when pepper is used as a spice, the effect is small Salt is a much more effective preservative, and salt-cured meats were common fare, especially in winter. However, pepper and other spices probably did play a role in improving the taste of long-preserved meats.

Its exorbitant price during the Middle Ages—and the monopoly on the trade held by Italy—was one of the inducements which led the Portuguese to seek a sea route to India. In 1498, Vasco da Gama became the first European to reach India by sea; asked by Arabs in Calicut (who spoke Spanish and Italian) why they had come, his representative replied, "we seek Christians and spices." Though this first trip to India by way of the southern tip of Africa was only a modest success, the Portuguese quickly returned in greater numbers and used their superior naval firepower to eventually gain complete control of trade on the Arabian sea. It was given additional legitimacy (at least from a European perspective) by the 1494 Treaty of Tordesillas, which granted Portugal exclusive rights to the half of the world where black pepper originated.

The Portuguese proved unable to maintain their stranglehold on the spice trade for long. The old Arab and

Venetian trade networks successfully smuggled enormous quantities of spices through the patchy Portuguese blockade, and pepper once again flowed through Alexandria and Italy, as well as around Africa. In the 17th century, the Portuguese lost almost all of their valuable Indian Ocean possessions to the Dutch and the English. The pepper ports of Malabar fell to the Dutch in the period 1661-1663.

As pepper supplies into Europe increased, the price of pepper declined (though the total value of the import trade generally did not). Pepper, which in the early Middle Ages had been an item exclusively for the rich, started to become more of an everyday seasoning among those of more average means. Today, pepper accounts for one-fifth of the world's spice trade.

China

It is possible that black pepper was known in China in the 2nd century BC, if poetic reports regarding an explorer named *Tang Meng* are correct. Sent by Emperor Wu to what is now south-west China, Tang Meng is said to have come across something called *jujiang* or "sauce-betel". He was told it came from the markets of Shu, an area in what is now the Sichuan province. The traditional view among historians is that "sauce-betel" is a sauce made from betel leaves, but arguments have been made that it actually refers to pepper, either long or black.

In the 3rd century CE, black pepper made its first definite appearance in Chinese texts, as *hujiao* or "foreign pepper". It does not appear to have been widely known at the time, failing to appear in a 4th-century work describing a wide variety of spices from beyond China's southern border, including long pepper. By the 12th century, however, black pepper had become a popular ingredient in the cuisine of the wealthy and powerful, sometimes taking the place of China's native Sichuan pepper (the tongue-numbing dried fruit of an unrelated plant).

Marco Polo testifies to pepper's popularity in 13th-century China when he relates what he is told of its consumption in the city of Kinsay (Zhejiang): "... Messer Marco heard it stated by one of the Great Kaan's officers of customs that the quantity of pepper introduced daily for consumption into the city of Kinsay amounted to 43 loads, each load being equal to 223 lbs." Marco Polo is not considered a very reliable source regarding China, and this second-hand data may be even more suspect, but if this estimated 10,000 pounds (4,500 kg) a day for one city is anywhere near the truth, China's pepper imports may have dwarfed Europe's.

As Medicine

Like many eastern spices, pepper was historically both a seasoning and a medicine. Long pepper, being stronger, was often the preferred medication, but both were used.

Black peppercorns figure in remedies in Ayurveda, Siddha and Unani medicine in India. The 5th century *Syriac Book of Medicines* prescribes pepper (or perhaps long pepper) for such illnesses as constipation, diarrhea, earache, gangrene, heart disease, hernia, hoarseness, indigestion, insect bites, insomnia, joint pain, liver problems, lung disease, oral abscesses, sunburn, tooth decay, and toothaches Various sources from the 5th century onward also recommend pepper to treat eye problems, often by applying salves or poultices made with pepper directly to the eye. There is no current medical evidence that any of these treatments has any benefit; pepper applied directly to the eye would be quite uncomfortable and possibly damaging.

Pepper has long been believed to cause sneezing; this is still believed true today. Some sources say that piperine, a substance present in black pepper, irritates the nostrils, causing the sneezing some say that it is just the effect of the fine dust in ground pepper, and some say that pepper is not in fact a very effective sneeze-producer at all. Few, if any, controlled studies have been carried out to answer the question. It has been shown that piperine can dramatically increase absorption of selenium, vitamin B and beta-carotene as well as other nutrients.

As a medicine, Pepper appears in the Buddhist Samaññaphala Sutta, chapter five, as one of the few medicines allowed to be carried by a monk.

Pepper contains small amounts of safrole, a mildly carcinogenic compound Also, it is eliminated from the diet of patients having abdominal surgery and ulcers because of its irritating effect upon the intestines, being replaced by what is referred to as a bland diet.

Flavour

Pepper gets its spicy heat mostly from the piperine compound, which is found both in the outer fruit and in the seed. Refined piperine, milligram-for-milligram, is about one per cent as hot as the capsaicin in chilli peppers. The outer fruit layer, left on black pepper, also contains important odour-contributing terpenes including pinene, sabinene, limonene, caryophyllene, and linalool, which give citrusy, woody, and floral notes. These scents are mostly missing in white pepper, which is stripped of the fruit layer. White pepper can gain some different odours (including musty notes) from its longer fermentation stage.

Pepper loses flavour and aroma through evaporation, so airtight storage helps preserve pepper's original spiciness longer. Pepper can also lose flavour when exposed to light, which can transform piperine into nearly tasteless isochavicine. Once ground, pepper's aromatics can evaporate quickly; most culinary sources recommend grinding whole peppercorns immediately before use for this reason. Handheld pepper mills (or "pepper grinders"), which mechanically grind or crush whole peppercorns, are used for this, sometimes instead of pepper shakers, dispensers of preground pepper. Spice mills such as pepper mills were found in European kitchens as early as the 14th century, but the mortar and pestle used earlier for crushing pepper remained a popular method for centuries after as well.

World Trade

Peppercorns are, by monetary value, the most widely traded spice in the world, accounting for 20 per cent of all spice imports in 2002. The price of pepper can be volatile, and this figure fluctuates a great deal year to year; for example, pepper made up 39 per cent of all spice imports in 1998. By weight, slightly more chilli peppers are traded worldwide than peppercorns. The International Pepper Exchange is located in Kochi, India.

As of 2008, Vietnam is the world's largest producer and exporter of pepper, producing 34% of the worlds *Piper nigrum* crop as of 2008. Other major producers include Indonesia (9%), India (19%), Brazil (13%), Malaysia (8%), Sri Lanka (6%), Thailand (4%), and China (6%). Global pepper production peaked in 2003 with over 3,550,000 t (3,910,000 short tons), but has fallen to just over 2,710,000 t (2,990,000 short tons) by 2008 due to a series of issues including poor crop management, disease and weather. Vietnam dominates the export market, using almost none of its production domestically; however its 2007 crop fell by nearly 10% from the previous year to about 90,000 t (99,000 short tons). Similar crop yields occurred in 2007 across the other pepper producing nations as well.

10

Vanilla

Vanilla is native of the Atlantic coast from Mexico to Brazil. It is grown on a plantation scale in Java, Mauritius, Madagascar, Tahiti, Seycheles, Zanzibar, Brazil and Jamaica and other islands of the West Indies. Malagassy Republic grows 70 to 80 per cent of the world's crop of Vanilla bean followed by Reunion. U.S.A. is the largest importer.

This spice was introduced to India as early as 1835. Its commercial cultivation in India is now restricted to Wynad of Kerala and Nilgiris of Tamil Nadu. The demand for natural vanilla is on the higher side. It is an orchid, belonging to the family Orchidaceae. There are two important species of vanilla viz. *V. planifolia* and *V. pompana.*

The former species produces short thick pods whereas the latter one has the largest pods. V.planifotia has opposite, sessile leave of 10 to 23 cm long which are oblong in shape. Climate and SoilVanilla requires a warm climate with frequent rains and prefers an annual rainfall of 150-300 cm. Partially uncleared jungle lands are ideal for establishing vanilla plantations. In such locations, it would be necessary to retain the natural shade provided by lofty trees which allows penetration of sunlight to the ground level and to leave the soil or the rich humus layer on the top undisturbed.

However, vanilla is cultivated in varied types of soils from sandy loam to laterites.PropagationThe crop is usually established by planting shoot cuttings. If possible cuttings with 18 to 24 internodes should be used as they come to flower earlier than shorter cuttings. But the length of the cuttings are to be adjusted depending on the availability of the planting material and the area to be planted. However, cuttings with less than five to sic inernodes and shorter than 60 cm in length should be avoided when planted directly in the main field.

For raising rooted cutting in polybag even two nodes cutting can be used. It can also be propagated by using tissue culture methods. However, care should be taken to use plantlets not less than 30 cm in length. The leaves of the fourth to fifth nodes from the tip are removed and the cutting is kept loosely rolled up in a cool, shaded place for tow to three weeks.

When ready for insertion, the cutting must be handled very carefully. The lower three to four internodes are placed in a shallow trench 3-4 cm deep and about 10cm wide. The evacuated soil is used to loosely fill this trench.

This operation is usually carried out at the beginning of the rainy season. Land preparationPreparing the soil for prospective pepper or vanilla plantations must take into account the need to supply each vine with a support or stake upon which it can climb. Later it will be seen that these supports are divided into two categories non-living and living.

In the former, site preparation is unaffected because it is possible to put the non-living support, for example a wooden stake, in place at any time after the soil has been cultivated by general ploughing or hole preparation. Where living supports are used, these must be established before taking the cuttings from the pepper or vanilla plants.

The supports most often used for pepper are either plants which are already in the plantation or trees from original forest growth, left in place during land clearance. In the latter case, the fact that the supports are already present makes it essential that the holes at the foot of each support are made by hand.

Fig. 10.1

Planting

Vanilla, being a climbing vine requires support for growing. It flourishes well in partial shade of about 50 per cent sunlight and low branching trees with rough bark and small leaves are grown for this purpose. Some of the trees now being used include Glyricidia, Erythrina, Jatropha carcas, Plumeria alba and Casuarna equisetifolia. If the support selected is a legume, it will be able to enrich the soil also.

The growth of live standards is to be adjusted as to make them branch at a height of 120 to 150 cm, to facilitate training of the vines around the branching shoots. The standards are planted at a spacing of 2.5 to 3 metres between rows and two metres between rows and two metres within the row making a population of 1600 to 2000 trees per hectare. In high density planting use of 1m spacing has been used to plant around 4000 vies in an acre ... but after 5 years pruning and spacing will be required. If limb cuttings are used for planting supports the ideal time is with the onset of rains after the summer, and it should be atleast six months before planting vanilla cuttings. Vanilla is generally planted at a time when the weather is not too rainy or too dry.

The months of June July, August-September are ideal for vanilla cultivation. Cuttings for planting should be collected in advance, and after removing three or four basal leaves, dipped in one per cent Bordeaux mixture and kept in shade to loose moisture for about a week. Since establishment of cuttings is almost cent per cent, planting of single cutting per support is enough.The defoliated part of the vine is laid on the loose soil surface and covered with a thin layer of about two to three cm soil. The basal tip of the cutting should be kept just above the soil to prevent rotting. The growing end is gently tied to the support for climbing by the aerial roots.

The cuttings are shaded with tall dry grass, palm fronds or with other suitable materials. In dry soil, a light sprinkling of water helps for early establishment of cuttings. It takes about four to eight weeks for the cuttings to strike roots and to show initial signs of growth. Vanilla can also be planted as an intercrop in coconut and arecanut plantations.

Mulching

This term refers to the act of spreading, on a cultivated plot, a fairly dense layer of a material which is usually, but not necessarily, of vegetable origin. This layer which should be as durable as possible, protects the soil from run-off and exposure to the sun, regulates rainfall infiltration, slows down evaporation, arrests or at least considerably restricts wed growth and is generally favourable to growth and yield since it also adds humus to the soil on decomposition.

Mulching is used on many of the species studied, and is applied in various ways. mulching of vanilla is carried out as soon as possible, after planting. A mixture of grasses and leguminous species is recommended.TrainingIf the vine is permitted to grow up on a tree, it will rarely blossom, so long as it is growing upward. Hence, vines are allowed to grow upto 1.50 m and then trained horizontally on the branch of supports and latercoiled round them.

Fig. 10.2

The vines commence flowering in the second or third year depending on the length of cuttings used due to the peculiar structure of the flower, artificial pollination by hand is the rule for fruit setting. The procedure involved is simple and done easily by children and women. Using a pointed bamboo splinter or pin, another is pressed against the stigma with the help of thumb and thus smearing the pollen over it. Generally 85 to 100 per cent success is obtained by hand pollination.

Fig. 10.3

The ideal time for pollination is between 6 a. m to 1 a.m. Unfertilized flowers fall within two or three days. Normally 5 to 6 flowers per inflorescence and a total of not more than 10 to 12 inflorescences per vine are pollinated. The excess flower buds are nipped off to permit the development of other pods. Pods take six weeks to attain full size from fertilization but takes 4 to 10 months to reach full maturity depending upon the locations.Maintenance of plantationOnce established, the vines have to be given constant attention.

The plantation should be visited frequently to train the vines to grow at convenient level, to regulate the growth of the vines and the supports, to watch for disease and pests and to always keep leaf mulch around the vines. Any operation done in the plantation should not disturb the roots, which are mainly confined to the mulch and surface layer of soil. In vanilla plantations provided with living supports, adjusting the shading is linked with correct pruning of the supports, a task, which requires care and attention. In the first year, it is enough to prune the lateral branches so as to obtain a sufficiently high single trunk.

Further growth in height is then prevented by topping the tree, which encourages the formation of a canopy but still provides light shade. Leucaena leucocephala is very well suited to this approach, as the pruning, which is left at the base of the tree, provide the soil with nitrogen-rich organic matter.

With vanilla, the shading provided by the living support is often inadequate. It can be supplemented by planting a range of shade trees, for example, Albizzia lebbeck and Inga edulis.

When the support trees grow up, they are pruned early to induce branching. It is desirable to develop an umbrella shape for the trees to give better shade and protection to the growing vines.

If the trees do not drop off leaves they are pruned before the commencement of heavy rains to allow in more sunlight.

The pruned vegetation is chopped and applied as a mulch in the plantation. The way in which the vine is trained has an effect on flower production. If the vine is permitted to grown up on a tree it will rarely blossom so long as it is growing upward.

For convenience of cultural operation the vines are allowed to grow up to a height of 1.2 to 1.5 metre and then trained horizontally on the branch of supports and later coiled round them. Alternatively two bamboo splits can be tied to two adjacent support trees and can be utilized for training the vines. Coiling of vines in this manner helps to accumulate carbohydrate and other flower forming materials, beyond the bend and to induce flower production in this portion of the vine.Plant Protection :Vanilla plants are, in general, free from any major pests and disease incidence.

However, conditions leading to weakened plants by drought, lack of nutrients, too much sun, over pollination and bean production certainly favour the incidence of diseases. Environmental conditions favouring diseases are excessive moisture, prolonged rainy weather, insufficient drainage, too much shade, damage to roots and over planting of vanilla. Fungal diseases like shoot tip rot, stem and bean rot caused by *Phytophthora sp.* as well as immature bean dropping are sometimes noticed. Fusarium oxysporum causes another kind of stem rot. Incidence of diseases can be reduced by maintaining conditions leading to vigorous growth of vines such as adequate shade, heavy mulch especially during the dry season, moderate to light pollination, irrigation during extended dry periods, application of fertilizers and providing adequate drainage. Over crowding of vines in a single support tree also should be avoided.

Fig. 10.4

The disease affected portions should be removed regularly and fungicides such as one per cent Bordeaux Mixture or 0.2 per cent Indofil-MA5 (200 g in 100 litres of water) may be applied in a need based manner to reduce the spread of diseases. Among insect pests, a few small

Lamellicorn beetles (*Hopliaretusa and Saula ferruginea Grest*) and an ash-gray weevil (*Cratopus retuse*) bite holes in the flowers and often destroys the column. In addition to these, there are a few caterpillars and certain earwigs, snails and slugs, which live on tender parts of the plant such as shoot, flower buds, immature beans etc. Grasshoppers and crabs are also found to cut growing tip of plants during the establishment stage of the plantation. Chickens, sometimes, cause considerable damage to the roots while scratching the mulch kept around the plants. Regular surveillance and removal of pests can reduce their damage to a great extent.

Harvesting and Curing

When immature, the bean is dark green in colour, but when ripe yellowing commences from its distal end. This is the optimum time for harvesting the bean. If left on the vine the bean turns yellw on the remaining portion and starts splitting, giving out a small quantity of oil reddish brown in colour, called the Balsam of Vanilla. Eventually they become dry, brittle and finally become scentless. Therefore, the artificial methods are employed to cure vanilla. Vanillin is developed as a result of the enzyme action on the glucosides contained in the beans during the process of curing. Basically any curing method involves the following four stages.

Quality Requirements

The primary quality determinant for cured vanilla beans is the aroma/flavour character. Other factors of significance in quality assessment are the general appearance, flexibility, the length and the vanillin content. The relative importance of these various quality attributes is dependent upon the intended end-use of the cured beans.

Traditionally, the appearance, the flexibility and size characteristics have been of importance since there is fairly close relationship between these factors and the aroma/

flavour quality. Top quality beans are long, fleshy, supple, very dark brown to black in colour, somewhat oily in appearance, strongly aromatic and free from scars and blemishes. Low-quality beans are usually hard, dry, thin, brown or reddish-brown in colour and possess a poor aroma. The moisture content of top grade beans is high (30 to 40 per cent), whereas it may be as little as 10 per cent in the lower grades. At one time, the presence of a surface coating of naturally exuded vanillin crystals ('frosting') was regarded as an indicator of good quality, though this is no longer considered so.

Traditional Curing Methods

A number of procedures have been evolved for the curing of vanilla but they are all characterised by four phases:

(a) *'Killing' or wilting:* This stops further vegetative development in the fresh bean and initiates the onset of enzymatic reactions responsible for the production of aroma and flavour. Killing is indicated by the development of a brown coloration in the bean.

(b) *'Sweating':* This involves raising the temperature of the killed beans to promote the desired enzymatic reactions and to provoke a first, fairly rapid drying to prevent harmful fermentations. During this operation, the beans acquire a deeper brown coloration and become quite supple, and the development of an aroma becomes perceptible.

(c) The third stage entails slow drying at ambient temperature, usually in the shade, until the beans have reached about one-third of their original.

(d) In the final stage, known as 'conditioning', the beans are stored in closed boxes for a period of three months or longer to permit the full development of the desired aroma and flavour.

The two most important of the various traditional procedures for curing vanilla beans are those of Mexico and the Indian Ocean islands producing 'Bourbon' vanilla.

Mexican Curing Methods

The two main traditional forms of curing employed in Mexico are the sun-wilting and the oven-wilting procedures. The former is the oldest known method of curing and the latter was introduced around 1850. Both methods are still widely used by the specialist curing firms in Mexico which process the vast bulk of the vanilla crop. The harvesting period in Mexico extends from

November to January and curing by either method takes around five to six months before the product is ready for the market. '*Sun-wilting*'- On arrival at the curing house, the fresh beans may be set aside in a store for a few days until required and during this time the beans start to shrivel. The fresh beans first have their peduncles removed and are then sorted according to their degree of maturity, size and into unsplit and split types. This is done as the various sorts cure at different rates. Beans, which are already beginning to darken, are removed, wiped with castor oil and are cured separately.

The beans are killed by exposing them to the sun for a period of about five hours on the day after sorting. The fresh beans are spread out on dark blankets resting on a cement patio or on wooden racks. In the afternoon, the beans become too hot to hold by hand and are then covered by the edges of the blanket. In the mid-to late afternoon before the beans have begun to cool, the thick ends of the beans are laid towards the center of the blanket and rolled up. The blanket rolls are immediately taken indoors and are placed in blanket-lined, air tight mahogany boxes to undergo their first ' sweating'. Blankets and matting are placed over the sweating boxes to prevent loss of heat. After 12 to 24 hours, the beans are removed and inspected. Most of the beans will have begun to acquire a dark-brown colour indicating a good 'killing'. Beans which have retained their original green colour or which have an uneven coloration are separated and are subjected to oven-wilting. Those beans, which have been properly killed, are next subjected to a process involving periodic 'sunnings' and sweatings. 'Sunning' entails spreading the beans on blankets and exposing them to the sun for two to three hours during the hottest part of the day when weather conditions are favourable. During the remaining part of the day, unless a sweating is to be undertaken, the beans are stored indoors on wooden racks in a well-ventilated room. There are two distinct phases to this sunning/sweating stage. The first phase involves a fairly rapid drying in which the beans are given 'sunnings' virtually every day and several overnight sweatings until they become supple. This takes about five to six days.

A preliminary sorting into lots corresponding to the various grades is usually carried out at this juncture. This is followed by further 'sunnings' and additional but less frequent sweatings. In practice, 'sunnings' are not carried out every day in this second phase since, apart from constraints imposed by the weather, too rapid drying is considered to be detrimental to quality. Some 20 to 30 days after killing, most of the beans become very supple and acquire characteristics close to those of the final product and are ready for the next stage of very slow drying indoors. The total number of sweatings undertaken during the 'sunning/ sweating' operation can vary between four and eight. Those beans, which require a large number of sunnings and sweatings generally, provide a low-quality product. Very slow drying indoors lasts for approximately one month and a further sorting into grades is usually carried out during this time. The beans are regularly inspected and those, which have achieved the requisite state of dryness, are immediately removed from the racks for 'conditioning'. The overall sweating and drying operation may take up to eight weeks from the time of 'killing', according to the prevailing weather conditions. Small and split beans are usually ready for conditioning earlier than perfect, large beans. Beans removed for conditioning are sorted again and are straightened by he fingers. This operation is also useful in that it spreads the oil, which exudes during the curing process and gives the beans their characteristic luster. The beans are next tied into bundles of about fifty with black string. The bundles are wrapped in waxed paper and are placed in waxed paper lined, metal conditioning boxes. Conditioning lasts for at least three months and during this period the beans are regularly inspected. Mouldy beans are removed for treatment and those, which are not developing the required aroma may be re-subjected to 'sunnings and sweatings'.

At the end of the conditioning period, the beans are given a final grading and are packed for shipment. 'Oven-wilting'- In this procedure, use is made of a specially constructed brick or cement room, known as a calorifico, which serves as an autoclave. The room measures approximately 4 × 4 × 4 metres and incorporates a wood-fired heater, which is stoked from the outside. It is fitted with a small access door and has wooden racks fitted along the walls. The beans to be killed by this method are divided into piles of up to 1000 and are then rolled up in a blanket, which is finally covered with matting to form a malleta.

The malletas are moistened with water and are placed on the shelves in the calorifico. Water is poured onto the solid floor to maintain a high humidity, the door is closed and the heating fire is lit. In about 12 hours, the temperature inside the calorifico reaches 60 °C. After a further 16 hours, a temperature of 70 °C is attained and this is maintained for another 8 hours. The malletas are removed after a total of 36 hours in the calorifico. If the temperature cannot be raised above 65 °C, then the total period of autoclaving is extended to 48 hours. On removal from the calorifico, the matting is quickly stripped from the malletas and the blanket wrapped beans are placed in sweating boxes. After 24 hours, the beans are removed and inspected. The killed beans are then subjected to repeated sunnings and sweatings, described above under 'Sun-wilting'. Should the weather be overcast, the killed beans are stored on racks indoors in a well-ventilated room until sunning is possible. However, if the weather does not improve within three days, the batch is reprocessed through the calorifico and sweating box.

Bourbon Curing Method

Bourbon vanilla is the name given to the product from the former French possessions in the Indian Ocean, which employ a curing technique first developed on the island of Reunion, formerly known as Bourbon. Production of Bourbon-type vanilla is now dominated by Madagascar, with the Comoro Islands and Reunion as smaller but important sources. The Bourbon curing technique is distinguished from those of Mexico in that 'killing' is achieved by scalding the beans in hot water and fewer sweatings are undertaken.

The Bourbon product usually has higher moisture content than the corresponding Mexican grade and is frequently frosted. As in Mexico, curing of vanilla is carried out by specialist firms rather than by the vanilla growers. Slight variations in the curing technique are practiced in the various producing islands and the following is a description of the procedure evolved on Madagascar. On arrival at the curing factory, the beans are sorted according to the degree of maturity, size, and into split and unsplit types. Batches of beans, weighing 25 to 30 kg, are loaded into openwork cylindrical baskets, which are then plunged into containers full of hot water heated to 63 to 65 °C over a wood fire. Batches of beans, which will eventually make up the top three qualities, are immersed for 2 to 3 minutes, while smaller and split beans are treated for less than 2 minutes. The warm beans are rapidly drained, wrapped in a dark cotton cloth and are placed in a cloth-lined sweating box. After 24 hours, the beans are removed and inspected to separate those, which have not been properly killed.

The next stage of sun-drying is carried out on a plot of dry, easily drained ground, at some distance from roads to avoid contamination by dust. The killed beans are spread out on dark cloths resting on slatted platforms, constructed from bamboo and raised 70 cm above the ground. After one hour of direct exposure to the sun, the edges of the cloth are folded over the beans to retain the heat. The cloth-covered beans are then left for a further two hours in the sun before the blanket is rolled up and taken indoors. This procedure is repeated for 6 to 8 days until the beans become quite supple. The third stage involves slow drying in the shade for a period of 2 to 3 months. The beans are spread on racks, mounted on Supports and are spaced 12 cm apart in a well-ventilated room. During this slow drying operation, the beans are sorted regularly and those which have dried to the requisite moisture content are immediately removed for conditioning. In some localities in the Bourbon producing areas, where the weather is frequently inclement during the sun-and indoor-drying periods of curing, ovens set at 45 to 50 °C have traditionally been used. Conditioning of the beans is carried out in a similar manner to that described for Mexico and takes about 3 months for completion. The overall curing process for Bourbon vanilla lasts for 5 to 8 months. The main nds from June to early October.

A modification to the traditional Bourbon curing method was devised in Puerto Rico in the 1940s and was adopted by the vanilla co-operative at Castaner. On arrival at the factory, the beans are sorted into split and unsplit types and are then killed as soon as possible. Prior to killing, the beans are wiped with a damp cloth. Scalding entails three 10-second immersions at 30-second intervals in a water bath at 80 °C. After draining, the beans are wrapped in a blanket and are placed in a sweating box. Killing is followed by daily two-hour sunnings and overnight sweatings for about seven days until the beans become supple. The next stage of indoor air-drying is continued until the beans reach one-third of their original weight. The beans are then bundled and conditioned in tin boxes until they dry to one-quarter of their original weight. By contrast to Bourbon vanilla from the Indian Ocean producers, Puerto Rican vanilla scalded at 80 °C rarely frosts. When the weather is unsuitable for sunning, the beans are sweated in a closed oven at 45 °C containing a pan of water.

Other methods for V. fragrans The Guadeloupe technique entails killing by making scars with a pin along the faces of the bean and then exposing the beans, wrapped in a blanket, to the sun for a few hours. The pin, which should be sterilised regularly, is fitted into a cork to protrude no more than 2 mm. After killing, the curing process is similar to that of Mexico. Two other methods, which tend to provide a poor-quality product, are the 'Guiana method' and the 'Peruvian process'. The' Guiana method' involves killing the beans by placing them in the ashes of a fire until they begin to shrivel. On removal, the beans are wiped clean, rubbed with olive oil, the lower ends are tied with string to prevent splitting, and they are then left to dry in the open air. In the 'Peruvian process', the beans are killed by immersion in boiling water and are then tied at the ends and hung up in the open air. After drying for about twenty days, the beans are lightly smeared with castor oil and are tied in bundles a few days later. No distinctive local method of curing appears to have been evolved in Java. Modifications of the Mexican and Bourbon methods were commonly used but in general less care seems to have been taken in curing and grading. The quality of the Java product has never compared favourably with those of Mexico or the Bourbon producers.

Curing of Tahiti Vanilla

Since *V. tahitensis* is indehiscent, the beans are not killed artificially but are harvested when mature. The tip of the bean turning brown characterises this. The curing is carried out by specialist firms, which employ a method bearing similarities to the Mexican procedure. On receipt by the curing firms, the beans are placed in piles, which are turned daily.

Beans, which are entirely brown, indicating that vegetative life has ceased, are removed for sweating and drying. The 'killed' beans are spread out on blankets resting on raised, wooden racks and are exposed to the sun for three to four hours. The warm beans are then rolled up in the blanket and are placed in a sweating box overnight. This process is repeated for fifteen to twenty days with progressively less frequent overnight sweatings. Finally, the beans are left outside in layers 10 cm deep to dry in the wind. When at the requisite state of dryness, beans are removed from the racks and are placed in large crates.

Most beans are sorted and sold shortly after drying has been completed and without any lengthy 'conditioning' period. The main harvest is collected during February and March and drying is usually completed during July and August. If the beans are kept for a long period before sale, they are stored in tins.

Yield

The yield of vanilla varies depending upon the age of vines and the method of cultivation. Normally it starts yielding from the third year and the yield goes on increasing till the seventh or eighth year. Thereafter the yield slowly starts declining till the vines are replanted after another seven to ten years. In one acre you can plant about 3000 vanilla plants.

Each plant is expected to yield about 500-800 grams of green beans per year. Under reasonable level of management, the yield range of a middle aged plantation will be about 500 kg-1000 kgs of green beans per acre. For every 5 kgs of green beans you can get aroun 1 kgs of cured beans.

Market for Vanilla

The main application of natural vanilla is for flavouring ice creams and soft drinks. It is estimated that nearly 300 tonnes of vanilla beans is used in USA every year in the preparation of cola type drinks. The major industrial purchasers of vanilla are pharma companies and soft drink companies like Coke and Pepsi. However the fact remains that market for natural vanilla essence is today largely only confined to the West. World production of vanilla beans is approximately 3000 tonnes per annum. Madagascar provides about 50 per cent of the world supply and the rest is from Indonesia. Comoro and Reunion.papua new guinea and India. Production in Indonesia is nearly 500 tonnes. The present international demand from vanilla is about 19,000 tonnes.India has just come into the market for production. Our production last year was a meagre 60 tonnes only.

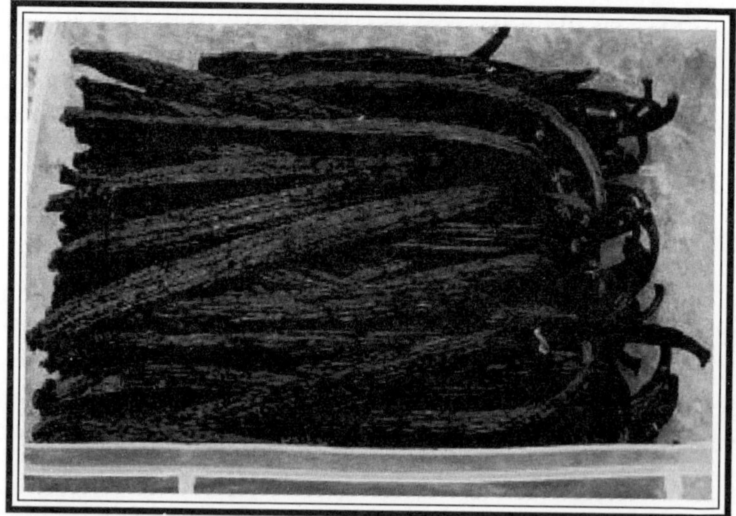

Fig. 10.5

Vanilla imports are dominated by three countries- USA, France and Germany. Importers in Germany and France are suppliers to other markets especially in Europe. Europe imports generally high quality beans while USA accepts low quality beans also. There is an understanding between Bourbon vanilla producing countries viz. Madagascar, Comoro and Reunion, and importers of France and Germany in the marketing of vanilla beans.

11

Banana

Banana is the common name for a fruit and also the herbaceous plants of the genus Musa which produce this commonly eaten fruit. They are native to the tropical region of Southeast Asia. Bananas are likely to have been first domesticated in Papua New Guinea. Today, they are cultivated throughout the tropics.

Fig. 11.1

Banana plants are of the family Musaceae. They are cultivated primarily for their fruit, and to a lesser extent for the production of fibre and as orna-mental plants. As the banana plants are normally tall and fairly sturdy they are often mistaken for trees, but their main or upright stem is actually a pseudostem (literally "fake stem"). For some species this pseudostem can reach a height of up to 2–8 m, with leaves of up to 3.5 m in length. Each pseudostem can produce a bunch of yellow, green or even red bananas before dying and being replaced by another pseudostem.

The banana fruit grow in hanging clusters, with up to 20 fruit to a tier (called a hand), and 3-20 tiers to a bunch. The total of the hanging clusters is known as a bunch, or commercially as a "banana stem", and can weigh from 30-50 kg. The fruit averages 125 g, of which approximately 75% is water and 25% dry matter content. Each individual fruit (known as a banana or 'finger') has a protective outer layer (a peel or skin) with a fleshy edible inner portion. Both skin and inner part can be eaten raw or cooked. Western cultures generally eat the inside raw and throw away the skin while some Asian cultures generally eat both the skin and inside cooked. Typically, the fruit has numerous strings (called 'phloem bundles') which run between the skin and inner part. Bananas are a valuable source of vitamin B6, vitamin C, and potassium.

Bananas are grown in at least 107 countries In popular culture and commerce, "banana" usually refers to soft, sweet "dessert" bananas. The bananas from a group of cultivars with firmer, starchier fruit are called plantains. Bananas may also be cut and dried and eaten as a type of chip. Dried bananas are also ground into banana flour.

Although the wild species have fruits with numerous large, hard seeds, virtually all culinary bananas have seedless fruits. Bananas are classified either as dessert bananas (meaning they are yellow and fully ripe when eaten) or as green cooking bananas. Almost all export bananas are of the dessert types; however, only about 10-15% of all production is for export, with the United States and European Union being the dominant buyers.

The banana plant is a pseudostem that grows to 6 to 7.6 metres (20-25 feet) tall, growing from a corm. Leaves are spirally arranged and may grow 2.7 metres (9 ft) long and 60 cm (2 ft) wide. The banana plant is the largest of all herbaceous flowering plants. The large leaves grow whole, but are easily torn by the wind, resulting in the familiar frond look.

A single, sterile, male banana flower, also known as the *banana heart* is normally produced by each stem (though on rare occasions more can be produced - a single plant in the Philippines has five. Banana hearts are used as a vegetable in Southeast Asia, steamed, in salads, or eaten raw. The female flowers are produced further up the stem and produce the actual fruit without requiring fertilization. The fruit has been described as a "leathery berry" In cultivated varieties, the seeds have degenerated nearly to non-existence; their remnants are tiny black specks in the interior of the fruit. The ovary is inferior to the flower; because of their stiff stems and the positioning of the ovary and flower, bananas grow sticking up, not hanging down.

Some sources assert that the genus of the banana, *Musa*, is named for Antonio Musa, physician to the Emperor Augustus. Others say that Linnaeus, who gave the genus its name in 1750, simply adapted an Arabic word for banana, *mauz* The word *banana* itself comes from the Arabic word *banan*, which means "finger" The genus contains numerous species; several produce edible fruit, while others are cultivated as ornamentals.

Properties

Bananas come in a variety of sizes and colours when ripe, including yellow, purple, and red. Bananas can be eaten raw though some varieties are generally cooked first. Depending upon cultivar and ripeness, the flesh can vary in taste from starchy to sweet, and texture from firm to mushy. Unripe or green bananas and plantains are used for cooking various dishes such as banana pudding and are the staple starch of many tropical populations. Banana sap is extremely sticky and can be used as a practical adhesive. Sap can be obtained from the pseudostem, from the fruit peelings, or from the fruit flesh.

Most production for local sale is of green cooking bananas and plantains, as ripe dessert bananas are easily damaged while being transported to market. Even when transported only within their country of origin, ripe bananas suffer a high rate of damage and loss.

The commercial dessert cultivars most commonly eaten in temperate countries (species *Musa acuminata* or the hybrid *Musa paradisiaca,* a cultigen) are imported in large quantities from the tropics. They are popular in part because, being a non-seasonal crop, they are available fresh year-round. In global commerce, by far the most important of these banana cultivars is 'Cavendish', which accounts for the vast bulk of bananas exported from the tropics. The Cavendish gained popularity in the 1950s after the previously mass produced cultivar, Gros Michel, became commercially unviable due to Panama disease, a fungus which attacks the roots of the banana plant.

The most important properties making 'Cavendish' the main export banana are related to transport and shelf life rather than taste; major commercial cultivars rarely have a superior flavour compared to the less widespread cultivars. Export bananas are picked green, and then usually ripened in ripening rooms when they arrive in their country of destination. These are special rooms made air-tight and filled with ethylene gas to induce ripening. Bananas can be ordered by the retailer "ungassed", however, and may show up at the supermarket still fully green. While these bananas will ripen more slowly, the flavor will be notably richer and the banana peel can be allowed to reach a yellow/brown speckled phase, and yet retain a firm flesh inside. Thus, shelf life is somewhat extended.

The vivid yellow colour normally associated with supermarket bananas is in fact a side-effect of the artificial ripening process. Cavendish bananas that have been allowed to ripen naturally on the plant have a greenish-yellow appearance which changes to a brownish-yellow as they ripen further. Although both the flavour and texture of "tree ripened" bananas is generally regarded as superior to any type green-picked fruit, once natural ripening has commenced the shelf life is typically only 7-10 days, making commercial distribution impractical. For most people the only practical means of obtaining such fruit is growing it themselves, however this is also somewhat problematic, as the bananas all tend to ripen at once and have very poor keeping properties.

The flavour and texture of bananas are also affected by the temperature at which they ripen. Bananas are refrigerated to between 13.5 and 15 °C (57 and 59 °F) during transportation. At lower temperatures, the ripening of bananas permanently stalls, and the bananas will eventually turn gray as cell walls break down. The skins of ripe bananas will quickly turn black in the 4°C environment of a domestic refrigerator, although the fruit inside remains unaffected.

It should be noted that *Musa paradisiaca* is also the generic name for the common plantain, a coarser and starchier variant not to be confused with *Musa acuminata* or the Cavendish variety.

In addition to the fruit, the flower of the banana plant (also known as *banana blossom* or *banana heart*) is used in Southeast Asian, Tamil, Bengali, and Kerala (India) cuisine, either served raw with dips or cooked in soups and curries. The tender core of the banana plant's trunk is also used in Bengali and Kerala cooking, and notably in the Burmese dish mohinga. Bananas fried with batter is a popular dessert in Malaysia, Singapore, and Indonesia. Banana fritters can be served with ice cream as well. Bananas are also eaten deep fried, baked in their skin in a split bamboo, or steamed in glutinous rice wrapped in a banana leaf in Burma where bunches of green bananas surrounding a green coconut in a tray form an important part of traditional offerings to the Buddha and the Nats. The juice extract prepared from the tender core is used to treat kidney stones.

The leaves of the banana plant are large, flexible, and waterproof. They are used many ways, including as umbrellas and to wrap food for cooking or storage Banana leaves are also used to serve food in India and other Asian countries.

Banana chips are a snack produced from dehydrated or fried banana or plantain slices, which have a dark brown color and an intense banana taste. Bananas have also been used in the making of jam. Unlike other fruits, it is difficult to extract juice from bananas because when compressed a banana simply turns to pulp.

In India, juice is extracted from the corm and used as a home remedy for the treatment of jaundice, sometimes with the addition of honey.

Trade

Bananas and plantains constitute a major staple food crop for millions of people in developing countries. In most tropical countries, green (unripe) bananas used for cooking represent the main cultivars. Cooking bananas are very similar to potatoes in how they are used. Both can be fried, boiled, baked, or chipped and have similar taste and texture when served. One green cooking banana has about the same calorie content as one potato.

In 2003, India led the world in banana production, representing approximately 23% of the worldwide crop, most of which was for domestic consumption. The four leading banana exporting countries were Ecuador, Costa Rica, the Philippines, and Colombia, which together accounted for about two-thirds of the world's exports, each exporting more than 1 million tons. Ecuador alone provided more than 30% of global banana exports, according to FAO statistics.

The vast majority of producers are small-scale farmers growing the crop either for home consumption or for local markets. Because bananas and plantains will produce fruit year-round, they provide an extremely valuable source of food during the hunger season (that period of time when all the food from the previous harvest has been consumed, and the next harvest is still some time away). It is for these reasons that bananas and plantains are of major importance to food security.

Bananas are among the most widely consumed foods in the world. Most banana farmers receive a low unit price for their produce as supermarkets buy enormous quantities and receive a discount for that business. Competition amongst supermarkets has led to reduced margins in recent years which in turn has led to lower prices for growers. Chiquita, Del Monte, Dole, and Fyffes grow their own bananas in Ecuador, Colombia, Costa Rica, Guatemala, and Honduras. Banana plantations are capital intensive and demand high expertise, so the majority of independent growers are large and wealthy landowners of these countries. This has led to bananas being available as a "fair trade" or Rainforest Alliance certified item in some countries.

The banana has an extensive trade history beginning with the founding of the United Fruit Company (now Chiquita) at the end of the nineteenth century. For much of the 20th century, bananas and coffee dominated the export economies of Central America. In the 1930s, bananas and coffee made up as much as 75% of the region's exports. As late as 1960, the two crops accounted for 67% of the exports from the region. Though the two were grown in similar regions, they tended not to be distributed together. The United Fruit Company based its business almost entirely on the banana trade, as the coffee trade proved too difficult for it to control. The term "banana republic" has been broadly applied to most countries in Central America, but from a strict economic perspective only Costa Rica, Honduras, and

Panama were actual "banana republics", countries with economies dominated by the banana trade.

The countries of the European Union have traditionally imported many of their bananas from the former European island colonies of the Caribbean, paying guaranteed prices above global market rates. As of 2005, these arrangements were in the process of being withdrawn under pressure from other major trading powers, principally the United States. The withdrawal of these indirect subsidies to Caribbean producers is expected to favour the banana producers of Central America, in which American companies have an economic interest.

The United States has minimal banana production. 14,000 tons of bananas were grown in Hawaii in 2001 Bananas have also been grown in Florida and southern California.

Early Cultivation

The domestication of bananas took place in southeastern Asia. Many species of wild bananas still exist in New Guinea, Malaysia, Indonesia, and the Philippines. Recent archaeological and palaeoenvironmental evidence at Kuk Swamp in the Western Highlands Province of Papua New Guinea suggests that banana cultivation there goes back to at least 5000 BCE, and possibly to 8000 BCE. This would make the New Guinean highlands the place where bananas were first domesticated. It is likely that other species of wild bananas were later also domesticated elsewhere in southeastern Asia. Southeast Asia is the region of primary diversity of the banana. Areas of secondary diversity are found in Africa, indicating a long history of banana cultivation in the region.

Some recent discoveries of banana phytoliths in Cameroon dating to the first millennium BCE have triggered an as yet unresolved debate about the antiquity of banana cultivation in Africa. There is linguistic evidence that bananas were already known in Madagascar around that time The earliest evidence of banana cultivation in Africa before these recent discoveries dates to no earlier than late 6th century AD. In this view, bananas were introduced to the east coast of Africa by Muslim Arabs.

The banana may have been present in isolated locations of the Middle East on the eve of the rise of Islam. There is some textual evidence that the prophet Muhammad was familiar with it. The spread of Islam was followed by the far reaching diffusion of bananas. There are numerous references to it in Islamic texts (such as poems and hadiths) beginning in the ninth century. By the tenth century the banana appears in texts from Palestine and Egypt. From there it diffused into north Africa and Muslim Spain. In fact, during the medieval ages, bananas from Granada were considered amongst the best in the Arab world. In 650, Islamic conquerors brought the banana to Palestine.

Bananas were introduced to the Americas by Portuguese sailors who brought the fruits from West Africa in the 1500s The word banana is of West African origin, and passed into English via Spanish or Portuguese.

Plantation Cultivation

In the 15th and 16th century, Portuguese colonists started banana plantations in the Atlantic Islands, Brazil, and western Africa. As late as the Victorian Era, bananas were not widely known in Europe, although they were available via merchant trade Jules Verne references bananas with detailed descriptions so as not to confuse readers in his book *Around the World in Eighty Days* (1872).

In the early 20th century, bananas began forming the basis of large commercial empires, exemplarized by the United Fruit Company, which created immense banana plantations especially in Central and South America. These were usually extremely commercially exploitative, and the term "Banana republic" was coined for states like Honduras and Guatemala, representing the fact that "servile dictatorships" were created and abetted by these companies and their political backers, for example in the USA.

Cultivation

While the original bananas contained rather large seeds, triploid (and thus seedless) cultivars have been selected for human consumption. These are propagated asexually from offshoots of the plant. The plant is allowed to produce 2 shoots at a time; a larger one for fruiting immediately and a smaller "sucker" or "follower" that will produce fruit in 6–8 months time. The life of a banana plantation is 25 years or longer, during which time the individual stools or planting sites may move slightly from their original positions as lateral rhizome formation dictates.

Cultivated bananas are *parthenocarpic*, which makes them sterile and unable to produce viable seeds. Lacking seeds, another form of propagation is required. This normally involves removing and transplanting part of the underground stem (called a corm). Usually this is done by carefully removing a sucker (a vertical shoot that develops from the base of the banana pseudostem) with some roots intact. However, small sympodial corms, representing not yet elongated suckers, are easier to transplant and can be left out of the ground for up to 2 weeks; they require minimal care and can be boxed together for shipment.

Contrary to what is widely believed, it is not actually necessary to include any of the corm or root structure to propagate bananas; severed suckers with no root material attached can be successfully propagated in damp sand, although this takes somewhat longer.

In some countries, bananas are also commercially propagated by means of tissue culture. This method is preferred since it ensures disease-free planting material.

When using vegetative parts such as suckers for propagation, there is a risk of transmitting diseases (especially the devastating Panama disease).

Pests, Diseases, and Natural Disasters

While in no danger of outright extinction, the most common edible banana cultivar 'Cavendish' (extremely popular in Europe and the Americas) could become unviable for large-scale cultivation in the next 10-20 years. Its predecessor 'Gros Michel', discovered in the 1820s, has already suffered this fate. Like almost all bananas, it lacks genetic diversity, which makes it vulnerable to diseases, which threaten both commercial cultivation and the small-scale subsistence farming. Some commentators have further remarked that those variants which could replace what much of the world considers a "typical banana" are so different that most people would not consider them the same fruit, and blame the decline of the banana on monogenetic cultivation driven by short-term commercial exploitation motives.

Major Diseases

The fungus enters the plants through the roots and moves up with water into the trunk and leaves, producing gels and gums. These plug and cut off the flow of water and nutrients, causing the plant to wilt. Prior to 1960 almost all commercial banana production centered on the cultivar. 'Gros Michel', which was highly susceptible to fusarium wilt and collapse, exposing the rest of the plant to lethal amounts of sunlight. The cultivar 'Cavendish' was chosen as a replacement for 'Gros Michel' because out of the resistant cultivars it was viewed as producing the highest quality fruit. However, more care is required for shipping the 'Cavendish' banana, and its quality compared to 'Gros Michel' is debated.

However, according to current references, a deadly form of Panama disease is infecting the world's Cavendish banana plants. All are genetically identical, which causes problems when it comes to disease resistance. However, researchers are experimenting with hundreds of feral varieties to find out which one(s) are resistant.

- *Tropical Race 4* - a reinvigorated strain of Panama disease first discovered in 1993. This is a virulent form of fusarium wilt that has wiped out 'Cavendish' in several southeast Asian countries. It has yet to reach the Americas; however, soil fungi can easily be carried on boots, clothing, or tools. This is how Tropical Race 4 moves from one plantation to another and is its most likely route into Latin America. The Cavendish cultivar is highly susceptible to TR4, and over time, Cavendish is almost certain to be eliminated from commercial production by this disease. Unfortunately, the only known defense to TR4 is genetic resistance.
- *Black Sigatoka* - a fungal leaf spot disease first observed in Fiji in 1963 or 1964. Black Sigatoka (also known as Black Leaf Streak) has spread to banana plantations throughout the tropics due to infected banana leaves being used as packing material. It affects all of the main cultivars of bananas and plantains, impeding photosynthesis by turning parts of their leaves black, and eventually killing the entire leaf. Being starved for energy, fruit production falls by 50% or more, and the bananas that do grow suffer premature ripening, making them unsuitable for export. The fungus has shown ever increasing resistance to fungicidal treatment, with the current expense for treating 1 hectare exceeding $1000 per year. In addition to the financial expense there is the question of how long such intensive spraying can be justified environmentally. Several resistant cultivars of banana have been developed, but none has yet received wide scale commercial acceptance due to taste and texture issues.

- *Banana Bunchy Top Virus* (*BBTV*) - this virus is spread from plant to plant by aphids. It causes stunting of the leaves resulting in a "bunched" appearance. Generally, a banana plant infected with the virus will not set fruit, although mild strains exist in many areas which do allow for some fruit production. These mild strains are often mistaken for malnourishment, or a disease other than BBTV. There is no cure for BBTV, however its effect can be minimised by planting only tissue cultured plants (In-vitro propagation), controlling the aphids, and immediately removing and destroying any plant from the field that shows signs of the disease.

Even though it is no longer viable for large scale cultivation, 'Gros Michel' is not extinct and is still grown in areas where Panama disease is not found. Likewise, 'Cavendish' is in no danger of extinction, but it may leave the shelves of the supermarkets for good if diseases make it impossible to supply the global market. It is unclear if any existing cultivar can replace 'Cavendish' on a scale needed to fill current demand, so various hybridisation and genetic engineering programs are working on creating a disease-resistant, mass-market banana.

In Australia

Australia is relatively free of plant diseases and therefore prohibits imports. When Cyclone Larry wiped out Australia's domestic banana crop in 2006, bananas became relatively expensive, due to both low supply domestically and the existence of laws prohibiting banana imports. Prices have since fallen as production has reverted back to a steady rate.

In East Africa

Most bananas grown worldwide are used for local consumption. In the tropics, bananas, especially cooking bananas, represent a major source of food, as well as a major source of income for smallholder farmers. It is in the East

African highlands that bananas reach their greatest importance as a staple food crop. In countries such as Uganda, Burundi, and Rwanda per capita consumption has been estimated at 450 kg per year, the highest in the world. Ugandans use the same word "matooke" to describe both banana and food.

In the past, the banana was a highly sustainable crop with a long plantation life and stable yields year round. However with the arrival of the Black sigatoka fungus, banana production in eastern Africa has fallen by over 40%. For example, during the 1970s, Uganda produced 15 to 20 tonnes of bananas per hectare. Today, production has fallen to only 6 tonnes per hectare.

The situation has started to improve as new disease resistant cultivars have been developed by the International Institute of Tropical Agriculture and NARO such as the FHIA-17 (known in Uganda as the Kabana 3). These new cultivars taste different from the traditionally grown banana which has slowed their acceptance by local farmers. However, by adding mulch and animal manure to the soil around the base of the banana plant, these new cultivars have substantially increased yields in the areas where they have been tried.

The International Institute of Tropical Agriculture and NARO, funded by the Rockefeller Foundation and CGIAR have started trials for genetically modified banana plants that are resistant to both Black sigatoka and banana weevils. It is developing cultivars specifically for smallholder or subsistence farmers.

Allergic Reactions

There are two forms of banana allergy. One is oral allergy syndrome which causes itching and swelling in the mouth or throat within one hour after ingestion and is related to birch tree and other pollen allergies. The other is related to latex allergies and causes urticaria and potentially serious upper gastrointestinal symptoms.

Fibre

The banana plant has long been a source of fibre for high quality textiles. In Japan, the cultivation of banana for clothing and household use dates back to at least the 13th century. In the Japanese system, leaves and shoots are cut from the plant periodically to ensure softness. The harvested shoots must first be boiled in lye to prepare the fibres for the making of the yarn. These banana shoots produce fibres of varying degrees of softness, yielding yarns and textiles with differing qualities for specific uses. For example, the outermost fibres of the shoots are the coarsest, and are suitable for tablecloths, whereas the softest innermost fibres are desirable for kimono and kamishimo. This traditional Japanese banana cloth making process requires many steps, all performed by hand.

In another system employed in Nepal, the trunk of the banana plant is harvested instead, small pieces of which are subjected to a softening process, mechanical extraction of the fibres, bleaching, and drying. After that, the fibres are sent to the Kathmandu Valley for the making of high end rugs with a textural quality similar to silk. These banana fibre rugs are woven by the traditional Nepalese hand-knotted methods, and are sold RugMark certified.

Paper

Banana fibre is also used in the production of banana paper. Banana paper is used in two different senses: to refer to a paper made from the bark of the banana plant, mainly used for artistic purposes, or paper made from banana fibre, obtained from an industrialized process, from the stem and the non usable fruits. This paper can be either hand-made or made by industrialized machine.

Storage and Transport

In the current world marketing system, bananas are grown in the tropics. The fruit therefore has to be transported over long distances and storage is necessary. To gain maximum life, bunches are harvested before the fruit is fully mature. The fruit is carefully handled, transported quickly to the seaboard, cooled, and shipped under sophisticated refrigeration. The basis of this procedure is to prevent the bananas producing ethylene which is the natural ripening agent of the fruit. This sophisticated technology allows storage and transport for 3-4 weeks at 13 degrees Celsius. On arrival at the destination, the bananas are held at about 17 degrees Celsius and treated with a low concentration of ethylene. After a few days, the fruit has begun to ripen and it is distributed for retail sale. It is important to note that unripe bananas can not be held in the home refrigerator as they suffer from the cold. After ripening some bananas can be held for a few days at home. They can be stored indefinitely frozen, then eaten like an ice pop or cooked as a banana mush.

Recent studies have suggested that the presence of carbon dioxide (which is produced by the fruit) extends the life and the addition of an ethylene absorbent further extends the life even at high temperatures. This effect can be exploited by packing the fruit in a polyethylene bag and including an ethylene absorbent, potassium permanganate, on an inert carrier. The bag is then sealed with a band or string. This treatment has been shown to more than double the life of the bananas at a range of temperatures and can give a life of up to 3-4 weeks without the need for refrigeration.

Peels

The depiction of a person slipping on a banana peel has been a staple of physical comedy for generations. A 1906 comedy record produced by Edison Records features a popular character of the time, "Cal Stewart", claiming to describe his own such incident.

Symbols

Bananas are also humorously used as a phallic symbol due to similarities in size and shape. This is typified by the artwork of the debut album of The Velvet Underground, which features a banana on the front cover, yet on the original LP version, the design allowed the listener to 'peel' this banana to find a pink, phallic structure on the inside.

Blue Fluorescence, a Recent Discovery

Ripe bananas exhibit a blue fluorescence when exposed to ultraviolet (UV) light (Black light). This property has been overlooked for a long time. Green bananas do not show any sign of fluorescence. The cause is attributed by the authors to the degradation of chlorophyll giving rise to the accumulation of a fluorescent product in the skin of the fruit. The chlorophyll breakdown product is stabilized by a propionate ester group. Banana-tree leaves also fluoresce in the same way. A possible consequence in nature is that animals capable of seeing in the UV spectrum would also be able to more quickly detect the ripened fruits.

12

Sugarcane

Sugarcane (Saccharum) is a genus of 6 to 37 species (depending on taxonomic interpretation) of tall perennial grasses (family Poaceae, tribe Andropogoneae), native to warm temperate to tropical regions of the Old World. They have stout, jointed, fibrous stalks that are rich in sugar and measure 2 to 6 metres tall. All of the sugar cane species interbreed, and the major commercial cultivars are complex hybrids.

Cultivation and Uses

About 195 countries grow the crop to produce 1,324.6 million tons (more than six times the amount of sugar beet produced). As of the year 2005, the world's largest producer of sugar cane by far is Brazil followed by India. Uses of sugar cane include the production of sugar, Falernum, molasses, rum, soda, cachaça (the national spirit of Brazil) and ethanol for fuel. The bagasse that remains after sugar cane crushing may be burned to provide both heat - used in the mill - and electricity, typically sold to the consumer electricity grid. It may also, because of its high cellulose content, be used as raw material for paper, cardboard, and eating utensils branded as "environmentally friendly" as it is made from a by-product of sugar production.

History of Sugarcane

Sugarcane was originally from tropical South Asia and Southeast Asia Different species likely originated in different locations with *S. barberi* originating in India and *S. edule* and *S. officinarum* coming from New Guinea The thick stalk stores energy as sucrose in the sap. From this juice, sugar is extracted by evaporating the water. Crystallized sugar was reported 5000 years ago in India.

Around the eighth century A.D., Arabs introduced sugar to the Mediterranean, Mesopotamia, Egypt, North Africa, and Spain. By the tenth century, sources state, there was no village in Mesopotamia that didn't grow sugar cane. It was among the early crops brought to the Americas by Spaniards. Brazil is currently the biggest sugar cane producing country.

A *boiling house* was used in the 17th through 19th centuries to make sugarcane juice into raw sugar. These houses were add-ons to the sugar plantations in the western colonies. This process was often conducted by the African slaves, under very poor conditions. The boiling house was made of cut stone. The furnaces were rectangular boxes of brick or stone with openings near to one side, and at the bottom to stoke the fire and pull out the ashes. At the top of each furnace were up to seven copper kettles or boilers, each one smaller than the previous one and hotter. The cane juice was placed in the first copper kettle which was the largest. The juice was then heated and a little lime added to remove impurities. The juice was then skimmed then channeled to the other copper kettles. The last kettle, which was called the 'teache' was where the cane juice became syrup. It was then put into cooling troughs where the sugar crystals hardened around a sticky core of molasses. The raw sugar was then shoveled from the cooling trough into hogsheads (wooden barrels) where they were put in the curing house.

Sugarcane was, and still is, extensively grown in the Caribbean, where it was first brought by Christopher Columbus during his second voyage to The Americas, initially to the island of Hispaniola (modern day Haiti and the Dominican Republic). In colonial times, sugar was a major product of the triangular trade of New World raw materials, European manufactures, and African slaves. France found its sugarcane islands so valuable it effectively traded its portion of Canada, famously dubbed "a few acres of snow," to Britain for their return of Guadeloupe, Martinique and St. Lucia at the end of the Seven-year' War. The Dutch similarly kept Suriname, a sugar colony in South America, instead of seeking the return of the New Netherlands (New Amsterdam). Cuban sugarcane produced sugar that received price supports from and a guaranteed market in the USSR; the dissolution of that country forced the closure of most of Cuba's sugar industry. Sugarcane remains an important part of the economy of Belize, Barbados, Haiti along with the Dominican Republic, Guadeloupe, Jamaica, and other islands. The sugarcane industry is a major export for the Caribbean, but it is expected to collapse with the removal of European preferences by 2009.

Sugarcane production greatly influenced many tropical Pacific islands, including Okinawa and most particularly Hawaii and Fiji. In these islands, sugar cane came to dominate the economic and political landscape after the arrival of powerful European and American agricultural business, which promoted immigration from various Asian countries for workers to tend and harvest the crop. Sugar-industry policies eventually established the ethnic makeup of the island populations that now exist, profoundly affecting modern politics and society in the islands.

Fig. 12.1

Brazil is a major grower of sugarcane, which is used to produce sugar and provide the ethanol used in making gasoline-ethanol blends (gasohol) for transportation fuel. In India, sugarcane is sold as jaggery and also refined into sugar, primarily for consumption in tea and sweets, and for the production of alcoholic beverages.

Cultivation

Sugarcane cultivation requires a tropical or subtropical climate, with a minimum of 600 mm (24 in) of annual moisture. It is one of the most efficient photosynthesizers in the plant kingdom. It is a C-4 plant, able to convert up to 2 per cent of incident solar energy into biomass In prime growing regions, such as Peru, Brazil, Bolivia, Colombia, Australia, Ecuador, Cuba, the Philippines and Hawaii, sugarcane can produce 20 kg for each square meter exposed to the sun.

Sugarcane is propagated from cuttings, rather than from seeds; although certain types still produce seeds, modern methods of stem cuttings have become the most common method of reproduction. Each cutting must contain at least one bud, and the cuttings are usually planted by hand. Once planted, a stand of cane can be harvested several times; after each harvest, the cane sends up new stalks, called ratoons. Usually, each successive harvest gives a smaller yield, and eventually the declining yields justify replanting. Depending on agricultural practice, two to ten harvests may be possible between plantings.

Sugarcane is harvested mostly by hand and sometimes mechanically. Hand harvesting accounts for more than half of the world's production, and is especially dominant in the developing world. When harvested by hand, the field is first set on fire. The fire spreads rapidly, burning away dry dead leaves, and killing any venomous snakes hiding in the crop, but leaving the water-rich stalks and roots unharmed. With cane knives or machetes, harvesters then cut the standing cane just above the ground. A skilled harvester can cut 500 kg of sugarcane in an hour.

With mechanical harvesting, a sugarcane combine (or chopper harvester), a harvesting machine originally developed in Australia, is used. The Austoft 7000 series was the original design for the modern harvester and has now been copied by other companies including Cameco and John Deere. The machine cuts the cane at the base of the stalk, separates the cane from its leaves, and deposits the cane into a haulout transporter while blowing the thrash back onto the field. Such machines can harvest 100 tonnes of cane each hour, but cane harvested using these machines must be transported to the processing plant rapidly; once cut, sugarcane begins to lose its sugar content, and damage inflicted on the cane during mechanical harvesting accelerates this decay.

Pests

The most important sugarcane pests are the larvae of some butterfly/moth species, including the turnip moth, the sugarcane borer (*Diatraea saccharalis*), the Mexican rice borer (*Eoreuma loftini*), leaf-cutting ants, termites; spittlebugs (especially *Mahanarva fimbriolata* and *Deois flavopicta*), and the beetle *Migdolus fryanus*. The planthopper *Eumetopina flavipes* is an insect which acts as a vector for the phytoplasma.

Processing

Traditionally, sugarcane has been processed in two stages. Sugarcane mills, located in sugarcane-producing regions, extract sugar from freshly harvested sugarcane, resulting in raw sugar for later refining, and in "mill white" sugar for local consumption. Sugar refineries, often located in heavy sugar-consuming regions, such as North America, Europe, and Japan, then purify raw sugar to produce refined white sugar, a product that is more than 99 per cent pure sucrose. These two stages are slowly becoming blurred. Increasing affluence in the sugar-producing tropics has led to an increase in demand for refined sugar products in those areas, where a trend toward combined milling and refining has developed.

Milling

Sugarcane first has to be moved to a mill which is usually located close to the area of cultivation. Small rail networks are a common method of transporting the cane to a mill.Once the factories acquire the cane it will be subjected to the quality test. In Sri Lanka cane will be evaluated according to the brix and trash percentage.

Sugar Crystals

In a sugar mill, sugarcane is washed, chopped, and shredded by revolving knives. The shredded cane is repeatedly mixed with water and crushed between rollers;

the collected juices (called garapa in Brazil) contain 10-15 per cent sucrose, and the remaining fibrous solids, called bagasse, are burned for fuel. Bagasse makes a sugar mill more than self-sufficient in energy; the surplus bagasse can be used for animal feed, in paper manufacture, or burned to generate electricity for the local power grid.

The cane juice is next mixed with lime to adjust its pH to 7. This mixing arrests sucrose's decay into glucose and fructose, and precipitates out some impurities. The mixture then sits, allowing the lime and other suspended solids to settle out, and the clarified juice is concentrated in a multiple-effect evaporator to make a syrup about 60 per cent by weight in sucrose. This syrup is further concentrated under vacuum until it becomes supersaturated, and then seeded with crystalline sugar. Upon cooling, sugar crystallizes out of the syrup. A centrifuge is used to separate the sugar from the remaining liquid, or molasses. Additional crystallizations may be performed to extract more sugar from the molasses; the molasses remaining after no more sugar can be extracted from it in a cost-effective fashion is called blackstrap.

Raw sugar has a yellow to brown colour. If a white product is desired, sulfur dioxide may be bubbled through the cane juice before evaporation; this chemical bleaches many color-forming impurities into colourless ones. Sugar bleached white by this *sulfitation* process is called "mill white", "plantation white", and "crystal sugar". This form of sugar is the form most commonly consumed in sugarcane-producing countries. Traditionally, sugarcane has been processed in two stages. Sugarcane mills, located in sugarcane-producing regions, extract sugar from freshly harvested sugarcane, resulting in raw sugar for later refining, and in "mill white" sugar for local consumption. Sugar refineries, often located in heavy sugar-consuming regions, such as North America, Europe, and Japan, then purify raw sugar to produce refined white sugar, a product that is more than 99 per cent pure sucrose. These two stages are slowly becoming blurred. Increasing affluence in the sugar-producing tropics has led to an increase in demand for refined sugar products in those areas, where a trend toward combined milling and refining has developed.

Refining

The Santa Elisa sugarcane processing plant, one of the largest and oldest in Brazil, is located in Sertãozinho, Brazil.

Evaporator with baffled pan and foam dipper for making ribbon cane syrup. Three Rivers Historical Society Museum at Browntown, South Carolina.

In sugar refining, raw sugar is further purified. It is first mixed with heavy syrup and then centrifuged clean. This process is called 'affination'; its purpose is to wash away the outer coating of the raw sugar crystals, which is less pure than the crystal interior. The remaining sugar is then dissolved to make a syrup, about 70 per cent by weight solids.

The sugar solution is clarified by the addition of phosphoric acid and calcium hydroxide, which combine to precipitate calcium phosphate. The calcium phosphate particles entrap some impurities and absorb others, and then float to the top of the tank, where they can be skimmed off. An alternative to this "phosphatation" technique is 'carbonatation,' which is similar, but uses carbon dioxide and calcium hydroxide to produce a calcium carbonate precipitate.

After any remaining solids are filtered out, the clarified syrup is decolorized by filtration through a bed of activated carbon; bone char was traditionally used in this role, but its use is no longer common. Some remaining colour-forming impurities adsorb to the carbon bed. The purified syrup is then concentrated to supersaturation and repeatedly crystallized under vacuum, to produce white refined sugar. As in a sugar mill, the sugar crystals are separated from the molasses by centrifuging. Additional sugar is recovered by blending the remaining syrup with the washings from affination and again crystallizing to produce brown sugar. When no more sugar can be economically recovered, the final molasses still contains 20-30 per cent sucrose and 15-25 per cent glucose and fructose.

To produce granulated sugar, in which the individual sugar grains do not clump together, sugar must be dried. Drying is accomplished first by drying the sugar in a hot rotary dryer, and then by conditioning the sugar by blowing cool air through it for several days.

Ribbon Cane Syrup

Ribbon cane is a subtropical type that was once widely grown in southern United States, as far north as coastal North Carolina. The juice was extracted with horse or mule-powered crushers; the juice was boiled, like maple syrup, in a flat pan, and then used in the syrup form as a sweetener for other foods. It is not a commercial crop nowadays, but a few growers try to keep alive the old traditions and find ready sales for their product. Most sugarcane production in the United States occurs in Florida and Louisiana, and to a lesser extent in Hawaii and Texas.

Cane Ethanol

This is generally available as a by-product of sugar mills producing sugar. It can be used as a fuel, mainly as a biofuel alternative to gasoline, and is widely used in cars in Brazil. It is steadily becoming a promising alternative to gasoline throughout much of the world and thus instead of sugar may be produced as a primary product out of sugar canes processing.

A textbook on renewable energy describes the energy transformation:

- At present, 74 tons of raw sugar cane are produced annually per hectare in Brazil. The cane delivered to the processing plant is called burned and cropped (b&c) and represents 77% of the mass of the raw cane. The reason for this reduction is that the stalks are separated from the leaves (which are burned and whose ashes are left in the field as fertilizer) and from the roots that remain in the ground to sprout for the next crop. Average cane production is, therefore, 58 tons of b&c per hectare per year.

- Each ton of b & c yields 740 kg of juice (135 kg of sucrose and 605 kg of water) and 260 kg of moist bagasse (130 kg of dry bagasse). Since the higher heating value of sucrose is 16.5 MJ/kg, and that of the bagasse is 19.2 MJ/kg, the total heating value of a ton of b&c is 4.7 GJ of which 2.2 GJ come from the sucrose and 2.5 from the bagasse.
- Per hectare per year, the biomass produced corresponds to 0.27 TJ. This is equivalent to 0.86 W per square meter. Assuming an average insolation of 225 W per square meter, the photosynthetic efficiency of sugar cane is 0.38%.

  The 135 kg of sucrose found in 1 ton of b&c are transformed into 70 liters of ethanol with a combustion energy of 1.7 GJ. The practical sucrose-ethanol conversion efficiency is, therefore, 76% (compare with the theoretical 97%).
- One hectare of sugar cane yields 4000 liters of ethanol per year (without any additional energy input because the bagasse produced exceeds the amount needed to distill the final product). This however does not include the energy used in tilling, transportation, and so on. Thus, the solar energy-to-ethanol conversion efficiency is 0.13%.

Sugarcane as Food

In most countries where sugarcane is cultivated, there are several foods and popular dishes derived from it, such as:

- Direct consumption of raw sugarcane cylinders or cubes, which are chewed to extract the juice, and the bagasse is spat out Freshly extracted juice (garapa, *guarab, guarapa, guarapo, papelón, 'aseer asab,* Ganna sharbat, mosto or *caldo de cana*) by hand or electrically operated small mills, with a touch of lemon and ice, makes a popular drink.
- Molasses, used as a sweetener and as a syrup accompanying other foods, such as cheese or cookies.
- Rapadura, a candy made of flavored solid brown sugar in Brazil, which can be consumed in small hard blocks, or in pulverized form (flour), as an add-on to other desserts.
- Sugarcane is also used in rum production, especially in the Caribbean.
- Cane sugar syrup was the traditional sweetener in soft drinks for many years, but has been largely supplanted (in the US at least) by high-fructose corn syrup, which is less expensive, but is considered by some to not taste quite like the sugar it replaces.
- Jaggery - solidified molasses of sugarcane, known as Gur or Gud in South Asia. Traditionally produced by heat evaporating sugarcane juice until it is a thick sludge and then letting it cool in buckets used as molds. Modern production methods make use of partial freeze drying to give reduce caramelization and give it lighter color. It is used as sweetener in cooking traditional meal entrees as well as sweets and desserts.

Nitrogen Fixation

Some sugarcane varieties are known to be capable of fixing atmospheric nitrogen in association with a bacterium, Acetobacter diazotrophicus. Unlike legumes and other nitrogen fixing plants which form root nodules in the soil in association with bacteria, Acetobacter diazotrophicus lives within the intercellular spaces of the sugarcane's stem.

13

Coffee

Coffee is a brewed beverage prepared from roasted seeds, commonly called coffee beans, of the coffee plant. Caffeinated coffee has a stimulating effect in humans. Today, coffee is one of the most popular beverages world-wide.

Fig. 13.1

Coffee was first consumed in the ninth century, when it was discovered in the highlands of Ethiopia. From there, it spread to Egypt and Yemen, and by the 15th century, had reached Azerbaijan, Persia, Turkey, and northern Africa. From the Muslim world, coffee spread to Italy, then to the rest of Europe, to Indonesia, and to the Americas.

Coffee berries, which contain the coffee bean, are produced by several species of small evergreen bush of the genus Coffea. The two most commonly grown species are Coffea canephora (also known as Coffea robusta) and Coffea arabica. These are cultivated in Latin America, Southeast Asia, and Africa. Once ripe, coffee berries are picked, processed, and dried. The seeds are then roasted, undergoing several physical and chemical changes. They are roasted to varying degrees, depending on the desired flavor. They are then ground and brewed to create coffee. Coffee can be prepared and presented in a variety of ways.

Coffee has played an important role in many societies throughout modern history. In Africa and Yemen, it was used in religious ceremonies. As a result, the Ethiopian Church banned its secular consumption until the reign of Emperor Menelik II of Ethiopia It was banned in Ottoman Turkey in the 17th century for political reasons, and was associated with rebellious political activities in Europe.

Coffee is an important export commodity. In 2004, coffee was the top agricultural export for 12 countries, and in 2005, it was the world's seventh-largest legal agricultural export by value.

Some controversy is associated with coffee cultivation and its impact on the environment. Many studies have examined the relationship between coffee consumption and certain medical conditions; whether the overall effects of coffee are positive or negative is still disputed.

Etymology

The term was introduced to Europe via the Ottoman Turkish, kahver, which is, in turn, derived from the Arabic: qahweh The origin of the Arabic term is derived either from the name of the Kaffa region in western Ethiopia, where coffee was cultivated, or by a truncation of qahwat al-bunn, meaning "wine of the bean" in Arabic. The English word coffee first came to be used in the early to mid-1600s, but early forms of the word date to the last decade of the 1500s. In Ethiopia's neighbor Eritrea, "bunn" (also meaning "wine of the bean" in Tigrinya) is used Also the Amharic and Afan Oromo name for coffee is bunna.

History

Coffee use can be traced at least to as early as the ninth century, when it appeared in the highlands of Ethiopia. According to legend, Ethiopian shepherds were the first to observe the influence of the caffeine in coffee beans when the goats appeared to "dance" and to have an increased level of energy after consuming wild coffee berries. The legend names the shepherd "Kaldi." From Ethiopia, coffee spread to Egypt and Yemen It was in Arabia that coffee beans were first roasted and brewed, similar to how it is done today. By the 15th century, it had reached the rest of the Middle East, Persia, Turkey, and northern Africa.

Fig. 13.2

In 1583, Leonhard Rauwolf, a German physician, gave this description of coffee after returning from a ten-year trip to the Near East.

"A beverage as black as ink, useful against numerous illnesses, particularly those of the stomach. Its consumers take it in the morning, quite frankly, in a porcelain cup that is passed around and from which each one drinks a cupful. It is composed of water and the fruit from a bush called bunnu." From the Muslim world, coffee spread to Italy. The thriving trade between Venice and North Africa, Egypt, and the Middle East brought many goods, including coffee, to the Venetian port. From Venice, it was introduced to the rest of Europe. Coffee became more widely accepted after it was deemed a Christian beverage by Pope Clement VIII in 1600, despite appeals to ban the "Muslim drink." The first European coffee house opened in Italy in 1645 The Dutch were the first to import coffee on a large scale, and they were among the first to defy the Arab prohibition on the exportation of plants or unroasted seeds when Pieter van den Broeck smuggled seedlings from Aden into Europe in 1616. The Dutch later grew the crop in Java and Ceylon. The first exports of Indonesian coffee from Java to the Netherlands occurred in 1711. Through the efforts of the British East India Company, coffee became popular in England as well. It was introduced in France in 1657, and in Austria and Poland after the 1683 Battle of Vienna, when coffee was captured from supplies of the defeated Turks.

When coffee reached North America during the Colonial period, it was initially not as successful as it had been in Europe. During the Revolutionary War, however, the demand for coffee increased so much that dealers had to hoard their scarce supplies and raise prices dramatically; this was also due to the reduced availability of tea from British merchants After the War of 1812, during which Britain temporarily cut off access to tea imports, the Americans' taste for coffee grew, and high demand during the American Civil War together with advances in brewing technology secured the position of coffee as an everyday commodity in the United States.

Noted as one of the world's largest, most valuable legally traded commodities (after oil), coffee has become a vital cash crop for many Third World countries. Over one hundred million people in developing countries have become dependent on coffee as their primary source of income Coffee has become the primary export and backbone for African countries like Uganda, Burundi, Rwanda, and Ethiopia as well as many Central American countries.

Biology

The *Coffea* plant is native to subtropical Africa and southern Asia It belongs to a genus of ten species of flowering plants of the family *Rubiaceae*. It is an evergreen shrub or small tree that may grow 5 metres tall when unpruned. The leaves are dark green and glossy, usually 100-150 milimetres long and 60 milimetres wide. It produces clusters of fragrant white flowers that bloom simultaneously. The fruit berry is oval, about 15 milimeters long and green when immature, but ripens to yellow, then crimson, becoming black on drying. Each berry usually contains two seeds, but from 5–10% of the berries have only one; these are called peaberries. Berries ripen in seven to nine months.

Cultivation

Coffee is usually propagated by seeds. The traditional method of planting coffee is to put 20 seeds in each hole at the beginning of the rainy season; half are eliminated naturally. Coffee is often intercropped with food crops, such as corn, beans, or rice, during the first few years of cultivation.

The two main cultivated species of the coffee plant are *Coffea canephora* and *Coffea arabica*. Arabica coffee (from *C. arabica*) is considered more suitable for drinking than robusta coffee (from *C. canephora*); robusta tends to be bitter and have less flavor than arabica. For this reason, about three-quarters of coffee cultivated worldwide is *C. arabica*.

However, *C. canephora* is less susceptible to disease than *C. arabica* and can be cultivated in environments where *C. arabica* will not thrive. Robusta coffee also contains about 40-50% more caffeine than arabica For this reason, it is used as an inexpensive substitute for arabica in many commercial coffee blends. Good quality robustas are used in some espresso blends to provide a better foam head and to lower the ingredient cost Other cultivated species include *Coffea liberica* and *Coffea esliaca,* believed to be indigenous to Liberia and southern Sudan, respectively.

Most arabica coffee beans originate from either Latin America, eastern Africa, Arabia, or Asia. Robusta coffee beans are grown in western and central Africa, throughout southeast Asia, and to some extent in Brazil. Beans from different countries or regions usually have distinctive characteristics such as flavor, aroma, body, and acidity These taste characteristics are dependent not only on the coffee's growing region, but also on genetic subspecies (varietals) and processing Varietals are generally known by the region in which they are grown, such as Colombian, Java or Kona.

Production

Brazil is the world leader in production of green coffee, followed by Vietnam and Colombia. Originally, coffee farming was done in the shade of trees, which provided habitat for many animals and insects This method is commonly referred to as the traditional shaded method. Many farmers have decided to switch their production method to sun cultivation, a method in which coffee is grown in rows under full sun with little or no forest canopy. This causes berries to ripen more rapidly and bushes to produce higher yields, but requires the clearing of trees and increased use of fertilizer and pesticides. Traditional coffee production, on the other hand, causes berries to ripen more slowly and produce lower yields, compared to the sun cultivation method, but the quality of the coffee is allegedly superior.

In addition, the traditional shaded method is environmentally friendly and serves as a habitat for many species. Opponents of sun cultivation say environmental problems such as deforestation, pesticide pollution, habitat destruction, and soil and water degradation are the side effects of these practices. -grown" and organic coffees, which it says are sustainably harvested However, while certain types of shaded coffee cultivation systems show greater biodiversity than full-sun systems, they still compare poorly to native forest in terms of habitat value.

Another issue concerning coffee is its use of water. According to New Scientist, it takes about 140 litres of water to grow the coffee beans needed to produce one cup of coffee, and the coffee is often grown in countries where there is a water shortage, such as Ethiopia.

Economics

Brazil remains the largest coffee exporting nation, but in recent years, Vietnam has become a major producer of robusta beans Indonesia is the third-largest exporter and the largest producer of washed arabica coffee. Robusta coffees, traded in London at much lower prices than New York's arabica, are preferred by large industrial clients, such as multinational roasters and instant coffee producers because of the lower cost.

The concept of fair trade labelling, which guarantees coffee growers a negotiated preharvest price, began with the Max Havelaar Foundation's labeling program in the Netherlands. In 2004, 24,222 metric tons (of 7,050,000 produced worldwide) were fair trade; in 2005, 33,991 metric tons out of 6,685,000 were fair trade, an increase from 0.34% to 0.51% A number of studies have shown that fair trade coffee has a positive impact on the communities that grow it. A study in 2002 found that fair trade strengthened producer organizations, improved returns to small producers, and positively affected their quality of life A 2003 study concluded that fair trade has "greatly improved the well-being of small-scale coffee farmers and their families" by providing access to credit and external development funding and greater access to training, giving them the ability to improve the quality of their coffee The families of fair trade producers were also more stable than those who were not involved in fair trade, and their children had better access to education. A 2005 study of Bolivian coffee producers concluded that fair trade certification has had a positive impact on local coffee prices, economically benefiting all coffee producers.

Coffee as a Commodity

Coffee is also bought and sold by roasters, investors and price speculators as a tradable commodity. Coffee futures contracts for Grade 3 washed arabicas are traded on the New York Mercantile Exchange (NYMEX) under ticker symbol KT, with contract deliveries occurring every year in March, May, July, September, and December. Higher and lower grade arabica coffees are sold through other channels. Futures contracts for robusta coffee are traded on the London Liffe exchange and, since 2007, on the New York ICE exchange.

PROCESSING

Roasting

Coffee berries and their seeds undergo several processes before they become the familiar roasted coffee. First, coffee berries are picked, generally by hand. Then they are sorted by ripeness and color and the flesh of the berry is removed, usually by machine, and the seeds—usually called beans—are fermented to remove the slimy layer of mucilage still present on the bean. When the fermentation is finished, the beans are washed with large quantities of fresh water to remove the fermentation residue, which generates massive amounts of highly polluted coffee wastewater. Finally, the seeds are dried, sorted, and labeled as green coffee beans.

A traditional way to let the coffee beans dry is to let them sit on a cement patio and rake over the beans till dry. Other companies use cylinders to pump in heated air to dry the coffee beans.

The next step in the process is the roasting of the green coffee. Coffee is usually sold in a roasted state, and all coffee is roasted before it is consumed. It can be sold roasted by the supplier, or it can be home roasted The roasting process influences the taste of the beverage by changing the coffee bean both physically and chemically. The bean decreases in weight as moisture is lost and increases in volume, causing it to become less dense. The density of the bean also influences the strength of the coffee and requirements for packaging. The actual roasting begins when the temperature inside the bean reaches 200 °C, though different varieties of beans differ in moisture and density and therefore roast at different rates. During roasting, caramelization occurs as intense heat breaks down starches in the bean, changing them to simple sugars that begin to brown, changing the color of the bean Sucrose is rapidly lost during the roasting process and may disappear entirely in darker roasts. During roasting, aromatic oils, acids, and caffeine weaken, changing the flavor; at 205 °C, other oils start to develop One of these oils is *caffeol*, created at about 200 °C, which is largely responsible for coffee's aroma and flavor.

Depending on the colour of the roasted beans as perceived by the human eye, they will be labeled as light, medium light, medium, medium dark, dark, or very dark. A more accurate method of discerning the degree of roast involves measuring the reflected light from roasted beans illuminated with a light source in the near infrared spectrum. This elaborate light meter uses a process known as spectroscopy to return a number that consistently indicates the roasted coffee's relative degree of roast or flavor development. Such devices are routinely used for quality assurance by coffee-roasting businesses.

Darker roasts are generally smoother, because they have less fiber content and a more sugary flavour. Lighter roasts have more caffeine, resulting in a slight bitterness, and a stronger flavor from aromatic oils and acids otherwise destroyed by longer roasting times. A small amount of chaff is produced during roasting from the skin left on the bean after processing. Chaff is usually removed from the beans by air movement, though a small amount is added to dark roast coffees to soak up oils on the beans. Decaffeination may also be part of the processing that coffee seeds undergo. Seeds are decaffeinated when they are still green. Many methods can remove caffeine from coffee, but all involve either soaking beans in hot water or steaming them, then using a solvent to dissolve caffeine-containing oils. Decaffeination is often done by processing companies, and the extracted caffeine is usually sold to the pharmaceutical industry.

Storage

Once roasted, coffee beans must be stored properly to preserve the fresh taste of the bean. Ideally, the container must be airtight and kept cool. In order of importance, air, moisture, heat, and light are the environmental factors responsible for deteriorating flavor in coffee beans.

Folded-over bags, a common way consumers often purchase coffee, are generally not ideal for long-term storage because they allow air to enter. A better package contains a one-way valve, which prevents air from entering.

Preparation

Coffee beans must be ground and brewed in order to create a beverage. Grinding the roasted coffee beans is done at a roastery, in a grocery store, or in the home. They are most commonly ground at a roastery and then packaged and sold to the consumer, though "whole bean" coffee can be ground at home. Coffee beans may be ground in several ways. A burr mill uses revolving elements to shear the bean; an electric grinder smashes the beans with blunt blades moving at high speed; and a mortar and pestle crushes the beans.

The type of grind is often named after the brewing method for which it is generally used. Turkish grind is the finest grind, while coffee percolator or French press are the coarsest grinds. The most common grinds are between the extremes; a medium grind is used in most common home coffee brewing machines.

Coffee may be brewed by several methods: boiled, steeped, or pressured. Brewing coffee by boiling was the earliest method, and Turkish coffee is an example of this method It is prepared by powdering the beans with a mortar and pestle, then adding the powder to water and bringing it to a boil in a pot called a cezve or, in Greek, a briki. This produces a strong coffee with a layer of foam on the surface.

Machines such as percolators or automatic coffeemakers brew coffee by gravity. In an automatic coffeemaker, hot water drips onto coffee grounds held in a coffee filter made of paper or perforated metal, allowing the water to seep through the ground coffee while absorbing its oils and essences. Gravity causes the liquid to pass into a carafe or pot while the used coffee grounds are retained in the filter In a percolator, boiling water is forced into a chamber above a filter by steam pressure created by boiling. The water then passes downward through the grounds due to gravity, repeating the process until shut off by an internal timer or, more commonly, a thermostat that turns off the heater when the entire pot reaches a certain temperature. This thermostat also serves to keep the coffee warm (it turns on when the pot cools), but requires the removal of the basket holding the grounds after the initial brewing to avoid additional brewing as the pot reheats. Purists do not feel that this repeated boiling is conducive to achieving the best-flavoured coffee.

Coffee may also be brewed by steeping in a device such as a French press (also known as a *cafetière* or coffee press). Ground coffee and hot water are combined in a coffee press and left to brew for a few minutes. A plunger is then depressed to separate the coffee grounds, which remain at the bottom of the container. Because the coffee grounds are in direct contact with the water, all the coffee oils remain in the beverage, making it stronger and leaving more sediment than in coffee made by an automatic coffee machine.

The espresso method forces hot (but not boiling) pressurized water through ground coffee. As a result of brewing under high pressure (ideally between 9-10 atm), the espresso beverage is more concentrated (as much as 10 to 15 times the amount of coffee to water as gravity-brewing methods can produce) and has a more complex physical and chemical constitution. A well-prepared espresso has a reddish-brown foam called *crema* that floats on the surface The drink "Americano" is popularly thought to have been named after American soldiers in WW II who found the European way of drinking espresso too strong; baristas would cut the espresso with hot water for them.

Presentation

Once brewed, coffee may be presented in a variety of ways. Drip brewed, percolated, or French-pressed/cafetière coffee may be served with no additives or sugar (colloquially known as black) or with milk, cream, or both. When served cold, it is called iced coffee.

Espresso-based coffee has a wide variety of possible presentations. In its most basic form, it is served alone as a "shot" or in the more watered-down style café américano—a shot or two of espresso with hot water. The Americano should be served with the espresso shots on top of the hot water to preserve the crema. Milk can be added in various forms to espresso: steamed milk makes a cafè latte equal parts espresso and milk froth make a cappuccino, and a dollop of hot foamed milk on top creates a caffè macchiato. The use of steamed milk to form patterns such as hearts or maple leaves is referred to as latte art.

A number of products are sold for the convenience of consumers who do not want to prepare their own coffee. Instant coffee is dried into soluble powder or freeze-dried into granules that can be quickly dissolved in hot water. Canned coffee has been popular in Asian countries for many years, particularly in Japan and South Korea. Vending machines typically sell varieties of flavored canned coffee, much like brewed or percolated coffee, available both hot and cold. Japanese convenience stores and groceries also have a wide availability of bottled coffee drinks, which are typically lightly sweetened and preblended with milk. Bottled coffee drinks are also consumed in the United States Liquid coffee concentrates are sometimes used in large institutional situations where coffee needs to be produced for thousands of people at the same time. It is described as having a flavor about as good as low-grade robusta coffee, and costs about 10¢ a cup to produce. The machines used can process up to 500 cups an hour, or 1,000 if the water is preheated.

TYPES OF POPULAR COFFEE BEVERAGES

Social Aspects

Coffee was initially used for spiritual reasons. At least 1,000 years ago, traders brought coffee across the Red Sea into Arabia (modern-day Yemen), where Muslim monks began cultivating the shrub in their gardens. At first, the Arabians made wine from the pulp of the fermented coffee berries. This beverage was known as *qishr* (*kisher* in modern usage) and was used during religious ceremonies.

Coffee became the substitute beverage in spiritual practices where wine was forbidden. Coffee drinking was briefly prohibited by Muslims as *haraam* in the early years of the 16th century, but this was quickly overturned. Use in religious rites among the Sufi branch of Islam led to coffee's being put on trial in Mecca: it was accused of being a heretical substance, and its production and consumption were briefly repressed. It was later prohibited in Ottoman Turkey under an edict by the Sultan Murad IV. Coffee, regarded as a Muslim drink, was prohibited by Ethiopian Orthodox Christians until as late as 1889; it is now considered a national drink of Ethiopia for people of all faiths. Its early association in Europe with rebellious political activities led to its banning in England, among other places.

A contemporary example of coffee prohibition can be found in The Church of Jesus Christ of Latter-day Saints The organization claims that it is both physically and spiritually unhealthy to consume coffee This comes from the Mormon doctrine of health, given in 1833 by Mormon founder Joseph Smith in a revelation called the Word of Wisdom. It does not identify coffee by name, but includes the statement that "hot drinks are not for the belly," which has been interpreted to forbid both coffee and tea.

Quite a number of members of the Seventh-day Adventist Church also avoid caffeinated drinks. In its teachings, the Church requires members to avoid tea and coffee and other stimulants. Studies conducted on Adventists have shown a small but statistically significant association between coffee consumption and mortality from ischemic heart disease, other cardiovascular disease, all cardiovascular diseases combined, and all causes of death.

Health and Pharmacology

Coffee ingestion on average is about a third of that of tap water in North America and Europe Worldwide, 6.7 million metric tons of coffee were produced annually in 1998–2000, and the forecast is a rise to 7 million metric tons annually by 2010.

Scientific studies have examined the relationship between coffee consumption and an array of medical conditions. Findings are contradictory as to whether coffee has any specific health benefits, and results are similarly conflicting regarding the negative effects of coffee consumption.

Coffee consumption has been linked to breast size reduction, and taking regular hits of caffeine reduces the risk of breast cancer Coffee appears to reduce the risk of Alzheimer's disease, Parkinson's disease, heart disease, diabetes mellitus type 2, cirrhosis of the liver and gout. A longitudinal study in 2009 showed that moderate drinkers of coffee (3-5 cups per day) had lower chances of getting Dementia, in addition to Alzheimer's disease It increases the risk of acid reflux and associated diseases. Some health effects of coffee are due to its caffeine content, as the benefits are only observed in those who drink caffeinated coffee while others appear to be due to other components For example, the antioxidants in coffee prevent free radicals from causing cell damage.

Coffee consumption can lead to iron deficiency anemia in mothers and infants Coffee also interferes with the absorption of supplemental iron.

American scientist Yaser Dorri has suggested that the smell of coffee can restore appetite and refresh olfactory receptors. He suggests that people can regain their appetite after cooking by smelling coffee beans, and that this method can also be used for research animals. Many high end perfume shops now offer coffee beans to refresh the receptors between perfume tests.

Over 1,000 chemicals have been reported in roasted coffee; more than half of those tested (19/28) are rodent carcinogens. Coffee's negative health effects are often blamed on its caffeine content. Research suggests that drinking caffeinated coffee can cause a temporary increase in the stiffening of arterial walls. Coffee is no longer thought to be a risk factor for coronary heart disease. Some studies suggest that it may have a mixed effect on short-term memory, by improving it when the information to be recalled is related to the current train of thought but making it more difficult to recall unrelated information About 10% of people with a moderate daily intake (235 mg per day) reported increased depression and anxiety when caffeine was withdrawn and about 15% of the general population report having stopped caffeine use completely, citing concern about health and unpleasant side effects

Caffeine Content

Depending on the type of coffee and method of preparation, the caffeine content of a single serving can vary greatly. On average, a single cup of coffee (about 207 milliliters or a single shot of espresso (about 30 mL) can be expected to contain the following amounts of caffeine:

- *Drip coffee:* 115–175 mg (0.56-0.85 mg/ml)
- *Espresso:* 60 mg (2 mg/ml)
- *Brewed/Pressed:* 80-135 mg (0.39-0.65 mg/ml)
- *Instant:* 65–100 mg (0.31-0.48 mg/ml)
- *Decaf, brewed:* 3-4 mg
- *Decaf, instant:* 2-3 mg.

14

Cocoa

Cocoa is the dried and fully fermented fatty seed of the cacao tree from which chocolate is made. "Cocoa" can often also refer to the drink commonly known as hot chocolate cocoa powder, the dry powder made by grinding cocoa seeds and removing the cocoa butter from the dark, bitter cocoa solids; or it may refer to the combination of both cocoa powder and cocoa butter together.

Fig. 14.1

A cacao pod has a rough leathery rind about 3 cm thick (this varies with the origin and variety of pod). It is filled with sweet, mucilaginous pulp called 'baba de cacao' in South America, enclosing 30 to 50 large almond-like seeds (beans) that are fairly soft and pinkish or purplish in colour.

The cacao tree is native to the Americas. It may have originated in the foothills of the Andes in the Amazon and Orinoco basins of South America where today, examples of wild cacao still can be found. However, it may have had a larger range in the past, evidence for which may be obscured because of its cultivation in these areas long before, as well as after, the Spanish arrived. It may have been introduced into Central America by the ancient Mayas, and cultivated in Mexico by the Olmecs, then by the Toltecs and later by the Aztecs. It was a common currency throughout Mesoamerica and the Caribbean before the Spanish conquest.

Cacao trees will grow in a limited geographical zone, of approximately 20 degrees to the north and south of the Equator. Nearly 70% of the world crop is grown in West Africa.

Cocoa was an important commodity in Pre-Columbian Mesoamerica. Spanish chroniclers of the conquest of Mexico by Hernán Cortés relate that when Montezuma II, emperor of the Aztecs, dined he took no other beverage than chocolate, served in a golden goblet and eaten with a golden spoon. Flavored with vanilla and spices, his chocolate was whipped into a froth that dissolved in the mouth. It is reported that Montezuma II may have consumed no fewer than 50 portions each day, and 200 more by the nobles of his court.

Chocolate was introduced to Europe by the Spaniards and became a popular beverage by the mid 1600s. They also introduced the cacao tree into the West Indies and the Philippines.

The cacao plant was first given its botanical name by Swedish natural scientist Carolus Linnaeus in his original classification of the plant kingdom, who called it *Theobroma* ("food of the gods") *cacao*.

There are three main varieties of cacao: Forastero, Criollo, and Trinitario. The first comprises 95% of the world production of cacao, and is the most widely used. Overall, the highest quality cocoa beans come from the Criollo variety, which is considered a delicacy Criollo plantations have lower yields than those of Forastero, and also tend to be less resistant to several diseases that attack the cocoa plant, hence very few countries still produce it. One of the largest producer of Criollo beans is Venezuela (Chuao and Porcelana). Hacienda San José, located in Paria/Venezuela, cultivates Criollo beans. The total area is of this hacienda is 320 hectares, of which 185 hectares are devoted to cacao with a density of 1.000 plants per hectare. Trinitario is a hybrid between Criollo and Forastero varieties. It is considered of much higher quality than the latter, but has higher yields and is more resistant to disease than the former. The Netherlands is the leading cocoa processing country, followed by the U.S.

Cocoa and its products (including chocolate) are used worldwide. Per capita consumption is poorly understood with numerous countries claiming the highest: various reports state that Switzerland, Belgium, and the UK have the highest consumption, but because there is no clear mechanism to determine how much of a country's production is consumed by residents and how much by visitors, this is all speculative.

The world's largest cocoa bean producing countries are as follows. The figure gives the production estimates for the 2006-2007 season from the International Cocoa Organization. The percentage is the proportion of the world's total of 3.5 million tonnes for the relevant period.

Harvesting

When the pods ripen, they are harvested from the trunks and branches of the Cocoa tree with a curved knife on a long pole. The pod itself is green when ready to harvest, rather than red or orange. Normally, red or orange pods are considered of a lesser quality because their flavours and aromas are poorer; these are used for industrial chocolate. The pods are either opened on the field and the seeds extracted and carried to the fermentation area on the plantation, or the whole pods are taken to the fermentation area.

Processing

The harvested pods are opened—typically with a machete—the pulp and cocoa seeds are removed and the rind is discarded. The pulp and seeds are then piled in heaps, placed in bins, or laid out on grates for several days. During this time, the seeds and pulp undergo "sweating", where the thick pulp liquefies as it ferments. The fermented pulp trickles away, leaving cocoa seeds behind to be collected. Sweating is important for the quality of the beans, which originally have a strong bitter taste. If sweating is interrupted, the resulting cocoa may be ruined; if underdone the cocoa seed maintains a flavor similar to raw potatoes and becomes susceptible to mildew. Some cocoa producing countries distill alcoholic spirits using the liquefied pulp.

The fermented beans are dried by spreading them out over a large surface and constantly raking them. In large plantations, this is done on huge trays under the sun or by using artificial heat. Small plantations may dry their harvest on little trays or on cowhides. Finally, the beans are trodden and shuffled about (often using bare human feet) and sometimes, during this process, red clay mixed with water is sprinkled over the beans to obtain a finer color, polish, and protection against molds during shipment to factories in the United States, the Netherlands, United Kingdom, and other countries. Drying in the sun is preferable to drying by artificial means, as no extraneous flavors such as smoke or oil are introduced which might otherwise taint the flavour.

CHOCOLATE PRODUCTION

Chocolate

To make 1 kg (2.2 pounds) of chocolate, about 300 to 600 beans are processed, depending on the desired cocoa content. In a factory, the beans are roasted. Next they are cracked and then de-shelled by a "winnower". The resulting pieces of beans are called nibs, and are ground using various methods into a thick creamy paste, known as chocolate liquor or cocoa paste. This "liquor" is then further processed into chocolate by mixing in (more) cocoa butter and sugar (and sometimes lecithin as an emulsifier and vanilla), and then refining, conching and tempering. Or it can be separated into cocoa powder and cocoa butter using a hydraulic press or the Broma process. This process produces around 50% cocoa butter and 50% cocoa powder. Standard cocoa powder has a fat content of approximately 10-12 per cent. Cocoa butter is used in chocolate bar manufacture, other confectionery, soaps, and cosmetics.

Fig. 14.2

Adding an alkali produces Dutch process cocoa powder, which is less acidic, darker and more mellow in flavor than what is generally available in most of the world. Regular (non-alkalized) cocoa is acidic, so when cocoa is treated with an alkaline ingredient, generally potassium carbonate, the pH increases. This process can be done at various stages during manufacturing, including during nib treatment, liquor treatment or press cake treatment.

Another process that helps develop the flavour is roasting. Roasting can be done on the whole bean before shelling or on the nib after shelling. The time and temperature of the roast affect the result: A "low roast" produces a more acid, aromatic flavor, while a high roast gives a more intense, bitter flavor lacking complex flavour notes.

Health Benefits of Cocoa Consumption

Chocolate and cocoa contain a high level of flavonoids, specifically epicatechin, which may have beneficial cardiovascular effects on health The ingestion of flavonol-rich cocoa is associated with acute elevation of circulating nitric oxide, enhanced flow-mediated vasodilation, and augmented microcirculation.

Prolonged intake of flavonol-rich cocoa has been linked to cardiovascular health benefits, though it should be noted that this refers to raw cocoa and to a lesser extent, dark chocolate, since flavanoids degrade during cooking and alkalizing processes. Milk chocolate's addition of whole milk reduces the overall cocoa content per ounce while increasing saturated fat levels, possibly negating some of cocoa's heart-healthy potential benefits. Nevertheless, studies have still found short term benefits in LDL cholesterol levels from dark chocolate consumption.

Hollenberg and colleagues of Harvard Medical School studied the effects of cocoa and flavanols on Panama's Kuna

Indian population, who are heavy consumers of cocoa. The researchers found that the Kuna Indians living on the islands had significantly lower rates of heart disease and cancer compared to those on the mainland who do not drink cocoa as on the islands. It is believed that the improved blood flow after consumption of flavanol-rich cocoa may help to achieve health benefits in hearts and other organs. In particular, the benefits may extend to the brain and have important implications for learning and memory.

Cocoa also contains large amounts of antioxidants such as epicatechins and polyphenols. According to research at Cornell University, cocoa powder has nearly twice the antioxidants of red wine, and up to three times the antioxidants found in green tea. Cocoa also contains magnesium, iron, chromium, vitamin C, zinc and others.

Foods rich in cocoa appear to reduce blood pressure but drinking green and black tea may not, according to an analysis of previously published research in the April 9, 2007 issue of Archives of Internal Medicine one of the JAMA/ Archives journals.

Non-human Animal Consumption

Chocolate is a food product with appeal not only to the human population, but to many different animals as well. However, chocolate and cocoa contain a high level of xanthines, specifically theobromine and to a much lesser extent caffeine, that are detrimental to the health of many animals, including dogs and cats. While these compounds have desirable effects in humans, they cannot be efficiently metabolized in many animals and can lead to cardiac and nervous system problems, and if consumed in high quantities, even lead to death. However, since the mid-2000s, some cocoa derivatives with a low concentration of xanthines, have been designed by specialized industry to be suitable for pet consumption, enabling the pet food industry to offer animal safe chocolate and cocoa flavored products. It results in products with a high concentration of fiber and proteins, while maintaining low concentrations of sugar and other carbohydrates, thus enabling it to be used to create healthy functional cocoa pet products.

Sustainable Cocoa

In the industrialized world, changing attitudes to cocoa products may cause a reduced demand for them in the future. Obesity, particularly among children, has become a major health problem and chocolate—a food product with a high calorie content-is considered to be part of the problem. Additionally, consumers are becoming increasingly interested in the environmental impact of the production of cocoa, as well as what they perceive as the negative social impact of its production.

Price instability makes it difficult for small-scale farmers to predict income levels from year to year. Efforts to diverisfy cropping patterns and improve production and marketing efficiencies can help to address this.

Roundtable for a Sustainable Cocoa Economy (RSCE)

This initiative, called the Roundtable for a Sustainable Cocoa Economy (RSCE), has developed from the growing requirement to face the challenges posed by sustainability. It was launched in 2007 by the International Cocoa Organization (ICCO) and is steered by an independent working group with representation of major stakeholders. The mission of the Roundtable is to establish a participatory and transparent process towards economic, environmental and social sustainability in the global cocoa economy. The 1st Roundtable in 2007 brought together more than 200 stakeholders representing 25 countries, including cocoa farmers, government officials from cocoa producing and consuming countries, traders, chocolate manufacturers, donor organizations and national and international NGOs.

Child Labour in the Cocoa Production Industry

- Children work in the cocoa production industry. According to an International Labor Organization (ILO) report, in 2002 more than 109,000 children were working on cocoa farms in Côte d'Ivoire (Ivory Coast), some of them in 'the worst forms of child labor'. The International Labor Organization later reported that 200,000 children were working in the cocoa industry in Ivory Coast in 2005.
- The first allegations that child slavery is used in cocoa production appeared in 1998. The 2005 International Labor Organization report failed to fully characterize this problem, but estimated that up to 6% of the 200,000 children involved in cocoa production could be the victims of human trafficking or slavery.

The Cocoa Protocol is an effort to end these practices. It has however been criticized by some groups including the International Labor Rights Fund as an industry initiative which falls short.

Organizations that Directly Support Sustainable Cocoa

Cocoa farmers in many countries lack information on production and marketing practices to help them improve their livelihoods. Organizations such as the World Cocoa Foundation helps to support sustainable cocoa efforts through public-private partnerships such as IITA's sustainable tree crops program (STCP) in cocoa growing regions. World Cocoa Foundation's regional programs in West Africa, Latin America and Southeast Asia have reach over 300,000 small scale cocoa farmers and their families. Graduates of WCF-supported farmer field schools report income improvements of 22–55 per cent or more, through improved cultivation and marketing practices.

Environmental Impact

The poverty of many cocoa farmers means that they can't afford to take the best care of the environment in their activities.

For decades, these farmers have encroached on forest, most of the time after the best trees had been cut down by logging companies. This has happened less in recent times, as there is less forest left and because many governments and communities take better care of the remaining forests.

Usually, use of current inputs, such as chemical fertilizers and pesticides, by cocoa farmers is limited. For this reason most have only limited knowledge of the most appropriate ways of using such inputs.

Cocoa Trading

Cocoa beans, Cocoa butter and cocoa powder are traded on two world exchanges: London and New York. The London market is based on West African cocoa and New York on cocoa predominantly from South East Asia. Cocoa is the world's smallest soft commodity market. The futures price of cocoa butter and cocoa powder is determined by multiplying the bean price by a ratio. The combined butter and powder ratio has tended to be around 3.5. If the combined ratio falls below 3.2 or so, production ceases to be economically viable and some factories cease extraction of butter and powder and trade exclusively in cocoa liquor.

15

Orange (Fruit)

An orange—specifically, the sweet orange—is the citrus *Citrus sinensis* (syn. *Citrus aurantium* L. var. dulcis L., or *Citrus aurantium* Risso) and its fruit. The orange is a hybrid of ancient cultivated origin, possibly between pomelo (*Citrus maxima*) and tangerine (*Citrus reticulata*). It is a small

Fig. 15.1

flowering tree growing to about 10 m tall with evergreen leaves, which are arranged alternately, of ovate shape with crenulate margins and 4-10 cm long. The orange fruit is a hesperidium, a type of berry.

Oranges originated in Southeast Asia. The fruit of Citrus sinensis is called sweet orange to distinguish it from Citrus aurantium, the bitter orange. In a number of languages, it is known as a "Chinese apple" (e.g. Dutch Sinaasappel, "China's apple", or "Apfelsine" in German). The name is thought to ultimately derive from the Dravidian and Telugu word for the orange tree, with its final form developing after passing through numerous intermediate languages.

Fruit

All citrus trees are of the single genus, *Citrus*, and remain largely interbreedable; that is, there is only one "superspecies" which includes grapefruits, lemons, limes and oranges. Nevertheless, names have been given to the various members of the genus, oranges often being referred to as *Citrus sinensis* and *Citrus aurantium*. Fruits of all members of the genus *Citrus* are considered berries because they have many seeds, are fleshy and soft, and derive from a single ovary. An orange seed is called a pip. The white thread-like material attached to the inside of the peel is called pith.

Persian Orange

The Persian orange, grown widely in southern Europe after its introduction to Italy in the 11th century, was bitter. Sweet oranges brought to Europe in the 15th century from India by Portuguese traders, quickly displaced the bitter, and are now the most common variety of orange cultivated. The sweet orange will grow to different sizes and colours according to local conditions, most commonly with ten *carpels*, or segments, inside.

Some South East Indo-European tongues name orange after Portugal, which was formerly the main source of imports of sweet oranges. Examples are Bulgarian *portokal* Greek *portokali* , Persian *porteghal* and Romanian *portocala*. Also in South Italian dialects (Neapolitan), orange is named *portogallo* or *purtualle*, literally "the Portuguese ones". Related names can also be found in other languages: Turkish *Portakal*, Arabic *al-burtuqal* Amharic *birtukan*, and Georgian *phortokhali*.

Portuguese, Spanish, Arab, and Dutch sailors planted citrus trees along trade routes to prevent scurvy. On his second voyage in 1493, Christopher Columbus brought the seeds of oranges, lemons and citrons to Haiti and the Caribbean. They were introduced in Florida (along with lemons) in 1513 by Spanish explorer Juan Ponce de Leon, and were introduced to Hawaii in 1792.

Navel Orange

A single mutation in 1820 in an orchard of sweet oranges planted at a monastery in Brazil yielded the navel orange, also known as the Washington, Riverside, or Bahie navel. The mutation causes navel oranges to develop a second orange at the base of the original fruit, opposite the stem. The second orange develops as a conjoined twin in a set of smaller segments embedded within the peel of the larger orange. From the outside, it looks similar to the human navel.

Because the mutation left the fruit seedless and, therefore, sterile, the only means available to cultivate more of this new variety is to graft cuttings onto other varieties of citrus tree. Two such cuttings of the original tree were transplanted to Riverside, California in 1870, which eventually led to worldwide popularity.

Today, navel oranges continue to be produced via cutting and grafting. This does not allow for the usual selective breeding methodologies, and so not only do the navel oranges of today have exactly the same genetic makeup as the original tree, and are therefore clones; in a sense, all navel oranges can be considered to be the fruit of that single over-a-century-old tree.

On rare occasions, however, further mutations can lead to new varieties.

Valencia Orange

The Valencia or Murcia orange is one of the sweet oranges used for juice extraction. It is a late-season fruit, and therefore a popular variety when the navel oranges are out of season. For this reason, the orange was chosen to be the official mascot of the 1982 FIFA World Cup, which was held in Spain. The mascot was called "Naranjito" ("little orange"), and wore the colours of the Spanish soccer team uniform.

Fig. 15.2

Blood Orange

The blood orange has streaks of red in the fruit, and the juice is often a dark burgundy colour. The fruit has found a niche as an interesting ingredient variation on traditional Seville marmalade, with its striking red streaks and distinct flavour. The scarlet navel is a variety with the same dual-fruit mutation as the navel orange.

Acidity

Like all citrus fruits, the *orange* is acidic, with a pH level of around 2.5-3; depending on the age, size and variety of the fruit. Although this is not, on average, as strong as the lemon, it is still quite strong on the scale - as strong as vinegar.

Production

Oranges grown for commercial production are generally grown in groves and are produced throughout the world. The top three orange-producing countries are Brazil, the United States, and Mexico. Oranges are sensitive to frost, and a common treatment to prevent frost damage when sub-freezing temperatures are expected, is to spray the trees with water, since as long as unfrozen water is turning to ice on the trees' branches, the ice that has formed stays just *at* the freezing point, giving protection even if air temperatures have dropped far lower.

Etymology

The word *orange* is derived from Sanskrit *naranga?* "orange tree." and in Telugu "Naringa". The Sanskrit word was borrowed into European languages through Persian *narang,* Armenian *narinj,* Arabic *naranj,* (Spanish *naranja* and Portuguese *laranja*), Late Latin *arangia,* Italian *arancia* or *arancio,* and Old French *orenge,* in chronological order. The first appearance in English dates from the 14th century. The forms starting with n- are older; this initial n- may have been mistaken as part of the indefinite article, in languages with articles ending with an -n sound (e.g., in French *une norenge* may have been taken as *une orenge*). The name of the colour is derived from the fruit, first appearing in this sense in 1542.

Some languages have different words for the bitter and the sweet orange, such as Modern Greek *nerantzi* and *portokali*, respectively. Or in Persian, the words are *narang* and *porteghal* (Portugal), in the same order. The reason is that the sweet orange was brought from China or India to Europe during the 15th century by the Portuguese. For the same reason, some languages refer to it as *Applesin* (or variants), which means "Apple from China," while the bitter orange was introduced through Persia.

Juice and other Products

Oranges are widely grown in warm climates worldwide, and the flavours of oranges vary from sweet to sour. The fruit is commonly peeled and eaten fresh, or squeezed for its juice. It has a thick bitter rind that is usually discarded, but can be processed into animal feed by removing water, using pressure and heat. It is also used in certain recipes as flavouring or a garnish. The outer-most layer of the rind can be grated or thinly veneered with a tool called a zester, to produce orange zest. Zest is popular in cooking because it contains the oil glands and has a strong flavour similar to the fleshy inner part of the orange. The white part of the rind, called the *pericarp* or *albedo* and including the pith, is a source of pectin and has nearly the same amount of vitamin C as the flesh.

Products made from oranges include

- Orange juice is one of the commodities traded on the New York Board of Trade. Brazil is the largest producer of orange juice in the world, followed by the USA. It is made by squeezing the fruit on a special instrument called a "*juicer*" or a "*squeezer*." The juice is collected in a small tray underneath. This is mainly done in the home, and in industry is done on a much larger scale.

- Frozen orange juice concentrate is made from freshly squeezed and filtered orange juice.
- Sweet orange oil is a by-product of the juice industry produced by pressing the peel. It is used as a flavouring of food and drink and for its fragrance in perfume and aromatherapy Sweet orange oil consists of about 90% d-Limonene, a solvent used in various household chemicals, such as to condition wooden furniture, and along with other citrus oils in grease removal and as a hand-cleansing agent. It is an efficient cleaning agent which is promoted as being environmentally friendly and preferable to petroleum distillates. However, d-Limonene is classified as toxic or very toxic in several countries Its smell is considered more pleasant by some than those of other cleaning agents. Although once thought to cause renal cancer in rats, limonene now is known as a significant chemopreventive agent with potential value as a dietary anti-cancer tool in humans. There is no evidence for carcinogenicity or genotoxicity in humans. The IARC classifies *d*-limonene under Class 3: *not classifiable as to its carcinogenicity to humans*.
- The orange blossom, which is the state flower of Florida, is traditionally associated with good fortune, and was popular in bridal bouquets and head wreaths for weddings for some time. The petals of orange blossom can also be made into a delicately citrus-scented version of rosewater. Orange blossom water (aka orange flower water) is a common part of both French and Middle Eastern cuisines, used most often as an ingredient in desserts. The orange blossom gives its touristic nickname to the *Costa del Azahar* ("Orange-blossom coast"), the Castellon seaboard.

- In Spain, fallen blossoms are dried and then used to make tea.
- In the United States, orange flower water is used to make orange blossom scones.
- Orange blossom honey, or actually citrus honey, is produced by putting beehives in the citrus groves during bloom, which also pollinates seeded citrus varieties. Orange blossom honey is highly prized, and tastes much like orange.
- Marmalade, a conserve usually made with Seville oranges. All parts of the orange are used to make marmalade: the pith and pips are separated, and typically placed in a muslin bag where they are boiled in the juice (and sliced peel) to extract their pectin, aiding the setting process.
- Orange peel is used by gardeners as a slug repellent.
- Orange leaves can be boiled to make tea.

16

Cotton

Cotton is a soft, staple fibre that grows in a form known as a boll around the seeds of the cotton plant a shrub native to tropical and subtropical regions around the world, including the Americas, India and Africa. The fibre most often is spun into yarn or thread and used to make a soft, breathable

Fig. 16.1

textile, which is the most widely used natural-fibre cloth in clothing today. The English name, which began to be used circa 1400, derives from the Arabic (al) qutn meaning cotton.

Cotton plants as imagined and drawn by John Mandeville in the fourteenth century.

Cotton was cultivated by the inhabitants of the Indus Valley Civilization by the 5th millennium BCE - 4th millennium BCE The Indus cotton industry was well developed and some methods used in cotton spinning and fabrication continued to be used until the modern Industrialization of India. Well before the Common Era the use of cotton textiles had spread from India to the Mediterranean and beyond:

> "Cotton has been spun, woven, and dyed since prehistoric times. It clothed the people of ancient India, Egypt, and China. Hundreds of years before the Christian era cotton textiles were woven in India with matchless skill, and their use spread to the Mediterranean countries. In the 1st cent. Arab traders brought fine muslin and calico to Italy and Spain. The Moors introduced the cultivation of cotton into Spain in the 9th cent. Fustians and dimities were woven there and in the 14th cent. in Venice and Milan, at first with a linen warp. Little cotton cloth was imported to England before the 15th cent., although small amounts were obtained chiefly for candlewicks. By the 17th cent. the East India Company was bringing rare fabrics from India. Native Americans skillfully spun and wove cotton into fine garments and dyed tapestries. Cotton fabrics found in Peruvian tombs are said to belong to a pre-Inca culture. In color and texture the ancient Peruvian and Mexican textiles resemble those found in Egyptian tombs."

The earliest cultivation of cotton discovered thus far in the Americas occurred in Mexico, some 5,000 years ago. The indigenous species was *Gossypium hirsutum* which is today the most widely planted species of cotton in the world, constituting about 90% of all production worldwide. The greatest diversity of wild cotton species is found in Mexico, followed by Australia and Africa.

In Iran (Persia), the history of cotton dates back to Achaemenid era (5th century B.C.), however there are few sources about the implantation of cotton in Pre-Islamic Iran. The implantation of cotton was common in Merv, Ray and Pars of Iran (Persia). In the poems of Persian poets, specially Ferdowsi's Shahname, there are many referrals to Cotton ("Panbe" in Persian). Marco Polo (13th century) refers to the major products of Persia (Iran), including Cotton. John Chardin a famous french traveler of 17th century who has visited the Safavid Persia, has approved the vast cotton farms of Persia.

In Peru, cultivation of the indigenous cotton species *Gossypium barbadense* was the backbone of the development of coastal cultures such as the Norte Chico, Moche and Nazca. Cotton was grown upriver, made into nets and traded with fishing villages along the coast for large supplies of fish. The Spanish who came to Mexico in the early 1500s found the people growing cotton and wearing clothing made of it.

During the late medieval period, cotton became known as an imported fibre in northern Europe, without any knowledge of how it was derived, other than that it was a plant; noting its similarities to wool, people in the region could only imagine that cotton must be produced by plant-borne sheep. John Mandeville, writing in 1350, stated as fact the now-preposterous belief: "There grew there [India] a wonderful tree which bore tiny lambs on the endes of its branches. These branches were so pliable that they bent down to allow the lambs to feed when they are hungrie" This aspect is retained in the name for cotton in many European languages, such as German *Baumwolle*, which translates as "tree wool" (*Baum* means "tree"; *Wolle* means "wool"). By the end of the 16th century, cotton was cultivated throughout the warmer regions in Asia and the Americas.

India's cotton-processing sector gradually declined during British expansion in India and the establishment of colonial rule during the late 18th and early 19th centuries. This was largely due to the East India Company's exposing of India to foreign competition, which made cotton processing and manufacturing workshops in India uncompetitive. Indian markets increasingly supplied only raw cotton and were obliged to purchase manufactured textiles from Britain.

The advent of the Industrial Revolution in Britain provided a great boost to cotton manufacture, as textiles emerged as Britain's leading export. In 1738 Lewis Paul and John Wyatt, of Birmingham, England, patented the Roller Spinning machine, and the flyer-and-bobbin system for drawing cotton to a more even thickness using two sets of rollers that travelled at different speeds. Later, the invention of the spinning jenny in 1764 and Richard Arkwright's spinning frame (based on the Roller Spinning Machine) in 1769 enabled British weavers to produce cotton yarn and cloth at much higher rates. From the late eighteenth century onwards, the British city of Manchester acquired the nickname *"cottonopolis"* due to the cotton industry's omnipresence within the city, and Manchester's role as the heart of the global cotton trade. Production capacity was further improved by the invention of the cotton gin by Eli Whitney in 1793. Improving technology and increasing control of world markets allowed British traders to develop a commercial chain in which raw cotton fibres were (at first) purchased from colonial plantations, processed into cotton cloth in the mills of Lancashire, and then re-exported on British ships to captive colonial markets in West Africa, India, and China.

Fig. 16.2

By the 1840s, India was no longer capable of supplying the vast quantities of cotton fibres needed by mechanized British factories, while shipping bulky, low-price cotton from India to Britain was time-consuming and expensive. This, coupled with the emergence of American cotton as a superior type (due to the longer, stronger fibres of the two domesticated native American species, *Gossypium hirsutum* and *Gossypium barbadense*), encouraged British traders to purchase cotton from plantations in the United States and the Caribbean. This was also much cheaper as it was produced by unpaid slaves. By the mid 19th century, "King Cotton" had become the backbone of the southern American economy. In the United States, cultivating and harvesting cotton became the leading occupation of slaves.

During the American Civil War, American cotton exports slumped due to a Union blockade on Southern ports, also because of a strategic decision by the Confederate Government to cut exports, hoping to force Britain to recognize the Confederacy or enter the war, prompting the main purchasers of cotton, Britain and France, to turn to Egyptian cotton. British and French traders invested heavily in cotton plantations and the Egyptian government of Viceroy Isma'il took out substantial loans from European bankers and stock exchanges. After the American Civil War ended in 1865, British and French traders abandoned Egyptian cotton and returned to cheap American exports, sending Egypt into a deficit spiral that led to the country declaring bankruptcy in 1876, a key factor behind Egypt's annexation by the British Empire in 1882.

During this time cotton cultivation in the British Empire, especially India, greatly increased to replace the lost production of the American South. Through tariffs and other restrictions the British government discouraged the production of cotton cloth in India; rather the raw fibre was sent to England for processing. The Indian patriot Mahatma Gandhi described the process:

- English people buy Indian cotton in the field, picked by Indian labor at seven cents a day, through an optional monopoly.
- This cotton is shipped on British bottoms, a three-week journey across the Indian Ocean, down the Red Sea, across the Mediterranean, through Gibraltar, across the Bay of Biscay and the Atlantic Ocean to London. One hundred per cent profit on this freight is regarded as small.
- The cotton is turned into cloth in Lancashire. You pay shilling wages instead of Indian pennies to your workers. The English worker not only has the advantage of better wages, but the steel companies of England get the profit of building the factories and machines. Wages; profits; all these are spent in England.
- The finished product is sent back to India at European shipping rates, once again on British ships. The captains,

officers, sailors of these ships, whose wages must be paid, are English. The only Indians who profit are a few lascars who do the dirty work on the boats for a few cents a day.

- The cloth is finally sold back to the kings and landlords of India who got the money to buy this expensive cloth out of the poor peasants of India who worked at seven cents a day.

In the United States, Southern cotton provided capital for the continuing development of the North. The cotton produced by enslaved African Americans not only helped the South but also enriched Northern merchants. Much of the Southern cotton was transshipped through the northern ports.

Cotton remained a key crop in the southern economy after emancipation and the end of the civil war in 1865. Across the South, sharecropping evolved, in which free black farmers worked on white-owned cotton plantations in return for a share of the profits. Cotton plantations required vast labour forces to hand-pick cotton, and it was not until the 1950s that reliable harvesting machinery was introduced into the South (prior to this, cotton-harvesting machinery had been too clumsy to pick cotton without shredding the fibres). During the early twentieth century, employment in the cotton industry fell as machines began to replace labourers, and as the South's rural labor force dwindled during the First and Second World Wars. Today, cotton remains a major export of the southern United States, and a majority of the world's annual cotton crop is of the long-staple American variety.

Tangüis Cotton

In 1901, Peru's cotton industry suffered because of a fungus plague caused by a plant disease known as "Cotton wilt" and "Fusarium wilt" (*Fusarium vasinfectum*) The plant disease, which spread throughout Peru, entered the plant by its roots and worked its way up the stem until the plant was completely dried up. Fermín Tangüis a Puerto Rican agricultürist who lived in Peru, studied some species of the plant that were affected by the disease to a lesser extent and experimented in germination with the seeds of various cotton plants. In 1911, after 10 years of experimenting and failures, Tangüis was able to develop a seed which produced a superior cotton plant resistant to the disease. The seeds produced a plant that had a 40% longer (between 29 mm and 33 mm) and thicker fibre that did not break easily and required little water The Tangüis cotton, as it became known, is the variety which is preferred by the Peruvian national textile industry. It constituted 75 per cent of all the Peruvian cotton production, both for domestic use and apparel exports. The Tangüis cotton crop was estimated at 225,000 bales that year.

Cultivation

Successful cultivation of cotton requires a long frost-free period, plenty of sunshine, and a moderate rainfall, usually from 600 to 1200mm (24 to 48 inches). Soils usually need to be fairly heavy, although the level of nutrients does not need to be exceptional. In general, these conditions are met within the seasonally dry tropics and subtropics in the Northern and Southern hemispheres, but a large proportion of the cotton grown today is cultivated in areas with less rainfall that obtain the water from irrigation. Production of the crop for a given year usually starts soon after harvesting the preceding autumn. Planting time in spring in the Northern hemisphere varies from the beginning of February to the beginning of June. The area of the United States known as the South Plains is the largest contiguous cotton-growing region in the world. It is heavily dependent on irrigation water drawn from the Ogallala Aquifer.

Cotton is a thirsty crop, and as water resources get tighter around the world, economies that rely on it face difficulties and conflict, as well as potential environmental problems. For example, cotton has led to desertification in areas of Uzbekistan, where it is a major export. In the days of the Soviet Union, the Aral Sea was tapped for agricultural irrigation, largely of cotton, and now salination is widespread.

Genetically Modified Cotton

Genetically modified (GM) cotton was developed to reduce the heavy reliance on pesticides. The bacterium *Bacillus thuringiensis (BT)* naturally produces a chemical harmful only to a small fraction of insects, most notably the larvae of moths and butterflies, beetles, and flies, and harmless to other forms of life. The gene coding for *BT* toxin has been inserted into cotton, causing cotton to produce this natural insecticide in its tissues. In many regions the main pests in commercial cotton are lepidopteran larvae, which are killed by the *BT* protein in the transgenic cotton that they eat. This eliminates the need to use large amounts of broad-spectrum insecticides to kill lepidopteran pests (some of which have developed pyrethroid resistance). This spares natural insect predators in the farm ecology and further contributes to non-insecticide pest management.

BT cotton is ineffective against many cotton pests, however, such as plant bugs, stink bugs, aphids, etc.; depending on circumstances it may still be desirable to use insecticides against these.

Genetically modified cotton is widely used throughout the world. However, researchers have recently published the first documented case of in-field pest resistance to GM cotton The International Service for the Acquisition of Agri-biotech Applications (ISAAA) said that, worldwide, GM cotton was planted on an area of 67,000 km^2 in 2002. This is 20% of the worldwide total area planted in cotton. The U.S. cotton crop was 73% GM in 2003.

The initial introduction of GM cotton proved to be a commercial and ecological disaster in Australia - the yields were far lower than predicted, and the cotton plants were cross-pollinated with other varieties of cotton. However, the introduction of a second variety of GM cotton led to 15% of Australian cotton being GM in 2003. 80% of the crop was genetically modified in 2004, when the original GM variety was banned.

Cotton has also been genetically modified for resistance to glyphosate (marketed as Roundup in the USA), an inexpensive and highly effective but broad-spectrum herbicide, during its early growth. This allows glyphosate to be used for weed control during the early growing season.

GM cotton acreage in India continues to grow at a rapid rate increasing from 50,000 hectares in 2002 to 3.8 million hectares in 2006. The total cotton area in India is about 9.0 million hectares (the largest in the world or, about 25% of world cotton area) so GM cotton is now grown on 42% of the cotton area. This makes India the country with the largest area of GM cotton in the world, surpassing China (3.5 million hectares in 2006). The major reasons for this increase is a combination of increased farm income ($225/ha) and a reduction in pesticide use to control the Cotton Bollworm.

Cotton has gossypol, a toxin that makes it inedible. However, scientists have silenced the gene that produces the toxin, making it a potential food crop.

Organic Cotton

Organic cotton is cotton that is grown without insecticide or pesticide. Worldwide, cotton is a pesticide-intensive crop, using approximately 25% of the world's insecticides and 10% of the world's pesticides. According to the World Health Organization (WHO), 20,000 deaths occur each year from pesticide poisoning in developing countries, many of these from cotton farming. Organic agriculture uses methods that are ecological, economical, and socially sustainable and denies the use of agrochemicals and artificial fertilizers. Instead, organic agriculture uses crop rotation, the growing of different crops than cotton in alternative years. The use of insecticides is prohibited; organic agriculture uses natural enemies to suppress harmful insects. The production of organic cotton is more expensive than the production of conventional cotton. Although toxic pollution from synthetic chemicals is eliminated, other pollution-like problems may remain, particularly run-off. Organic cotton is produced in organic agricultural systems that produce food and fibre according to clearly established standards. Organic agriculture prohibits the use of toxic and persistent chemical pesticides and fertilizers, as well as genetically modified organisms. It seeks to build biologically diverse agricultural systems, replenish and maintain soil fertility, and promote a healthy environment.

Pests and Weeds

The cotton industry relies heavily on chemicals such as fertilizers and insecticides, although a very small number of farmers are moving toward an organic model of production and organic cotton products are now available for purchase at limited locations. These are popular for baby clothes and diapers. Under most definitions, organic products do not use genetic engineering.

Historically, in North America, one of the most economically destructive pests in cotton production has been the boll weevil. Due to the US Department of Agriculture's highly successful Boll Weevil Eradication Program (BWEP), this pest has been eliminated from cotton in most of the United States. This program, along with the introduction of genetically engineered "*Bt* cotton" (which contains a bacteria gene that codes for a plant-produced protein that is toxic to a number of pests such as tobacco budworm, cotton bollworm, and pink bollworm), has allowed a reduction in the use of synthetic insecticides.

Mechanized Harvesting

Most cotton in the United States, Europe, and Australia is harvested mechanically, either by a cotton picker, a machine that removes the cotton from the boll without damaging the cotton plant, or by a cotton stripper, which strips the entire boll off the plant. Cotton strippers are used in regions where it is too windy to grow picker varieties of cotton, and usually after application of a chemical defoliant or the natural defoliation that occurs after a freeze. Cotton is a perennial crop in the tropics and without defoliation or freezing, the plant will continue to grow.

Competition from Synthetic Fibres

The era of manufactured fibres began with the development of Rayon in France in the 1890s. Rayon is derived from a natural cellulose and cannot be considered synthetic, but requires extensive processing in a manufacturing process and led the less expensive replacement of more naturally derived materials. A succession of new synthetic fibres were introduced by the chemicals industry in the following decades. Acetate in fibre form was developed in 1924. Nylon, the first fibre synthesized entirely from petrochemicals, was introduced as a sewing thread by DuPont in 1936, followed by Dupont's acrylic in 1944. Some garments were created from fabrics based on these fibres, such as women's hosiery from nylon, but it was not until the introduction of polyester into the fibre marketplace in the early 1950s that the market for cotton came under threat. The rapid uptake of polyester garments in the 1960s caused economic hardship in cotton exporting economies, especially in Central American countries such as Nicaragua where cotton production had boomed tenfold between 1950 and

1965 with the advent of cheap chemical pesticides. Cotton production recovered in the 1970s, but crashed to pre-1960 levels in the early 1990s.

Beginning as a self-help program in the mid-1960s, the Cotton Research and Promotion Program was organized by U.S. cotton producers in response to cotton's steady decline in market share. At that time, producers voted to set up a per-bale assessment system to fund the program, with built-in safeguards to protect their investments. With the passage of the Cotton Research & Promotion Act of 1966, the program joined forces and began battling synthetic competitors and re-establishing markets for cotton. Today, the success of this program has made cotton the best-selling fibre in the U.S. and one of the best-selling fibres in the world.

Administered by the Cotton Board and conducted by Cotton Incorporated, the Cotton Research & Promotion Program works to greatly increase the demand for and profitability of cotton through various research and promotion activities. It is funded by U.S. cotton producers and importers.

Uses

Cotton is used to make a number of textile products. These include terrycloth, used to make highly absorbent bath towels and robes; denim, used to make blue jeans; chambray, popularly used in the manufacture of blue work shirts (from which we get the term "blue-collar"); and corduroy, seersucker, and cotton twill. Socks, underwear, and most T-shirts are made from cotton. Bed sheets often are made from cotton. Cotton also is used to make yarn used in crochet and knitting. Fabric also can be made from recycled or recovered cotton that otherwise would be thrown away during the spinning, weaving, or cutting process. While many fabrics are made completely of cotton, some materials blend cotton with other fibres, including rayon and synthetic fibres such as polyester. It can either be used in knitted or woven fabrics, as it can be blended with elastine to make a stretchier thread for knitted fabrics, and things such as stretch jeans.

In addition to the textile industry, cotton is in fishnets, coffee filters, tents, gunpowder, cotton paper, and in bookbinding. The first Chinese paper was made of cotton fibre. Fire hoses were once made of cotton.

The cotton-seed which remains after the cotton is ginned is used to produce cottonseed oil, which, after refining, can be consumed by humans like any other vegetable oil. The cottonseed meal that is left generally is fed to ruminant livestock; the gossypol remaining in the meal is toxic to mongastric animals. Cottonseed hulls can be added to dairy cattle rations for roughage. During the American slavery period, cotton root bark was used in a folk remedy as an abortifacient, that is, to provoke abortion.

Cotton linters are fine, silky fibres which adhere to the seeds of the cotton plant after ginning. These curly fibres typically are less than 1/8 in (3 mm) long. The term also may apply to the longer textile fibre staple lint as well as the shorter fuzzy fibres from some upland species. Linters are traditionally used in the manufacture of paper and as a raw material in the manufacture of cellulose.

Shiny cotton is a processed version of the fibre that can be made into cloth resembling satin for shirts and suits. However, its hydrophobic property of not easily taking up water makes it unfit for the purpose of bath and dish towels (although examples of these made from shiny cotton are seen).

The term Egyptian cotton refers to the extra long staple cotton grown in Egypt and favored for the luxury and upmarket brands worldwide. During the U.S. Civil War, with heavy European investments, Egyptian-grown cotton became a major alternate source for British textile mills. Egyptian cotton is more durable and softer than American Pima cotton, which is why it is more expensive. Pima cotton is American cotton that is grown in the southwestern states of the U.S.

The International Cotton Trade

The United States, with sales of $4.9 billion, and Africa, with sales of $2.1 billion, are the largest exporters of raw cotton. Total international trade is $12 billion. Africa's share of the cotton trade has doubled since 1980. Neither area has a significant domestic textile industry, textile manufacturing having moved to developing nations in Eastern and South Asia such as India and China. In Africa cotton is grown by numerous small holders. Dunavant Enterprises, based in Memphis, Tennessee, is the leading cotton broker in Africa with hundreds of purchasing agents. It operates cotton gins in Uganda, Mozambique, and Zambia. In Zambia it often offers loans for seed and expenses to the 180,000 small farmers who grow cotton for it, as well as advice on farming methods. Cargill also purchases cotton in Africa for export.

The 25,000 cotton growers in the United States are heavily subsidized at the rate of $2 billion per year. The future of these subsidies is uncertain and has led to anticipatory expansion of cotton brokers' operations in Africa. Dunavant expanded in Africa by buying out local operations. This is only possible in former British colonies and Mozambique; former French colonies continue to maintain tight monopolies, inherited from their former colonialist masters, on cotton purchases at low fixed prices.

Leading Cotton-producing Countries

The five leading exporters of cotton are:

1. The United States;
2. Uzbekistan;
3. India;
4. Brazil; and
5. Burkina Faso.

The largest non-producing importers are Bangladesh, Indonesia, Thailand, Russia, and Taiwan.

In India, the States of Maharashtra (26.63%), Gujarat (17.96%) and Andhra Pradesh (13.75%) are the leading cotton producing States. These States have a predominantly tropical wet and dry climate.

In the United States, the State of Texas leads in total production while the state of California has the highest yield per acre in the world.

Fair Trade

Cotton is an enormously important commodity throughout the world. However, many farmers in developing countries receive a low price for their produce, or find it difficult to compete with developed countries.

This has led to an international dispute:

- On 27 September 2002 Brazil requested consultations with the US regarding prohibited and actionable subsidies provided to US producers, users and/or exporters of upland cotton, as well as legislation, regulations, statutory instruments and amendments thereto providing such subsidies (including export credits), grants, and any other assistance to the US producers, users and exporters of upland cotton.
- On 8 September 2004, the Panel Report recommended that the United States "withdraw" export credit guarantees and payments to domestic user and exporters, and "take appropriate steps to remove the adverse effects or withdraw" the mandatory price-contingent subsidy measures.

In addition to concerns over subsidies, the cotton industries of some countries are criticized for employing child labor and damaging workers' health by exposure to pesticides used in production. The international production and trade situation has led to 'fair trade' cotton clothing and footwear, joining a rapidly growing market for organic clothing, fair fashion or so-called 'ethical fashion'. The fair trade system was initiated in 2005 with producers from Cameroon, Mali and Senegal.

Critical Temperatures

- Favourable travel temperature range - no lower limit: 25 °C (77 °F)
- Optimum travel temperature: 20 °C (68 °F)
- Glow temperature: 205 °C (401 °F)
- Fire point: 210 °C (410 °F)
- Autoignition temperature: 407 °C (765 °F)
- Autoignition temperature (for oily cotton): 120 °C (248°F)

Cotton dries out, becomes hard and brittle and loses all elasticity at temperatures above 25°C (77°F). Extended exposure to light causes similar problems.

A temperature range of 25 °C (77 °F) to 35 °C (95°F) is the optimal range for mold development. At temperatures below 0°C (32 °F), rotting of wet cotton stops. Damaged cotton is sometimes stored at these temperatures to prevent further deterioration.

17

Tobacco

Tobacco is an agricultural product processed from the fresh leaves of plants in the genus Nicotiana. It can be consumed, used as an organic pesticide, and in the form of nicotine tartrate it is used in some medicines. In consumption it may be in the form of smoking, chewing, snuffing, dipping tobacco, or snus. Tobacco has long been in use as an entheogen in the Americas. However, upon the arrival of Europeans in North America, it quickly became popularized as a trade item and as a recreational drug. This popularization led to the development of the southern economy of the United States until it gave way to cotton. Following the American Civil War, a change in demand and a change in labor force allowed for the development of the cigarette. This new product quickly led to the growth of tobacco companies until the scientific controversy of the mid-1900s.

There are many species of tobacco, which are all encompassed by the plant genus Nicotiana. The word nicotiana (as well as nicotine) was named in honor of Jean Nicot, French ambassador to Portugal, who in 1559 sent it as a medicine to the court of Catherine de Medici.

Fig. 17.1

Because of the addictive properties of nicotine, tolerance and dependence develop. Absorption quantity, frequency, and speed of tobacco consumption are believed to be directly related to biological strength of nicotine dependence, addiction, and tolerance. The usage of tobacco, is an activity that is practiced by some 1.1 billion people, and up to 1/3 of the adult population The World Health Organization reports it to be the leading preventable cause of death worldwide and estimates that it currently causes 5.4 million deaths per year. Rates of smoking have leveled off or declined in developed countries, however they continue to rise in developing countries.

Tobacco is cultivated similar to other agricultural products. Seeds are sown in cold frames or hotbeds to prevent attacks from insects, and then transplanted into the fields. Tobacco is an annual crop, which is usually harvested in a large single-piece farm equipment. After harvest, tobacco is stored to allow for curing, which allow for the slow oxidation and degradation of carotenoids. This allows for the agricultural product to take on properties that are usually attributed to the "smoothness" of the smoke. Following this, tobacco is packed into its various forms of consumption which include smoking, chewing, sniffing, and so on.

Etymology

The Spanish word "tabaco" is thought to have its origin in Arawakan language, particularly, in the Taino language of the Caribbean. In Taino, it was said to refer either to a roll of tobacco leaves (according to Bartolome de Las Casas, 1552), or to the tabago, a kind of Y-shaped pipe for sniffing tobacco smoke (according to Oviedo; with the leaves themselves being referred to as Cohiba).

However, similar words in Spanish and Italian were commonly used from 1410 to define medicinal herbs, originating from the Arabic tabbaq, a word reportedly dating to the 9th century, as the name of various herbs.

Early Developments

Tobacco had already long been used in the Americas when European settlers arrived and introduced the practice to Europe, where it became popular. At high doses, tobacco can become hallucinogenic; accordingly, Native Americans never used the drug recreationally. Instead, it was often consumed as an entheogen; among some tribes, this was done only by experienced shamans or medicine men Eastern North American tribes would carry large amounts of tobacco in pouches as a readily accepted trade item and would often smoke it in pipes, either in defined ceremonies that were considered sacred, or to seal a bargain, and they would smoke it at such occasions in all stages of life, even in childhood It was believed that tobacco was a gift from the Creator and that the exhaled tobacco smoke was capable of carrying one's thoughts and prayers to heaven.

Popularization

Following the arrival of the Europeans, tobacco became increasingly popular as a trade item. It fostered the economy for the southern United States until it was replaced by cotton. Following the American civil war, a change in demand and a change in labor force allowed inventor James Bonsack to create a machine which automated cigarette production.

This increase in production allowed tremendous growth in the tobacco industry until the scientific revelations of the mid-1900s.

Contemporary

Following the scientific revelations of the mid-1900s, tobacco became condemned as a health hazard, and eventually became encompassed as a cause for cancer, as well as other respiratory and circulatory diseases. This led to the Tobacco Master Settlement Agreement (MSA) which settled the lawsuit in exchange for a combination of yearly payments to the states and voluntary restrictions on advertising and marketing of tobacco products.

As the industry's downward tumble continued, in the 1990s Brown & Williamsons cross-bred a strain of tobacco to produce Y1. This strain of tobacco contained an unusually high amount of nicotine, nearly doubling its content from 3.2-3.5% to 6.5%. This prompted Food and Drug Administration (FDA) to use this strain as evidence that tobacco companies were intentionally manipulating the nicotine content of cigarettes.

In 2003, in response to tobaccos growth in developing countries, the World Health Organization (WHO) successfully rallied 168 countries to sign the Framework Convention on Tobacco Control. The Convention is designed to push for effective legislation and its enforcement in all countries to reduce the harmful effects of tobacco. This led to the development of tobacco cessation products.

Fig. 17.2

Nicotiana

There are many species of tobacco, which are encompassed by the genus of herbs *Nicotiana*. It is part of the nightshade family (Solanaceae) indigenous to North and South America, Australia, south west Africa and the South Pacific.

Many plants contain nicotine, a powerful neurotoxin that is particularly harmful to insects. However, tobaccos contain a higher concentration of nicotine than most other plants. Unlike many other Solanaceae they do not contain tropane alkaloids, which are often poisonous to humans and other animals.

Despite containing enough nicotine and other compounds such as germacrene and anabasine and other piperidine alkaloids (varying between species) to deter most herbivores, a number of such animals have evolved the ability to feed on *Nicotiana* species without being harmed.

Nonetheless, tobacco is unpalatable to many species and therefore some tobacco plants (chiefly Tree Tobacco, *N. glauca*) have become established as invasive weeds in some places.

Types

There are a number of types of tobacco include but are not limited to:

- Aromatic Fire-cured, it is cured by smoke from open fires. In the United States, it is grown in northern middle Tennessee, central Kentucky and in Virginia. Fire-cured tobacco grown in Kentucky and Tennessee are used in some chewing tobaccos, moist snuff, some cigarettes, and as a condiment in pipe tobacco blends. Another fire-cured tobacco is Latakia and is produced from oriental varieties of *N. tabacum*. The leaves are cured and smoked over smoldering fires of local hardwoods and aromatic shrubs in Cyprus and Syria.
- Brightleaf tobacco, Brightleaf is commonly known as "Virginia tobacco", often regardless of which state they are planted. Prior to the American Civil War, most tobacco grown in the US was fire-cured dark-leaf. This type of tobacco was planted in fertile lowlands, used a robust variety of leaf, and was either fire cured or air cured. Most Canadian cigarettes are made from 100% pure Virginia tobacco.
- Burley tobacco, is an air-cured tobacco used primarily for cigarette production. In the U.S., burley tobacco plants are started from palletized seeds placed in polystyrene trays floated on a bed of fertilized water in March or April.
- Cavendish is more a process of curing and a method of cutting tobacco than a type of it. The processing and the cut are used to bring out the natural sweet taste in the tobacco. Cavendish can be produced out of any

tobacco type but is usually one of, or a blend of Kentucky, Virginia, and Burley and is most commonly used for pipe tobacco and cigars.

- Criollo tobacco is a type of tobacco, primarily used in the making of cigars. It was, by most accounts, one of the original Cuban tobaccos that emerged around the time of Columbus.
- Dokham, is a tobacco of Iranian origin mixed with leaves, bark, and herbs for smoking in a midwakh.
- Oriental tobacco, is a sun-cured, highly aromatic, small-leafed variety (*Nicotiana tabacum*) that is grown in Turkey, Greece, Bulgaria, and Macedonia. Oriental tobacco is frequently referred to as "Turkish tobacco", as these regions were all historically part of the Ottoman Empire. Many of the early brands of cigarettes were made mostly or entirely of Oriental tobacco; today, its main use is in blends of pipe and especially cigarette tobacco (a typical American cigarette is a blend of bright Virginia, burley and Oriental).
- Perique, A farmer called Pierre Chenet is credited with first turning this local tobacco into the Perique in 1824 through the technique of pressure-fermentation. Considered the truffle of pipe tobaccos, it is used as a component in many blended pipe tobaccos, but is too strong to be smoked pure. At one time, the freshly moist Perique was also chewed, but none is now sold for this purpose. It is typically blended with pure Virginia to lend spice, strength, and coolness to the blend.
- Shade tobacco, is cultivated in Connecticut and Massachusetts. Early Connecticut colonists acquired from the Native Americans the habit of smoking tobacco in pipes and began cultivating the plant commercially, even though the Puritans referred to it as the "evil weed". The industry has weathered some major

catastrophes, including a devastating hailstorm in 1929, and an epidemic of brown spot fungus in 2000, but is now in danger of disappearing altogether, given the value of the land to real estate speculators.

- White Burley, In 1865, George Webb of Brown County, Ohio planted Red Burley seeds he had purchased, and found that a few of the seedlings had a whitish, sickly look. The air-cured leaf was found to be more mild than other types of tobacco.
- Wild Tobacco, is native to the southwestern United States, Mexico, and parts of South America. Its botanical name is *Nicotiana rustica*.
- Y1 is a strain of tobacco that was cross-bred by Brown & Williamson to obtain an unusually high nicotine content. It became controversial in the 1990s when the United States Food and Drug Administration (FDA) used it as evidence that tobacco companies were intentionally manipulating the nicotine content of cigarettes.

Impact

Due to its long existence, tobacco has fostered many cultural items including: the usage of peace pipes, advertisements, movies. From its discovery tobacco has been highly regarded used in cultural ceremonies, for recreational purposes, and so forth. At the arrivals of the Europeans, tobacco was came to be regarded with wealth and knowledge. Smoking in public has for a long time been something reserved for men and when done by women has been associated with promiscuity. In Japan during the Edo period, prostitutes and their clients would often approach one another under the guise of offering a smoke and the same was true for 19th century Europe.

Following the civil war, the usage of tobacco, primarily in cigarettes became associated with masculinity, and power and is an iconic image associated with the stereotypical capitalist.From the mid-1900s and to today Tobacco is often rejected. This has spawned quitting-associations, negative-campaigns, and so forth. Bhutan is the only country in the world where tobacco sales are illegal.

Demographic

Research is limited mainly to tobacco smoking, which has been studied the more extensively than any other form of consumption. As of 2000, smoking is practiced by some 1.22 billion people, of which men are more likely to smoke than women (however the gender gap declines with age) poor more likely than rich, and people in developing countries or transitional economies are more likely than people in developed countries As of 2004, the World Health Organization (WHO) reports that of the 58.8 million deaths to occur globally 5.4 million are tobacco-attributed

Health

Tobacco use leads most commonly to diseases affecting the heart and lungs, with smoking being a major risk factor for heart attacks, chronic obstructive pulmonary disease (COPD), and cancer, particularly lung cancer, cancers of the larynx and mouth, and pancreatic cancer.

Fresh tobacco, processed tobacco, and tobacco smoke contain carcinogens. The current view on cancer is that carcinogenicity is a stochastic effect, where various environmental factors trigger the development of cancer. While exposure to a carcinogen increases the probability of cancer, the process remains random. For example, smoking tobacco is known to cause cancer in humans, but not all people who smoke necessarily develop smoking-related cancer. Additionally, in studies on humans, the large number of confounding variables makes it challenging to statistically distinguish their effects.

Economic

"Much of the disease burden and premature mortality attributable to tobacco use disproportionately affect the poor", and of the 1.22 billion smokers, 1 billion of them live in developing or transitional economies.

In Indonesia, the lowest income group spends 15% of its total expenditures on tobacco. In Egypt, more than 10% of households expediture in low-income homes is on tobacco. The poorest 20% of households in Mexico spend 11% of their income on tobacco.

The tobacco lobby gives money to politicians to vote in favor of deregulating tobacco. It is estimated that the United States tobacco lobby spends an average of $106,415 each day legislature meets; however the industry lost its support when the U.S. National Association of Attorneys General (NAAG) filed charges against the Tobacco Institute, a tobacco industry advocacy group This resulted in the Master Settlement Agreement, which forced the organization to disband and place all records on a website.

Production

Tobacco is cultivated similar to other agricultural products. Seeds were at first quickly scattered onto the soil. However, young plants came under increasing attack from flea beetles (*Epitrix cucumeris* or *Epitrix pubescens*), which caused destruction of half the tobacco crops in United States in 1876. By 1890 successful experiments were conducted that placed the plant in a frame covered by thin fabric. Today, tobacco is sown in cold frames or hotbeds, as their germination is activated by light.

In the United States, tobacco is often fertilized with the mineral apatite, which partially starves the plant of nitrogen to produce a more desired flavor. Apatite, however, contains radium, lead 210, and polonium 210 which are known radioactive carcinogens.

After the plants have reached relative maturity, they are transplanted into the fields, in which a relatively large hole is created in the tilled earth with a tobacco peg. Various mechanical tobacco planters where invented in the nineteenth and twentieth to automate the process: making the hole, fertilizing it, guiding the plant in-all in one motion.

Tobacco is cultivated annual, and can be harvested in several ways. In the oldest method, the entire plant is harvested at once by cutting off the stalk at the ground with a sickle. In the nineteenth century, bright tobacco began to be harvested by pulling individual leaves off the stalk as they ripened. The leaves ripen from the ground upwards, so a field of tobacco may go through several so-called "pullings," more commonly known as topping (topping always refers to the removal of the tobacco flower before the leaves are systematically removed and, eventually, entirely harvested. As the industrial revolution took hold, harvesting wagons used to transport leaves were equipped with man-powered stringers, an apparatus which used twine to attach leaves to a pole. In modern times large fields are harvested by a single piece of farm equipment, although topping the flower and in some cases the plucking of immature leaves is still done by hand.

Curing and subsequent aging allows for the slow oxidation and degradation of carotenoids in tobacco leaf. This produces certain compounds in the tobacco leaves very similar and give a sweet hay, tea, rose oil, or fruity aromatic flavor that contribute to the "smoothness" of the smoke. Starch is converted to sugar which glycates protein and is oxidized into advanced glycation endproducts (AGEs), a caramelization process that also adds flavor. Inhalation of these AGEs in tobacco smoke contributes to atherosclerosis and cancer. Levels of AGE's is dependent on the curing method used.

Tobacco can be cured through several methods which include but are not limited to:

- Air cured tobacco is hung in well-ventilated barns and allowed to dry over a period of four to eight weeks. Air-cured tobacco is low in sugar, which gives the tobacco smoke a light, sweet flavor, and high in nicotine. Cigar and burley tobaccos are air cured.
- Fire cured tobacco is hung in large barns where fires of hardwoods are kept on continuous or intermittent low smoulder and takes between three days and ten weeks, depending on the process and the tobacco. . Fire curing produces a tobacco low in sugar and high in nicotine. Pipe tobacco, chewing tobacco, and snuff are fire cured.
- Flue cured tobacco was originally strung onto tobacco sticks, which were hung from tier-poles in curing barns (Aus: kilns, also traditionally called Oasts). These barns have flues which run from externally fed fire boxes, heat-curing the tobacco without exposing it to smoke, slowly raising the temperature over the course of the curing. The process will generally take about a week. This method produces cigarette tobacco that is high in sugar and has medium to high levels of nicotine.
- Sun-cured tobacco dries uncovered in the sun. This method is used in Turkey, Greece and other Mediterranean countries to produce oriental tobacco. Sun-cured tobacco is low in sugar and nicotine and is used in cigarettes.

Consumption

- *Beedi* are thin, often flavored, south Asian cigarettes made of tobacco wrapped in a tendu leaf, and secured with colored thread at one end.
- *Chewing tobacco* is one of the oldest ways of consuming tobacco leaves. It is consumed orally, in two forms:

through sweetened strands, or in a shredded form. When consuming the long sweetened strands the tobacco is lightly chewed and compacted into a ball. When consuming the shredded tobacco, small amounts are placed at the bottom lip, between the gum and the teeth, where it is gently compacted, thus it can oftentimes be called *dipping tobacco*. Both methods stimulate the salve glands, which led to the development of the spittoon.

- *Cigars* are tightly rolled bundle of dried and fermented tobacco which is ignited so that its smoke may be drawn into the smoker's mouth.
- *Cigarettes* are a product consumed through the inhalation of smoke and manufactured out of cured and finely cut tobacco leaves and reconstituted tobacco, often combined with other additives, then rolled or stuffed into a paper-wrapped cylinder.
- *Creamy snuff* are tobacco paste, consisting of tobacco, clove oil, glycerin, spearmint, menthol, and camphor, and sold in a toothpaste tube. It is marketed mainly to women in India, and is known by the brand names Ipco (made by Asha Industries), Denobac, Tona, Ganesh. It is locally known as "mishri" in some parts of Maharashtra.
- *Dipping tobacco* are a form of smokeless tobacco. Dip is occasionally referred to as "chew", and because of this, it is commonly confused with chewing tobacco, which encompasses a wider range of products. A small clump of dip is 'pinched' out of the tin and placed between the lower or upper lip and gums.
- *Electronic cigarette* is an alternative to tobacco smoking, although no tobacco is consumed. It is a battery-powered device that provides inhaled doses of nicotine by delivering a vaporized propylene glycol/nicotine solution.

- *Gutka* are a preparation of crushed betel nut, tobacco, and sweet or savory flavorings. It is manufactured in India and exported to a few other countries. A mild stimulant, it is sold across India in small, individual-size packets.
- *Hookah* are a single or multi-stemmed (often glass-based) water pipe for smoking. Originally from India, the hookah has gained immense popularity, especially in the middle east. A hookah operates by water filtration and indirect heat. It can be used for smoking herbal fruits, tobacco, or cannabis.
- *Kreteks* are cigarettes made with a complex blend of tobacco, cloves and a flavoring "sauce". It was first introduced in the 1880s in Kudus, Java, to deliver the medicinal eugenol of cloves to the lungs.
- *Roll-Your-Own,* often called rollies or roll ups, are very popular particularly in European countries. These are prepared from loose tobacco, cigarette papers and filters all bought separately. They are usually much cheaper to make.
- *Pipe smoking* typically consists of a small chamber (the bowl) for the combustion of the tobacco to be smoked and a thin stem (shank) that ends in a mouthpiece (the bit). Shredded pieces of tobacco are placed into the chamber and ignited.
- *Snuff* are a generic term for fine-ground smokeless tobacco products. Originally the term referred only to dry snuff, a fine tan dust popular mainly in the eighteenth century. Snuff powder originated in the UK town of Great Harwood and was famously ground in the town's monument prior to local distribution and transport further up north to Scotland. There are two major varieties which include European (dry) and American (moist); although American snuff is often referred to as dipping tobacco.

- *Snus* is steam-cured moist powder tobacco product that is not fermented and does not induce salivation. It is consumed by placing it in the mouth against the gums for an extended period of time. It is a form of snuff that is used in a manner similar to American dipping tobacco, but does not require regular spitting.
- *Topical tobacco paste* are sometimes recommended as a treatment for wasp, hornet, fire ant, scorpion, and bee stings.

18

Grape

A grape is the non-climacteric fruit that grows on the perennial and deciduous woody vines of the genus Vitis. Grapes can be eaten raw or used for making jam, juice, jelly, vinegar, wine, grape seed extracts, raisins, and grape seed oil. Grapes are also used in some kinds of candy.

Fig. 18.1

Ancient Egyptian hieroglyphics show the cultivation of grapes. Scholars believe that ancient Greeks, Phoenicians and Romans also grew grapes both for eating and wine production. Later, the growing of grapes spread to Europe, North Africa, and eventually to the United States. Native grapes in North America grew along streams, however, the first cultivated grapes in California were grown by Spanish Franciscan Friars, looking to make a sacramental wine for the California Missions. The first table grape vineyard in California is credited to an early settler by the name of William Wolfskill in the Los Angeles area. As more settlers came to California, more and more varieties of European grapes were introduced. Some for winemaking, others for raisins and some for eating fresh. Today in the United States, approximately 98 per cent of commercially grown table grapes are from California.

Description

Grapes grow in clusters of 6 to 300, and can be crimson, black, dark blue, yellow, green and pink. "White" grapes are actually green in color, and are evolutionarily derived from the red grape. Mutations in two regulatory genes of white grapes turn off production of anthocyanins which are responsible for the color of red grapes Anthocyanins and other pigment chemicals of the larger family of polyphenols in red grapes are responsible for the varying shades of purple in red wines.

Grapevines

Most grapes come from cultivars of *Vitis vinifera*, the European grapevine native to the Mediterranean and Central Asia. Minor amounts of fruit and wine come from American and Asian species such as:

- *Vitis labrusca*, the North American table and grape juice grapevines (including the concord cultivar), sometimes used for wine. Native to the Eastern United States and Canada.

- *Vitis riparia*, a wild vine of North America, sometimes used for winemaking and for jam. Native to the entire Eastern U.S. and north to Quebec.
- *Vitis rotundifolia*, the muscadines, used for jams and wine. Native to the Southeastern United States from Delaware to the Gulf of Mexico.
- *Vitis amurensis*, the most important Asian species.

Distribution and Production

According to the Food and Agriculture Organization (FAO), 75,866 square kilometres of the world are dedicated to grapes. Approximately 71% of world grape production is used for wine, 27% as fresh fruit, and 2% as dried fruit. A portion of grape production goes to producing grape juice to be reconstituted for fruits canned "with no added sugar" and "100% natural". The area dedicated to vineyards is increasing by about 2% per year.

Seedless Grapes

Seedlessness is a highly desirable subjective quality in table grape selection, and seedless cultivars now make up the overwhelming majority of table grape plantings. Because grapevines are vegetatively propagated by cuttings, the lack of seeds does not present a problem for reproduction. It is, however, an issue for breeders, who must either use a seeded variety as the female parent or rescue embryos early in development using tissue culture techniques.

There are several sources of the seedlessness trait, and essentially all commercial cultivators get it from one of three sources: Thompson Seedless, Russian Seedless, and Black Monukka, all being cultivars of *Vitis vinifera*. There are currently more than a dozen varieties of seedless grapes. Several, such as Einset Seedless, Reliance and Venus, have been specifically cultivated for hardiness and quality in the relatively cold climates of north-eastern United States and southern Ontario.

An offset to the improved eating quality of seedlessness is the loss of potential health benefits provided by the enriched phytochemical content of grape seeds.

Raisins, Currants, and Sultanas

In most of Europe, dried grapes are universally referred to as 'raisins' or the local equivalent. In the UK, three different varieties are recognized, forcing the EU to use the term "Dried vine fruit" in official documents.

A *raisin* is any dried grape. While *raisin* is a French loanword, the word in French refers to the fresh fruit; *grappe* (from which the English *grape* is derived) refers to the bunch (as in *une grappe de raisins*).

A *currant* is a dried Zante grape, the name being a corruption of the French *raisin de Corinthe* (Corinth grape). Note also that *currant* has come to refer also to the blackcurrant and redcurrant, two berries unrelated to grapes.

A *sultana* was originally a raisin made from a specific type of grape of Turkish origin, but the word is now applied to raisins made from common grapes and chemically treated to resemble the traditional sultana.

HEALTH CLAIMS

French Paradox

Comparing diets among western countries, researchers have discovered that although the French tend to eat higher levels of animal fat, surprisingly the incidence of heart disease remains low in France, a phenomenon named the French Paradox and thought to occur from protective benefits of regularly consuming red wine. Apart from potential benefits of alcohol itself, including reduced platelet aggregation and vasodilation, polyphenols (e.g., resveratrol) mainly in the grape skin provide other suspected health benefits, such as:

- alteration of molecular mechanisms in blood vessels, reducing susceptibility to vascular damage
- decreased activity of angiotensin, a systemic hormone causing blood vessel constriction that would elevate blood pressure.
- increased production of the vasodilator hormone, nitric oxide (endothelium-derived relaxing factor).

Although adoption of wine consumption is not recommended by some health authorities, a significant volume of research indicates moderate consumption, such as one glass of red wine a day for women and two for men, may confer health benefits. Emerging evidence is that wine polyphenols like resveratrol provide physiological benefit whereas alcohol itself may have protective effects on the cardiovascular system.

Resveratrol

Grape phytochemicals such as resveratrol, a polyphenol antioxidant, have been positively linked to inhibiting cancer, heart disease, degenerative nerve disease, viral infections and mechanisms of Alzheimer's disease.

Protection of the genome through antioxidant actions may be a general function of resveratrol. In laboratory studies, resveratrol bears a significant transcriptional overlap with the beneficial effects of calorie restriction in heart, skeletal muscle and brain. Both dietary interventions inhibit gene expression associated with heart and skeletal muscle aging, and prevent age-related heart failure.

Resveratrol is the subject of several human clinical trials among which the most advanced is a one year dietary regimen in a Phase III study of elderly patients with Alzheimer's disease.

Synthesized by many plants, resveratrol apparently serves antifungal and other defensive properties. Dietary resveratrol has been shown to modulate the metabolism of lipids and to inhibit oxidation of low-density lipoproteins and aggregation of platelets.

Resveratrol is found in wide amounts among grape varieties, primarily in their skins and seeds which, in muscadine grapes, have about one hundred times higher concentration than pulp Fresh grape skin contains about 50 to 100 micrograms of resveratrol per gram.

Fig. 18.2

Anthocyanins and Other Phenolics

Anthocyanins tend to be the main polyphenolics in red grapes whereas flavan-3-ols (e.g., catechins) are the more abundant phenolic in white varieties. Total phenolic content, an index of dietary antioxidant strength, is higher in red varieties due almost entirely to anthocyanin density in red grape skin compared to absence of anthocyanins in white grape skin It is these anthocyanins that are attracting the efforts of scientists to define their properties for human health Phenolic content of grape skin varies with cultivar, soil composition, climate, geographic origin, and cultivation practices or exposure to diseases, such as fungal infections.

Red wine offers health benefits more so than white because many beneficial compounds are present in grape skin, and only red wine is fermented with skins. The amount of fermentation time a wine spends in contact with grape skins is an important determinant of its resveratrol content Ordinary non-muscadine red wine contains between 0.2 and 5.8 mg/L, depending on the grape variety, because it is fermented with the skins, allowing the wine to absorb the resveratrol. By contrast, a white wine contains lower phenolic contents because it is fermented after removal of skins.

Wines produced from muscadine grapes may contain more than 40 mg/L, an exceptional phenolic content In muscadine skins, ellagic acid, myricetin, quercetin, kaempferol, and trans-resveratrol are major phenolics Contrary to previous results, ellagic acid and not resveratrol is the major phenolic in muscadine grapes.

Seed Constituents

Since the 1980s, biochemical and medical studies have demonstrated significant antioxidant properties of grape seed oligomeric proanthocyanidins Together with tannins, polyphenols and polyunsaturated fatty acids, these seed constituents display inhibitory activities against several experimental disease models, including cancer, heart failure and other disorders of oxidative stress.

Grape seed oil from crushed seeds is used in cosmeceuticals and skincare products for many perceived health benefits. Grape seed oil is notable for its high contents of tocopherols (vitamin E), phytosterols, and polyunsaturated fatty acids such as linoleic acid, oleic acid and alpha-linolenic acid.

Concord Grape Juice

Commercial juice products from Concord grapes have been applied in medical research studies, showing potential benefits against the onset stage of cancer platelet aggregation and other risk factors of atherosclerosis, loss of physical performance and mental acuity during aging and hypertension in humans.

19

Coconut

The Coconut Palm (*Cocos nucifera*) is a member of the Family Arecaceae (palm family). It is the only species in the genus Cocos, and is a large palm, growing to 30 m tall, with pinnate

Fig. 19.1

leaves 4-6 m long, pinnae 60-90 cm long; old leaves break away cleanly leaving the trunk smooth. The term coconut refers to the seed of the coconut palm. An alternate spelling is cocoanut.

The coconut palm is grown throughout the tropical world, for decoration as well as for its many culinary and non-culinary uses; virtually every part of the coconut palm has some human uses.

The coconut has spread across much of the tropics, probably aided in many cases by seafaring people. The fruit is light and buoyant and presumably spread significant distances by marine currents. Fruits collected from the sea as far north as Norway have been found to be viable (and subsequently germinated under the right conditions). In the Hawaiian Islands, the coconut is regarded as a Polynesian introduction, first brought to the islands by early Polynesian voyagers from their homelands in the South Pacific. They are now almost ubiquitous between 26°N and 26°S.

The flowers of the coconut palm are polygamo-monoecious, with both male and female flowers in the same inflorescence. Flowering occurs continuously, with female flowers producing seeds. Coconut palms are believed to be largely cross-pollinated, although some dwarf varieties are self-pollinating. Coconuts also come with a liquid that is clear like water but sweet. The "Nut" of the coconut is edible and is in the shape of a ball or is on the inside sides of the coconut.

Origins

The origins of this plant are the subject of controversy, with most authorities claiming it is native to South Asia (particularly the Ganges Delta), while others claim its origin is in northwestern South America. Fossil records from New Zealand indicate that small, coconut-like plants grew there as long as 15 million years ago. Even older fossils have been uncovered in Kerala (Kerala means "land of coconut palms"), Rajasthan, Tamil Nadu, Maharashtra (India) and the oldest known so far in Khulna, Bangladesh.

Mention is made of coconuts in the 2nd-1st centuries BC in the Mahawamsa of Sri Lanka. The later Culawamasa states that King Aggabodhi I (575-608) planted a coconut garden of 3 yojanas length, possibly the earliest recorded coconut plantation.

Natural Habitat

The coconut palm thrives on sandy soils and is highly tolerant of salinity. It prefers areas with abundant sunlight and regular rainfall (150 cm to 250 cm annually), which makes colonizing shorelines of the tropics relatively straightforward Coconuts also need high humidity (70-80%+) for optimum growth, which is why they are rarely seen in areas with low humidity, like the Mediterranean, even where temperatures are high enough (regularly above 24 °C).

Coconut palms require warm conditions for successful growth, and are intolerant of cold weather. Optimum growth is with a mean annual temperature of 27 °C (80.6°F), and growth is reduced below 21 °C (69.8 °F). Some seasonal variation is tolerated, with good growth where mean summer temperatures are between 28-37 °C (82.4-98.6 °F), and survival as long as winter temperatures are above 4-12 °C (39.2-53.6 °F); they will survive brief drops to 0 °C (32 °F). Severe frost is usually fatal, although they have been known to recover from temperatures of -4 °C (24.8 °F). They may grow but not fruit properly in areas where there is not sufficient warmth, like Bermuda.

The conditions required for coconut trees to grow without any care are:

- mean daily temperature above 12-13 °C every day of the year;

- 50 year low temperature above freezing;
- mean yearly rainfall above 1000 mm.;
- no or very little overhead canopy since even small trees require a lot of sun.

The main limiting factor is that most locations that satisfy the first three requirements do not satisfy the fourth, except near the coast where the sandy soil and salt spray limit the growth of most other trees.

The range of the natural habitat of the coconut palm tree is delineated by the red line in map C1 to the right (based on information in Werth 1933 slightly modified by Niklas Jonsson).

Fig. 19.2

Cultivation

Coconut trees are very hard to establish in dry climates and cannot grow there without frequent irrigation; in drought conditions, the new leaves do not open well, and older leaves may become desiccated; fruit also tends to be shed.

Plant densities in Vanuatu for copra production are generally 9 metre, allowing a tree density of 100–160 trees per hectare.

Pests and Diseases

Coconuts are susceptible to the phytoplasma disease lethal yellowing. One recently selected cultivar, 'Maypan', has been bred for resistance to this disease. The fruit may also be damaged by eriophyid mites. The coconut is also used as a food plant by the larvae of many Lepidoptera (butterfly and moth) species, including the following *Batrachedra spp*: *B. arenosella, B. atriloqua* (feeds exclusively on *Cocos nucifera*), *B. mathesoni* (feeds exclusively on *Cocos nucifera*), and *B. nuciferae*.

Brontispa longissima (the "Coconut leaf beetle") feeds on young leaves and damages seedlings and mature coconut palms. On September 27, 2007, Philippines' Metro Manila and 26 provinces were quarantined due to having been infested with this pest (to save the $800-million Philippine coconut industry). In Kerala the major pests of Coconut are the Eriophyid mite, the Rhinoceros Beetle, the Red Palm Weevil and the Coconut Leaf caterpillar. The Eriophyid mite (*Eriophyes guerreronis*) is devastating and can cause damages up to 90% in coconut production. The immature nuts are infested and desapped by staying in the portion covered by the Perianth of the immature nut. Subsequently the nuts drop off or survive deformed. Spraying with Wettable Sulfur 0.4% alternately with neem based pesticides can give some relief, but is cumbersome and labor intensive. Research on this topic gave no results and the researchers from the Kerala Agricultural University and the Central Plantation Crop Research Institute, Kasaragode are still searching for a cure.

Growing in the United States

The only states in the U.S. where coconut palms can be grown and reproduced outdoors without irrigation are Hawaii and Florida. Coconut palms will grow from Bradenton southwards on Florida's west coast and Melbourne southwards on Florida's east coast. The occasional coconut palm is seen north of these areas in favoured microclimates in the Tampa-St. Petersburg-Clearwater metro area and around Cape Canaveral as well as the Orlando-Kissimmee-Daytona Beach metro area. They may likewise be grown in favoured microclimates in the Rio Grande Valley area of Deep South Texas near Brownsville and on Galveston Island. They may reach fruiting maturity, but are damaged or killed by the occasional winter freezes in these areas. While coconut palms flourish in south Florida, unusually bitter cold snaps can kill or injure coconut palms there as well. Only the Florida Keys and the coastlines provide safe havens from the cold as far as growing coconut palms on the U:S. mainland.

The farthest north in the United States a coconut palm has been known to grow outdoors is in Newport Beach, California along the Pacific Coast Highway. In order for coconut palms to survive in Southern California they need sandy soil and minimal water in the winter to prevent root rot, and would benefit from root heating coils.

Coconut Production in the Middle East

The main coconut producing area in the Middle East is the Dhofar region of Oman. Particular the area around Salalah maintains large coconut plantations similar to those found across the Arabian Sea.The large coconut grooves of Dhofar are already mentioned by the medieval Moroccan traveller Ibn Battuta in his writings known as Al Rihla. This is possible due to an annual rainy season known locally as Khareef. Coconut are also increasingly grown for decorative purposes along the coasts of UAE and Saudi Arabia with the help of irrigation. The UAE has however imposed strict laws on mature coconut tree imports from other countries to reduce the spreading of pests that can spread to other native palm trees such as the date palm.

Production

The Philippines is the world leader in coconut production (2007) followed by Indonesia and India in distant third.

Harvesting

In some parts of the world, trained pig-tailed macaques are used to harvest coconuts. Training schools for pig-tailed macaques still exist both in southern Thailand and in the Malaysian state of Kelantan. Competitions are held each year to find the fastest harvester.

Fruit

Botanically, a coconut is a simple dry nut known as a fibrous drupe. The husk, or mesocarp, is composed of fibers called coir and there is an inner stone, or endocarp. The endocarp is the hardest part. This hard endocarp, the outside of the coconut as sold in the shops of non-tropical countries, has three germination pores that are clearly visible on the outside surface once the husk is removed. It is through one of these that the radicle emerges when the embryo germinates. Adhering to the inside wall of the endocarp is the *testa,* with a thick albuminous endosperm (the coconut "meat"), the white and fleshy edible part of the seed.

Although coconut meat contains less fat than other dry nuts such as almonds, it is noted for its high amount of saturated fat Approximately 90% of the fat found in coconut meat is saturated, a proportion exceeding that of foods such as lard, butter, and tallow. However, there has been some debate as to whether or not the saturated fat in coconuts is healthier than the saturated fat found in other foods. Coconut meat also contains less sugar and more protein than popular fruits such as bananas, apples and oranges, and it is relatively high in minerals such as iron, phosphorus and zinc.

The endosperm surrounds a hollow interior space, filled with air and often a liquid referred to as coconut water, not to be confused with coconut milk. Coconut milk, called "santan" in Malay and "*Katas Ngungut*" in Kapampangan, is made by grating the endosperm and mixing it with (warm) water. The resulting thick, white liquid is used in much Asian cooking, for example, in curries. Coconut water from the unripe coconut can be drunk fresh. Young coconuts used for coconut water are called tender coconuts. The water of a tender coconut is liquid endosperm. It is sweet (mild) with aerated feel when cut fresh. Depending on the size a tender coconut could contain the liquid in the range of 300 to 1,000 ml.

When viewed on end, the endocarp and germination pores give the fruit the appearance of a *coco* (also Côca), a Portuguese word for a scary witch from Portuguese folklore, that used to be represented as a carved vegetable lantern, hence the name of the fruit The specific name *nucifera* is Latin for *nut-bearing*.

When the coconut is still green, the endosperm inside is thin and tender, often eaten as a snack. But the main reason to pick the fruit at this stage is to drink its water; a large unripe coconut contains up to one litre.

The meat in a young coconut is softer and more like gelatin than a mature coconut, so much so, that it is sometimes known as coconut jelly. When the coconut has ripened and the outer husk has turned brown, a few months later, it will fall from the palm of its own accord. At that time the endosperm has thickened and hardened, while the coconut water has become somewhat bitter. Coconuts sundried in Kozhikode in the State of Kerala, India for making copra, which is used for making coconut oil.

When the coconut fruit is still green the husk is very hard, but green coconuts only fall if they have been attacked by moulds, etc. By the time the coconut naturally falls, the husk has become brown, the coir has become drier and softer, and the coconut is less likely to cause damage when it drops. Still, there have been instances of coconuts falling from palms and injuring people, and claims of some fatalities. This was the subject of a paper published in 1984 that won the Ig Nobel Prize in 2001. Falling coconut deaths are often used as a comparison to shark attacks; the claim is often made that a person is more likely to be killed by a falling coconut than by a shark, yet, there is no evidence of people ever being killed in this manner. However, William Wyatt Gill, an early LMS missionary on Mangaia recorded a story in which Kaiara, the concubine of King Tetui, was killed by a falling green nut The offending palm was immediately cut down. This was around 1777, the time of Captain Cook's visit.

Husk

In Thailand the coconut husk is used as a potting medium because of its cost-effectiveness to produce healthy forest tree saplings. The process of husk extraction from the coir bypasses the retting process, using a custom-built coconut husk extractor designed by ASEAN-Canada Forest Tree Seed Centre (ACFTSC) in 1986. Fresh husks contains more tannin than old husks. Tannin produces negative effects on sapling growth.

Roots

Unlike some other plants, the palm tree has neither tap root nor root hairs; but has a fibrous root system.

Inflorescence

On the same inflorescence, the palm produces both the female and male flowers; thus the palm is monoecious

Uses

Nearly all parts of the coconut palm are useful, and the palms have a comparatively high yield, up to 75 fruits per year; it therefore has significant economic value. The name for the coconut palm in Sanskrit is *kalpa vriksha,* which translates as "the tree which provides all the necessities of life". In Malay, the coconut is known as *pokok seribu guna,* "the tree of a thousand uses". In the Philippines, the coconut is commonly given the title "Tree of Life".

A relatively young coconut which has been served in a hawker centre in Singapore with a straw with which to drink its coconut water.

Culinary

Culinary uses of the various parts of the palm include:

- The white, fleshy part of the seed, the coconut meat, is edible and used fresh or dried in cooking.
- Sport fruits are also harvested, primarily in the Philippines, where they are known as *macapuno.* They are sold in jars as "gelatinous mutant coconut" cut into balls or strands.
- The cavity is filled with coconut water which contains sugar, fiber, proteins, antioxidants, vitamins and minerals. Coconut water provides an isotonic electrolyte balance, and is a highly nutritious food source. It is used as a refreshing drink throughout the humid tropics and is also used in isotonic sports drinks. It can also be used to make the gelatinous dessert nata de coco. Mature fruits have significantly less liquid than young immature coconuts; barring spoilage, coconut water is sterile until opened.

- Coconut milk is made by processing grated coconut with hot water or milk, which extracts the oil and aromatic compounds. It should not be confused with the coconut water discussed above, and has a fat content of approximately 17%. When refrigerated and left to set, coconut cream will rise to the top and separate out the milk. The milk is used to produce virgin coconut oil by controlled heating and removing the oil fraction. Virgin coconut oil is found superior to the oil extracted from copra for cosmetic purposes.
- The leftover fiber from coconut milk production is used as livestock feed.
- The smell of coconuts comes from the pentyloxan-2-one molecule, known as delta-decalactone in the food and fragrance industry.
- The sap derived from incising the flower clusters of the coconut is drunk as neera, or fermented to produce palm wine, also known as "toddy" or, in the Philippines, *tuba*. The sap can also be reduced by boiling to create a sweet syrup or candy.
- Apical buds of adult plants are edible and are known as "palm-cabbage" or heart-of-palm. It is considered a rare delicacy, as the act of harvesting the bud kills the palm. Hearts of palm are eaten in salads, sometimes called "millionaire's salad".
- Ruku Raa is an extract from the young bud, a very rare type of nectar collected and used as morning break drink in the islands of Maldives reputed for its energetic power keeping the "raamen" (nectar collector) healthy and fit even over 80 and 90 years old. And by-products, a sweet honey-like syrup called *dhiyaa hakuru* is used as a creamy sugar for desserts.
- Newly germinated coconuts contain an edible fluff of marshmallow-like consistency called coconut sprout, produced as the endosperm nourishes the developing embryo.

- In the Philippines, rice is wrapped in coco leaves for cooking and subsequent storage - these packets are called puso.
- In Vietnam, coconut is grown in Ben Tre Province- the "Land of coconut" and people use it to make coconut candy, coconut caramel. Coconut water and coconut milk is also put in many dishes such as kho, chè, etc. especially in the Vietnam's Southern style of cooking.

Non-culinary

Extracting the fiber from the husk (Sri Lanka).

- Coconut water can be used as an intravenous fluid.
- Coir (the fibre from the husk of the coconut) is used in ropes, mats, brushes, caulking boats and as stuffing fiber; it is also used extensively in horticulture for making potting compost.
- Coconut oil can be rapidly processed and extracted as a fully organic product from fresh coconut flesh and used in many ways including as a medicine and in cosmetics, or as a direct replacement for diesel fuel.
- Copra is the dried meat of the seed and, after further processing, is a source of low grade coconut oil.
- The leaves provide materials for baskets and roofing thatch.
- Palmwood comes from the trunk and is increasingly being used as an ecologically-sound substitute for endangered hardwoods. It has several applications, particularly in furniture and specialized construction (notably in Manila's Coconut Palace).
- Hawaiians hollowed the trunk to form drums, containers, or even small canoes.
- The husk and shells can be used for fuel and are a good source of charcoal.

- Dried half coconut shells with husks are used to buff floors. In the Philippines, it is known as "bunot", and in Jamaica it is simply called "coconut brush".
- During the 1992 Barcelona Olympics, a large amount of coconut shells were imported by Spain from Kerala, India, to serve ice-creams and snacks.
- Activated carbon manufactured from coconut shell is considered superior to those obtained from other sources mainly because of small macropores structure which renders it more effective for the adsorption of gas/vapor and for the removal of color, oxidants, impurities and odor of compounds.
- A coconut is an essential element of several rituals associated with Hindus and the tradition of Hinduism. The coconut is often decorated with bright metals and other symbols associated with auspiciousness. It is offered during worship (*puja*) in the temples and at Hindu homes. A number of fishermen of India, irrespective of their religious affiliation and faith, offer it to the rivers and seas to propitiate the god Varuna, in hopes of having a bountiful catch. In Hindu wedding ceremonies, a nalikera is placed over the opening of a pot, representing a womb. Often Hindus initiate the beginning of any new activity by breaking nalikeras, to ensure the blessings of the gods and the successful completion of the activity. In tantric practices, nalikeras are sometimes used as substitutes for human skulls. The Hindu goddess of well-being and wealth, Lakshmi, is often shown holding a coconut.
- The Zulu Social Aid and Pleasure Club of New Orleans traditionally throws hand decorated coconuts—the most valuable of all Mardi Gras souvenirs—to parade revelers. The "Tramps" began the tradition ca. 1901. In 1987 a "coconut law" was signed by Gov. Edwards exempting from insurance liability any decorated coconut *handed* from a Zulu float.

- In the Philippines, dried half shells are used as a music instrument in a folk dance called *maglalatik*, a traditional dance about the conflicts for coconut meat within the Spanish era.
- Shirt buttons can be carved out of dried coconut shell. Coconut buttons are often used for Hawaiian Aloha shirts.
- The stiff leaflet midribs can be used to make cooking skewers, kindling arrows, or are bound into bundles, brooms and brushes.
- The roots are used as a dye, a mouthwash, and a medicine for dysentery. A frayed-out piece of root can also be used as a toothbrush.
- Half coconut shells are used in theatre Foley sound effects work, banged together to create the sound effect of a horse's hoofbeats. They were used in this way in the Monty Python film Monty Python and the Holy Grail.

  Making a rug from coconut fibre.
- The leaves can be woven to create effective roofing materials, or reed mats.
- Half coconut shells may be deployed as an improvised bra, especially for comedic effect or theatrical purposes. They were used in this way in the 1970s UK sitcom. It Ain't Half Hot Mum for example.
- Drained coconuts can be filled with gunpowder and used as Improvised explosive devices.
- In fairgrounds, a "coconut shy" is a popular target practice game, and coconuts are commonly given as prizes.
- A coconut can be hollowed out and used as a home for a rodent or small bird. Halved, drained coconuts can also be hung up as bird feeders, and after the flesh has gone, can be filled with fat in winter to attract tits.

- Fresh inner coconut husk can be rubbed on the lens of snorkelling goggles to prevent fogging during use.
- Dried coconut leaves can be burned to ash, which can be harvested for lime.
- Coconuts can be used as ammunition for homemade catapults.
- Dried half coconut shells are used as the bodies of musical instruments, including the Chinese yehu and banhu, and the Vietnamese.

  A wall made from coconut husks.
- Coconut is also commonly used as a traditional remedy in Pakistan to treat bites from rats.
- The "branches" (leaf petioles) are strong and flexible enough to make a switch. The use of coconut branches in corporal punishment was revived in the Gilbertese community on Choiseul in the Solomon Islands in 2005.

20

Tea

Tea refers to the agricultural products of the leaves, leaf buds, and internodes of the *Camellia sinensis* plant, prepared and cured by various methods. "Tea" also refers to the

Fig. 20.1

aromatic beverage prepared from the cured leaves by combination with hot or boiling water and is the colloquial name for the *Camellia sinensis* plant itself.

After water, tea is the most widely-consumed beverage in the world It has a cooling, slightly bitter, astringent flavor.

The four types of tea most commonly found on the market are black tea, oolong tea, green tea and white tea, all of which can be made from the same bushes, processed differently, and in the case of fine white tea, grown differently. Pu-erh tea, a double-fermented black tea, is also often classified as among the most popular types of tea.

The term "herbal tea" usually refers to an infusion or tisane of fruit or herbs that contains no *Camellia sinensis* The term "red tea" either refers to an infusion made from the South African rooibos plant, also containing no *Camellia sinensis*, or, in Chinese, Korean, Japanese and other East Asian languages, refers to black tea.

Cultivation

Camellia sinensis is an evergreen plant that grows mainly in tropical and sub-tropical climates. Nevertheless, some varieties can also tolerate marine climates and are cultivated as far north as Cornwall on the UK mainland and Seattle in the United States.

In addition to a zone 8 climate or warmer, tea plants require at least 50 inches of rainfall a year and prefer acidic soils Many high-quality tea plants are cultivated at elevations of up to 1500 meters (5,000 ft): at these heights, the plants grow more slowly and acquire a better flavor.

Only the top 1-2 inches of the mature plant are picked. These buds and leaves are called *flushes* A plant will grow a new flush every seven to ten days during the growing season.

A tea plant will grow into a tree if left undisturbed, but cultivated plants are pruned to waist height for ease of plucking.

Two principal varieties are used: the small-leaved China plant (*C. sinensis sinensis*), used for most Chinese, Formosan and Japanese teas (but not Pu-erh); and the large-leaved Assam plant (*C. sinensis assamica*), used in most Indian and other teas (but not Darjeeling). Within these botanical varieties, especially the small-leaved China plant, there are many traditional strains and modern clonal varieties. Leaf size is the chief criterion for the classification of tea plants: tea is classified into:

1. Assam type, characterized by the largest leaves;
2. China type, characterized by the smallest leaves; and
3. Cambod, characterized by leaves of intermediate size

Processing and Classification

A tea's type is determined by the processing through which it goes. Leaves of *Camellia sinensis* soon begin to wilt and oxidize if not dried quickly after picking. The leaves turn progressively darker as their chlorophyll breaks down and tannins are released. This process, *enzymatic oxidation,* is called *fermentation* in the tea industry, although it is not a true fermentation: it is not caused by micro-organisms, and is not an anaerobic process. The next step in processing is to stop the oxidation process at a predetermined stage by heating, which deactivates the enzymes responsible. With black tea this is done simultaneously with drying. Without careful moisture and temperature control during manufacture and packaging, the tea will grow fungi. The fungus causes real fermentation that will contaminate the tea with toxic and sometimes carcinogenic substances, as well as off-flavors, rendering the tea unfit for consumption.

Tea is traditionally classified based on the techniques with which it is produced and processed.

- White tea: Unwilted and unoxidized.
- Yellow tea: Unwilted and unoxidized but allowed to yellow.
- Green tea: Wilted and unoxidized.
- Oolong: Wilted, bruised, and partially oxidized.
- Black tea: Wilted, crushed, and fully oxidized.
- Post-fermented tea: Green Tea that has been allowed to ferment/compost.

Blending and Additives

Almost all teas in bags and most other teas sold in the West are blends. Blending may occur in the tea-planting area (as in the case of Assam), or teas from many areas may be blended. The aim is to obtain better taste, higher price, or both, as a more expensive, better-tasting tea may cover the inferior taste of cheaper varieties.

Some teas are not pure varieties, but have been enhanced through additives or special processing. Tea is highly receptive to inclusion of various aromas; this may cause problems in processing, transportation and storage, but also allows for the design of an almost endless range of scented and flavored variants, such as vanilla, caramel, and many others.

Content

Tea contains catechins, a type of antioxidant. In a fresh tea leaf, catechins can compose up to 30% of the dry weight. Catechins are highest in concentration in white and green teas, while black tea has substantially fewer due to its oxidative preparation. Tea also contains theanine and the stimulant caffeine at about 3% of its dry weight, translating to between 30 mg and 90 mg per 8 oz (250 ml) cup depending on type, brand and brewing method. Tea also contains small amounts of theobromine and theophylline, as well as fluoride, with certain types of brick tea made from old leaves and stems having the highest levels.

Dry tea has more caffeine by weight than coffee; nevertheless, more dried coffee is used than dry tea in preparing the beverage.

Tea has almost no carbohydrates, fat, or protein.

Origin and History

Camellia sinensis originated in southeast Asia, specifically around the intersection of latitude 29 °N and longitude 98 °E, the point of confluence of the lands of northeast India, north Burma, southwest China and Tibet. The plant was introduced to more than 52 countries, from this 'centre of origin'."

Based on morphological differences between the Assamese and Chinese varieties, botanists have long asserted a dual botanical origin for tea; however, statistical cluster analysis, the same chromosome number (2n=30), easy hybridization, and various types of intermediate hybrids and spontaneous polyploids all appear to demonstrate a single place of origin for *Camellia sinensis* — the area including the northern part of Burma, and Yunnan and Sichuan provinces of China.

Yunnan Province has also been identified as "the birthplace of tea ... the first area where humans figured out that eating tea leaves or brewing a cup could be pleasant". Fengqing County in the Lincang City Prefecture of Yunnan Province is said to be home to the world's oldest cultivated tea tree, some 3,200 years old.

Origin Myths

In one popular Chinese legend, Shennong, the legendary Emperor of China and inventor of agriculture and Chinese medicine was drinking a bowl of boiling water some time around 2737 BC when a few leaves were blown from a nearby tree into his water, changing the color. The emperor took a sip of the brew and was pleasantly surprised by its flavour and restorative properties. A variant of the legend tells that the emperor tested the medical properties of various herbs on himself, some of them poisonous, and found tea to work as an antidote. Shennong is also mentioned in Lu Yu's famous early work on the subject, *Cha Jing* A similar Chinese legend goes that the god of agriculture would chew the leaves, stems, and roots of various plants to discover medicinal herbs. If he consumed a poisonous plant, he would chew tea leaves to counteract the poison.

Tea and the Tang Dynasty

A rather gruesome legend dates back to the Tang Dynasty. In the legend, Bodhidharma, the founder of Chan Buddhism, accidentally fell asleep after meditating in front of a wall for nine years. He woke up in such disgust at his weakness that he cut off his own eyelids. They fell to the ground and took root, growing into tea bushes. Sometimes, another version of the story is told with Gautama Buddha in place of *Bodhidharma*.

Fig. 20.2

Varieties of Tea

Whether or not these legends have any basis in fact, tea has played a significant role in Asian culture for centuries as a staple beverage, a curative, and a status symbol. It is not surprising, therefore, that theories of its origin are often religious or royal in nature.

A Ming Dynasty painting by artist Wen Zhengming illustrating scholars greeting in a tea ceremony.

China

The Chinese have consumed tea for thousands of years. People of the Han Dynasty used tea as medicine (though the first use of tea as a stimulant is unknown). China is considered to have the earliest records of tea consumption with records dating back to the 10th century BC

Laozi (ca. 600-517 BC), the classical Chinese philosopher, described tea as "the froth of the liquid jade" and named it an indispensable ingredient to the elixir of life. Legend has it that master Lao was saddened by society's moral decay and, sensing that the end of the dynasty was near, he journeyed westward to the unsettled territories, never to be seen again. While passing along the nation's border, he encountered and was offered tea by a customs inspector named Yin Hsi. Yin Hsi encouraged him to compile his teachings into a single book so that future generations might benefit from his wisdom. This then became known as the Dao De Jing, a collection of Laozi's sayings. To honor Yin's generosity and its effect on the book's creation, a national custom of offering tea to guests began in China.

In 59 BC, Wang Bao wrote the first known book with instructions on buying and preparing tea, establishing that, at this time, tea was not only a medicine but an important part of diet.

In 220 , famed physician and surgeon Hua Tuo wrote *Shin Lun,* in which he describes tea's ability to improve mental functions: "to drink k'u t'u [bitter tea] constantly makes one think better.

During the Sui Dynasty (589-618 AD) tea was introduced to Japan by Buddhist monks.

The Tang Dynasty writer Lu Yu(729-804 AD)'s (simplified Chinese: traditional Chinese: pinyin: lùyu) *Cha Jing* (*The Classic of Tea*) (simplified Chinese: traditional Chinese:

pinyin: chá jing) is an early work on the subject. (See also Tea Classics) According to *Cha Jing* tea drinking was widespread. The book describes how tea plants were grown, the leaves processed, and tea prepared as a beverage. It also describes how tea was evaluated. The book also discusses where the best tea leaves were produced. Teas produced in this period were mainly tea bricks which were often used as currency, especially further from the center of the empire where coins lost their value.

During the Song Dynasty (960-1279), production and preparation of all tea changed. The tea of Song included many loose-leaf styles (to preserve the delicate character favored by court society), but a new powdered form of tea emerged. Steaming tea leaves was the primary process used for centuries in the preparation of tea. After the transition from compressed tea to the powdered form, the production of tea for trade and distribution changed once again. The Chinese learned to process tea in a different way in the mid-13th century. Tea leaves were roasted and then crumbled rather than steamed. This is the origin of today's loose teas and the practice of brewed tea.

Tea production in China, historically, was a laborious process, conducted in distant and often poorly accessible regions. This led to the rise of many apocryphal stories and legends surrounding the harvesting process. For example, one story that has been told for many years is that of a village where monkeys pick tea. According to this legend, the villagers stand below the monkeys and taunt them. The monkeys, in turn, become angry, and grab handfuls of tea leaves and throw them at the villagers. There are products sold today that claim to be harvested in this manner, but no reliable commentators have observed this firsthand, and most doubt that it happened at all For many hundreds of years the commercially-used tea tree has been, in shape, more of a bush than a tree "Monkey picked tea" is more likely a name of certain varieties than a description of how it was obtained.

In 1391, the Ming court issued a decree that only loose tea would be accepted as a "tribute". As a result, loose tea production increased and processing techniques advanced. Soon, most tea was distributed in full-leaf, loose form and steeped in earthenware vessels.

Tea Spreads to the World

The earliest record of tea in a more occidental writing is said to be found in the statement of an Arabian traveler, that after the year 879 the main sources of revenue in Canton were the duties on salt and tea. Marco Polo records the deposition of a Chinese minister of finance in 1285 for his arbitrary augmentation of the tea taxes. The travelers Giovanni Batista Ramusio (1559), L. Almeida (1576), Maffei (1588), and Teixeira (1610) also mentioned tea. In 1557, Portugal established a trading port in Macau and word of the Chinese drink "*chá*" spread quickly, but there is no mention of them bringing any samples home. In the early 17th century, a ship of the Dutch East India Company brought the first green tea leaves to Amsterdam from China. Tea was known in France by 1636. It enjoyed a brief period of popularity in Paris around 1648. The history of tea in Russia can also be traced back to the seventeenth century. Tea was first offered by China as a gift to Czar Michael I in 1618. The Russian ambassador tried the drink; he did not care for it and rejected the offer, delaying tea's Russian introduction by fifty years. In 1689, tea was regularly imported from China to Russia via a caravan of hundreds of camels traveling the year-long journey, making it a precious commodity at the time. Tea was appearing in German apothecaries by 1657 but never gained much esteem except in coastal areas such as Ostfriesland Tea first appeared publicly in England during the 1650s, where it was introduced through coffee houses. From there it was introduced to British colonies in America and elsewhere.

India

Tea had been known for millennia in India as a medicinal plant, but was not drunk for pleasure until the

British began to establish plantations in the 19th century. The Chinese variety is used for Darjeeling tea, and the Assamese variety, native to the Indian state of Assam, everywhere else. The British introduced tea-growing into India in 1836 and into Ceylon (Sri Lanka) in 1867. At first they used seeds from China, but later seeds from the Assam plant were used. Only black tea was produced until recent decades.

India was the top producer of tea for nearly a century, but was displaced by China as the top tea producer in the 21st century. Indian tea companies have acquired a number of iconic foreign tea enterprises including British brands Tetley and Typhoo. The per capita consumption of tea in India remains a modest 750 grams per person every year due to the large population base.

Potential Effects of Tea on Health

Tea leaves contain more than 700 chemicals, among which the compounds closely related to human health are flavanoides, amino acids, vitamins (C, E and K), caffeine and polysaccharides. Moreover, tea drinking has recently proven to be associated with cell-mediated immune function of the human body. Tea plays an important role in improving beneficial intestinal microflora, as well as providing immunity against intestinal disorders and in protecting cell membranes from oxidative damage. Tea also prevents dental caries due to the presence of fluorine. The role of tea is well established in normalizing blood pressure, lipid depressing activity, prevention of coronary heart diseases and diabetes by reducing the blood-glucose activity. Tea also possesses germicidal and germistatic activities against various gram-positive and gram negative human pathogenic bacteria. Both green and black tea infusions contain a number of antioxidants, mainly catechins that have anti-carcinogenic, anti-mutagenic and anti-tumoric properties.

In many cultures, tea is often had at high class social events, such as afternoon tea and the tea party. It may be consumed early in the day to heighten alertness; it contains theophylline and bound caffeine (sometimes called "theine"), although there are also decaffeinated teas. In many cultures such as Arab culture tea is a focal point for social gatherings. Moreover, the history of tea in Iran - in the Persian culture- is another to explore. One source cites: "the first thing you will be offered when a guest at an Iranian household is tea".

There are tea ceremonies which have arisen in different cultures, Japan's complex, formal and serene one being one of the most well known. Other examples are the Chinese tea ceremony which uses some traditional ways of brewing tea. One form of Chinese tea ceremony is the *Gongfu tea ceremony*, which typically uses small Yixing clay teapots and oolong tea.

Economics of Tea

Tea's world consumption easily equals all other manufactured drinks in the world — including coffee, chocolate, soft drinks, and alcohol — put together Most tea consumed outside East Asia is produced on large plantations in India or Sri Lanka, and is destined to be sold to large businesses. Opposite this large-scale industrial production there are many small "gardens", sometimes minuscule plantations, that produce highly sought-after teas prized by gourmets. These teas are both rare and expensive, and can be compared to some of the most expensive wines in this respect.

India is the world's largest tea-drinking nation although the per capita consumption of tea remains a modest 750 grams per person every year.

Production

In 2008 world tea production was 3.97 million tonnes annually. The largest producer was India, followed by China (the order has since reversed), followed by Kenya and Sri Lanka. China is the only country today to produce in industrial quantities all different kinds of tea (white tea, yellow tea, green tea, blue-green tea, red tea and black tea).

21

Flower

A flower, sometimes known as a bloom or blossom, is the reproductive structure found in flowering plants (plants of the division Magnoliophyta, also called angiosperms). The biological function of a flower is to mediate the union of male sperm with female ovum in order to produce seeds. The process begins with pollination, is followed by fertilization, leading to the formation and dispersal of the seeds. For the higher plants, seeds are the next generation, and serve as the primary means by which individuals of a species are dispersed across the landscape. The grouping of flowers on a plant are called the inflorescence.

Fig. 21.1

In addition to serving as the reproductive organs of flowering plants, flowers have long been admired and used by humans, mainly to beautify their environment but also as a source of food.

Flower Specialization and Pollination

Flowering plants usually face selective pressure to optimise the transfer of their pollen, and this is typically reflected in the morphology of the flowers and the behaviour of the plants. Pollen may be transferred between plants via a number of 'vectors'. Some plants make use of abiotic vectors - namely wind (anemophily) or, much less commonly, water (hydrophily). Others use biotic vectors including insects (entomophily), birds (ornithophily), bats (chiropterophily) or other animals. Some plants make use of multiple vectors, but many are highly specialised.

Cleistogamous flowers are self pollinated, after which they may or may not open. Many Viola and some Salvia species are known to have these types of flowers.

The flowers of plants that make use of biotic pollen vectors commonly have glands called nectaries that act as an incentive for animals to visit the flower. Some flowers have patterns, called nectar guides, that show pollinators where to look for nectar. Flowers also attract pollinators by scent and color. Still other flowers use mimicry to attract pollinators. Some species of orchids, for example, produce flowers resembling female bees in color, shape, and scent. Flowers are also specialized in shape and have an arrangement of the stamens that ensures that pollen grains are transferred to the bodies of the pollinator when it lands in search of its attractant (such as nectar, pollen, or a mate). In pursuing this attractant from many flowers of the same species, the pollinator transfers pollen to the stigmas—arranged with equally pointed precision—of all of the flowers it visits.

Anemophilous flowers use the wind to move pollen from one flower to the next. Examples include grasses, birch trees, ragweed and maples. They have no need to attract pollinators and therefore tend not to be "showy" flowers. Male and female reproductive organs are generally found in separate flowers, the male flowers having a number of long filaments terminating in exposed stamens, and the female flowers having long, feather-like stigmas. Whereas the pollen of animal-pollinated flowers tends to be large-grained, sticky, and rich in protein (another "reward" for pollinators), anemophilous flower pollen is usually small-grained, very light, and of little nutritional value to animals.

Morphology

Flowering plants are *heterosporangiate*, producing two types of reproductive spores. The pollen (male spores) and ovules (female spores) are produced in different organs, but the typical flower is a *bisporangiate strobilus* in that it contains both organs.

A flower is regarded as a modified stem with shortened internodes and bearing, at its nodes, structures that may be highly modified leaves. In essence, a flower structure forms on a modified shoot or *axis* with an apical meristem that does not grow continuously (growth is *determinate*). Flowers may be attached to the plant in a few ways. If the flower has no stem but forms in the axil of a leaf, it is called sessile. When one flower is produced, the stem holding the flower is called a peduncle. If the peduncle ends with groups of flowers, each stem that holds a flower is called a pedicel. The flowering stem forms a terminal end which is called the *torus* or receptacle. The parts of a flower are arranged in whorls on the torus. The four main parts:

- *Calyx*: the outer whorl of *sepals*; typically these are green, but are petal-like in some species.

- *Corolla*: the whorl of *petals*, which are usually thin, soft and colored to attract insects that help the process of pollination.
- *Androecium* (from Greek *andros oikia*: man's house): one or two whorls of stamens, each a filament topped by an another where pollen is produced. Pollen contains the male gametes.
- *Gynoecium* (from Greek *gynaikos oikia*: woman's house): one or more pistils. The female reproductive organ is the carpel. this contains an ovary with ovules (which contain female gametes). A pistil may consist of a number of carpels merged together, in which case there is only one pistil to each flower, or of a single individual carpel (the flower is then called *apocarpous*). The sticky tip of the pistil, the stigma, is the receptor of pollen. The supportive stalk, the style becomes the pathway for pollen tubes to grow from pollen grains adhering to the stigma, to the ovules, carrying the reproductive material.

Although the floral structure described above is considered the "typical" structural plan, plant species show a wide variety of modifications from this plan. These modifications have significance in the evolution of flowering plants and are used extensively by botanists to establish relationships among plant species. For example, the two subclasses of flowering plants may be distinguished by the number of floral organs in each whorl: dicotyledons typically having 4 or 5 organs (or a multiple of 4 or 5) in each whorl and monocotyledons having three or some multiple of three. The number of carpels in a compound pistil may be only two, or otherwise not related to the above generalization for monocots and dicots.

In the majority of species individual flowers have both pistils and stamens as described above. These flowers are described by botanists as being *perfect, bisexual,* or *hermaphrodite*. However, in some species of plants the flowers are *imperfect* or *unisexual*: having only either male (stamens) or female (pistil) parts. In the latter case, if an individual plant is either female or male the species is regarded as *dioecious*. However, where unisexual male and female flowers appear on the same plant, the species is considered *monoecious*.

Additional discussions on floral modifications from the basic plan are presented in the articles on each of the basic parts of the flower. In those species that have more than one flower on an axis—so-called *composite flowers*—the collection of flowers is termed an *inflorescence*; this term can also refer to the specific arrangements of flowers on a stem. In this regard, care must be exercised in considering what a "flower" is. In botanical terminology, a single daisy or sunflower for example, is not a flower but a flower *head*—an inflorescence composed of numerous tiny flowers (sometimes called florets). Each of these flowers may be anatomically as described above. Many flowers have a symmetry, if the perianth is bisected through the central axis from any point, symmetrical halves are produced—the flower is called regular or actinomorphic, e.g. rose or trillium. When flowers are bisected and produce only one line that produces symmetrical halves the flower is said to be irregular or zygomorphic. e.g. snapdragon or most orchids.

DEVELOPMENT

Flowering Transition

The transition to flowering is one of the major phase changes that a plant makes during its life cycle. The transition must take place at a time that will ensure maximal reproductive success. To meet these needs a plant is able to interpret important endogenous and environmental cues such as changes in levels of plant hormones and seasonable temperature and photoperiod changes. Many perennial and most biennial plants require vernalization to flower. The molecular interpretation of these signals through genes such as *Constans* and *FLC* ensures that flowering occurs at a time that is favorable for fertilization and the formation of seeds Flower formation is initiated at the ends of stems, and involves a number of different physiological and morphological changes. The first step is the transformation of the vegetative stem primordia into floral primordia. This occurs as biochemical changes take place to change cellular differentiation of leaf, bud and stem tissues into tissue that will grow into the reproductive organs. Growth of the central part of the stem tip stops or flattens out and the sides develop protuberances in a whorled or spiral fashion around the outside of the stem end. These protuberances develop into the sepals, petals, stamens, and carpels. Once this process begins, in most plants, it cannot be reversed and the stems develop flowers, even if the initial start of the flower formation event was dependent of some environmental cue once the process begins, even if that cue is removed the stem will continue to develop a flower.

Organ Development

The molecular control of floral organ identity determination is fairly well understood. In a simple model, three gene activities interact in a combinatorial manner to determine the developmental identities of the organ primordia within the floral meristem. These gene functions are called A, B and C-gene functions. In the first floral whorl only A-genes are expressed, leading to the formation of sepals. In the second whorl both A- and B-genes are expressed, leading to the formation of petals. In the third whorl, B and C genes interact to form stamens and in the center of the flower C-genes alone give rise to carpels. The model is based upon studies of homeotic mutants in *Arabidopsis thaliana* and snapdragon, *Antirrhinum majus*. For example, when there is a loss of B-gene function, mutant flowers are produced with sepals in the first whorl as usual, but also in the second whorl instead of the normal petal formation. In the third whorl the lack of B function but presence of C-function mimics the fourth whorl, leading to the formation of carpels also in the third whorl. See also The ABC Model of Flower Development.

Most genes central in this model belong to the MADS-box genes and are transcription factors that regulate the expression of the genes specific for each floral organ.

Fig. 21.2

Pollination

The primary purpose of a flower is reproduction. Since the flowers are the reproductive organs of plant, they mediate the joining of the sperm, contained within pollen, to the ovules - contained in the ovary. Pollination is the movement of pollen from the anthers to the stigma. The joining of the sperm to the ovules is called fertilization. Normally pollen is moved from one plant to another, but many plants are able to self pollinate. The fertilized ovules produce seeds that are the next generation. Sexual reproduction produces genetically unique offspring, allowing for adaptation. Flowers have specific designs which encourages the transfer of pollen from one plant to another of the same species. Many plants are dependent upon external factors for pollination, including: wind and animals, and especially insects. Even large animals such as birds, bats, and pygmy possums can be employed. The period of time during which this process can take place (the flower is fully expanded and functional) is called *anthesis*.

Attraction Methods

Plants can not move from one location to another, thus many flowers have evolved to attract animals to transfer pollen between individuals in dispersed populations. Flowers that are insect-pollinated are called *entomophilous*; literally "insect-loving" in Latin. They can be highly modified along with the pollinating insects by co-evolution. Flowers commonly have glands called *nectaries* on various parts that attract animals looking for nutritious nectar. Birds and bees have color vision, enabling them to seek out "colorful" flowers. Some flowers have patterns, called nectar guides, that show pollinators where to look for nectar; they may be visible only under ultraviolet light, which is visible to bees and some other insects. Flowers also attract pollinators by scent and some of those scents are pleasant to our sense of smell. Not all flower scents are appealing to humans, a number of flowers are pollinated by insects that are attracted to rotten flesh and have flowers that smell like dead animals, often called Carrion flowers including *Rafflesia*, the titan arum, and the North American pawpaw (*Asimina triloba*). Flowers pollinated by night visitors, including bats and moths, are likely to concentrate on scent to attract pollinators and most such flowers are white.

Still other flowers use mimicry to attract pollinators. Some species of orchids, for example, produce flowers resembling female bees in color, shape, and scent. Male bees move from one such flower to another in search of a mate.

Pollination Mechanism

The pollination mechanism employed by a plant depends on what method of pollination is utilized.

Most flowers can be divided between two broad groups of pollination methods:

- *Entomophilous*: flowers attract and use insects, bats, birds or other animals to transfer pollen from one flower to the next. Often they are specialized in shape and have an arrangement of the stamens that ensures that pollen grains are transferred to the bodies of the pollinator when it lands in search of its attractant (such as nectar, pollen, or a mate). In pursuing this attractant from many flowers of the same species, the pollinator transfers pollen to the stigmas—arranged with equally pointed precision—of all of the flowers it visits. Many flower rely on simple proximity between flower parts to ensure pollination. Others, such as the *Sarracenia* or lady-slipper orchids, have elaborate designs to ensure pollination while preventing self-pollination.
- *Anemophilous*: flowers use the wind to move pollen from one flower to the next, examples include the grasses, Birch trees, Ragweed and Maples. They have no need to attract pollinators and therefore tend not to be "showy" flowers. Whereas the pollen of entomophilous flowers tends to be large-grained, sticky, and rich in protein (another "reward" for pollinators), anemophilous flower pollen is usually small-grained, very light, and of little nutritional value to insects, though it may still be gathered in times of dearth. Honeybees and bumblebees actively gather anemophilous corn (maize) pollen, though it is of little value to them.

Some flowers are self pollinated and use flowers that never open or are self pollinated before the flowers open, these flowers are called cleistogamous. Many Viola species and some Salvia have these types of flowers.

Flower-pollinator Relationships

Many flowers have close relationships with one or a few specific pollinating organisms. Many flowers, for example, attract only one specific species of insect, and therefore rely on that insect for successful reproduction. This close relationship is often given as an example of coevolution, as the flower and pollinator are thought to have developed together over a long period of time to match each other's needs.

This close relationship compounds the negative effects of extinction. The extinction of either member in such a relationship would mean almost certain extinction of the other member as well. Some endangered plant species are so because of shrinking pollinator populations.

Fertilization and Dispersal

Some flowers with both stamens and a pistil are capable of self-fertilization, which does increase the chance of producing seeds but limits genetic variation. The extreme case of self-fertilization occurs in flowers that always self-fertilize, such as many dandelions. Conversely, many species of plants have ways of preventing self-fertilization. Unisexual male and female flowers on the same plant may not appear or mature at the same time, or pollen from the same plant may be incapable of fertilizing its ovules. The latter flower types, which have chemical barriers to their own pollen, are referred to as self-sterile or self-incompatible.

Evolution

While land plants have existed for about 425 million years, the first ones reproduced by a simple adaptation of their aquatic counterparts: spores. In the sea, plants — and some animals — can simply scatter out genetic clones of themselves to float away and grow elsewhere. This is how early plants reproduced. But plants soon evolved methods of protecting these copies to deal with drying out and other abuse which is even more likely on land than in the sea. The protection became the seed, though it had not yet evolved the flower. Early seed-bearing plants include the ginkgo and conifers. The earliest fossil of a flowering plant, *Archaefructus liaoningensis*, is dated about 125 million years old Several groups of extinct gymnosperms, particularly seed ferns, have been proposed as the ancestors of flowering plants but there is no continuous fossil evidence showing exactly how flowers evolved. The apparently sudden appearance of relatively modern flowers in the fossil record posed such a problem for the theory of evolution that it was called an "abominable mystery" by Charles Darwin. Recently discovered angiosperm fossils such as *Archaefructus*, along with further discoveies of fossil gymnosperms, suggest how angiosperm characteristics may have been acquired in a series of steps.

Recent DNA analysis (molecular systematics) show that *Amborella trichopoda*, found on the Pacific island of New Caledonia, is the sister group to the rest of the flowering plants, and morphological studies suggest that it has features which may have been characteristic of the earliest flowering plants.

The general assumption is that the function of flowers, from the start, was to involve other animals in the reproduction process. Pollen can be scattered without bright colors and obvious shapes, which would therefore be a liability, using the plant's resources, unless they provide some other benefit. One proposed reason for the sudden, fully developed appearance of flowers is that they evolved in an isolated setting like an island, or chain of islands, where the plants bearing them were able to develop a highly specialized relationship with some specific animal (a wasp, for example), the way many island species develop today. This symbiotic relationship, with a hypothetical wasp bearing pollen from one plant to another much the way fig wasps do today, could have eventually resulted in both the plant(s) and their partners developing a high degree of specialization. Island genetics is believed to be a common source of speciation, especially when it comes to radical adaptations which seem to have required inferior transitional forms. Note that the wasp example is not incidental; bees, apparently evolved specifically for symbiotic plant relationships, are descended from wasps.

Likewise, most fruit used in plant reproduction comes from the enlargement of parts of the flower. This fruit is frequently a tool which depends upon animals wishing to eat it, and thus scattering the seeds it contains.

While many such symbiotic relationships remain too fragile to survive competition with mainland animals and spread, flowers proved to be an unusually effective means of production, spreading (whatever their actual origin) to become the dominant form of land plant life.

While there is only hard proof of such flowers existing about 130 million years ago, there is some circumstantial evidence that they did exist up to 250 million years ago. A chemical used by plants to defend their flowers, oleanane, has been detected in fossil plants that old, including gigantopterids, which evolved at that time and bear many of the traits of modern, flowering plants, though they are not known to be flowering plants themselves, because only their stems and prickles have been found preserved in detail; one of the earliest examples of petrification.

The similarity in leaf and stem structure can be very important, because flowers are genetically just an adaptation of normal leaf and stem components on plants, a combination of genes normally responsible for forming new shoots. The most primitive flowers are thought to have had a variable number of flower parts, often separate from (but in contact with) each other. The flowers would have tended to grow in a spiral pattern, to be bisexual (in plants, this means both male and female parts on the same flower), and to be dominated by the ovary (female part). As flowers grew more advanced, some variations developed parts fused together, with a much more specific number and design, and with either specific sexes per flower or plant, or at least "ovary inferior".

Flower evolution continues to the present day; modern flowers have been so profoundly influenced by humans that many of them cannot be pollinated in nature. Many modern, domesticated flowers used to be simple weeds, which only sprouted when the ground was disturbed. Some of them tended to grow with human crops, and the prettiest did not get plucked because of their beauty, developing a dependence upon and special adaptation to human affection.

Symbolism

Many flowers have important symbolic meanings in Western culture. The practice of assigning meanings to flowers is known as floriography. Some of the more common examples include:

- Red roses are given as a symbol of love, beauty, and passion.

  Poppies are a symbol of consolation in time of death. In the UK, New Zealand, Australia and Canada, red poppies are worn to commemorate soldiers who have died in times of war.

- Irises Lily are used in burials as a symbol referring to "resurrection/life". It is also associated with stars (sun) and its petals blooming/shining. Daisies are a symbol of innocence.

Flowers within art are also representative of the female genitalia, as seen in the works of artists such as Georgia O'Keeffe, Imogen Cunningham, Veronica Ruiz de Velasco, and Judy Chicago, and in fact in Asian and western classical art. Many cultures around the world have a marked tendency to associate flowers with femininity.

The great variety of delicate and beautiful flowers has inspired the works of numerous poets, especially from the 18th-19th century Romantic era. Famous examples include William Wordsworth's *I Wandered Lonely as a Cloud* and William Blake's *Ah! Sun-Flower*.

Because of their varied and colorful appearance, flowers have long been a favorite subject of visual artists as well. Some of the most celebrated paintings from well-known painters are of flowers, such as Van Gogh's sunflowers series or Monet's water lilies. Flowers are also dried, freeze dried and pressed in order to create permanent, three-dimensional pieces of flower art.

The Roman goddess of flowers, gardens, and the season of Spring is Flora. The Greek goddess of spring, flowers and nature is Chloris.

In Hindu mythology, flowers have a significant status. Vishnu, one of the three major gods in the Hindu system, is often depicted standing straight on a lotus flower. Apart from the association with Vishnu, the Hindu tradition also considers the lotus to have spiritual significance. For example, it figures in the Hindu stories of creation.

Usage

In modern times, people have sought ways to cultivate, buy, wear, or otherwise be around flowers and blooming plants, partly because of their agreeable appearance and smell. Around the world, people use flowers for a wide range of events and functions that, cumulatively, encompass one's lifetime:

- For new births or Christenings.
- As a corsage or boutonniere to be worn at social functions or for holidays.
- As tokens of love or esteem.
- For wedding flowers for the bridal party, and decorations for the hall.

- As brightening decorations within the home.
- As a gift of remembrance for bon voyage parties, welcome home parties, and "thinking of you" gifts.
- For funeral flowers and expressions of sympathy for the grieving.

People therefore grow flowers around their homes, dedicate entire parts of their living space to flower gardens, pick wildflowers, or buy flowers from florists who depend on an entire network of commercial growers and shippers to support their trade.

Flowers provide less food than other major plants parts (seeds, fruits, roots, stems and leaves) but they provide several important foods and spices. Flower vegetables include broccoli, cauliflower and artichoke. The most expensive spice, saffron, consists of dried stigmas of a crocus. Other flower spices are cloves and capers. Hops flowers are used to flavour beer. Marigold flowers are fed to chickens to give their egg yolks a golden yellow color, which consumers find more desirable. Dandelion flowers are often made into wine. Bee Pollen, pollen collected from bees, is considered a health food by some people. Honey consists of bee-processed flower nectar and is often named for the type of flower, e.g. orange blossom honey, clover honey and tupelo honey.

Hundreds of fresh flowers are edible but few are widely marketed as food. They are often used to add color and flavor to salads. Squash flowers are dipped in breadcrumbs and fried. Edible flowers include nasturtium, chrysanthemum, carnation, cattail, honeysuckle, chicory, cornflower, Canna, and sunflower. Some edible flowers are sometimes candied such as daisy and rose.

Flowers can also be made into herbal teas. Dried flowers such as chrysanthemum, rose, jasmine, camomile are infused into tea both for their fragrance and medical properties. Sometimes, they are also mixed with tea leaves for the added fragrance.

Floriculture

Floriculture, or flower farming, is a discipline of horticulture concerned with the cultivation of flowering and ornamental plants for gardens and for floristry, comprising the floral industry. The development plant breeding of new varieties is a major occupation of floriculturists.

Floriculture crops include bedding plants, flowering plants, foliage plants or houseplants, cut cultivated greens, and cut flowers. As distinguished from nursery crops, floriculture crops are generally herbaceous. Bedding and garden plants consist of young flowering plants (annuals and perennials) and vegetable plants. They are grown in cell packs (in flats or trays), in pots, or in hanging baskets, usually inside a controlled environment, and sold largely for gardens and landscaping. Geraniums, impatiens, and petunias are the best-selling bedding plants. Chrysanthemums are the major perennial garden plant in the United States.

Flowering plants are largely sold in pots for indoor use. The major flowering plants are poinsettias, orchids, florist chrysanthemums, and finished florist azaleas. Foliage plants are also sold in pots and hanging baskets for indoor and patio use, including larger specimens for office, hotel, and restaurant interiors.

Cut flowers are usually sold in bunches or as bouquets with cut foliage. The production of cut flowers is specifically known as the cut flower industry. Farming flowers and foliage employs special aspects of floriculture, such as spacing, training and pruning plants for optimal flower harvest; and post-harvest treatment such as chemical treatments, storage, preservation and packaging. In Australia and the United States some species are harvested from the wild for the cut flower market.

22

Chilli Pepper

Chili pepper (chilli pepper, chilli, chili, chile) is the fruit of the plants from the genus Capsicum, members of the nightshade family, Solanaceae. Botany considers the plant a berry bush. Though chilis may be thought of as a vegetable, their culinary use is generally as a spice. It is the fruit that is usually harvested.

Fig. 22.1

Chili peppers and their cultivars originate in the Americas; they are now grown around the world because they are widely used as spices or vegetables in cuisine, and as medicine.

Chili peppers have been a part of the human diet in the Americas since at least 7500 BC. There is archaeological evidence at sites located in southwestern Ecuador that chili peppers were domesticated more than 6000 years ago, and is one of the first cultivated crops in the Americas that is self-pollinating. Chili peppers were domesticated at least in different parts of South and Middle America. Christopher Columbus was one of the first Europeans to encounter them (in the Caribbean), and called them "peppers" because of their similarity in taste (though not in appearance) with the Old World Black peppers of the *Piper* genus. Chilies were cultivated around the globe after Columbus Diego Álvarez Chanca, a physician on Columbus' second voyage to the West Indies in 1493, brought the first chili peppers to Spain, and first wrote about their medicinal effects in 1494. From Mexico, at the time the Spanish colony that controlled commerce with Asia, chili peppers spread rapidly into the Philippines and then to India, China, Korea and Japan. They were quickly incorporated into the local cuisines.

An alternate sequence for chili peppers' spread has the Portuguese getting the pepper from Spain, and thence to India, as described by Lizzie Collingham in her book *Curry* Collingham states in her book that the chili pepper figures heavily in the cuisine of the Goan region of India, which was the site of a Portuguese colony (e.g. Vindaloo, an Indian interpretation of a Portuguese dish). Collingham also describes the journey of chili peppers from India, through Central Asia and Turkey, to Hungary, where it became the national spice in the form of paprika.

There are speculations about pre-Columbian chili peppers in Europe. In an archaeological dig in the block of St. Botulf in Lund, archaeologists found a *Capsicum frutescens* in a layer dating to the 13th century. Hjelmqvist says that *Capsicum* was described by the Greek Theophrastus (370-286 BC). He mentions other antique sources. The Roman poet Martialis (around the 1st century) described "Piper crudum" (raw pepper) to be long and containing seeds. The description of the plants does not fit Black pepper *(Piper nigrum)*, which grows poorly in European climates.

The Black Habanero (*Chocolate Habanero, Habanero Negra*), is thought to be the closest to the original peppers that grew in the South American coastal plains. It is known to gourmets but rarely available, due in part to its long maturity. Seeds are available today but care is needed when purchasing as many sub species are sold under the same name.

Though there are only a few commonly used species, there are many cultivars and methods of preparing chili peppers that have different names for culinary use. Green and Red Bell peppers, for example, are the same cultivar of *C. annuum*; immature peppers being green. In the same species are the jalapeño, the poblano (when dried is referred to as ancho), New Mexico (which is also known as chile Colorado), Anaheim, Serrano, and other cultivars.

Peppers are commonly broken down into three groupings: bell peppers, sweet peppers, and hot peppers. Most popular pepper varieties are seen as falling into one of these categories or as a cross between them.

Intensity

The substances that gives chili peppers their intensity when ingested or applied topically are capsaicin (8-methyl-*N*-vanillyl-6-nonenamide) and several related chemicals, collectively called *capsaicinoids*. Capsaicin is the primary ingredient in pepper spray.

When consumed, capsaicinoids bind with pain receptors in the mouth and throat that are normally responsible for sensing heat. Once activated by the capsaicinoids, these receptors send a message to the brain that the person has consumed something hot. The brain responds to the burning sensation by raising the heart rate, increasing perspiration and release of endorphins.

The "heat" of chili peppers is measured in Scoville units (SHU), which is the amount of times a chilli extract must be diluted in water in order for it to lose its heat. Bell peppers rank at 0 (SHU), New Mexico green chilis at about 1,500 SHU, jalapeños at 3,000–6,000 SHU, and habaneros at 300,000 SHU. The record for the hottest chili pepper was assigned by the Guinness Book of Records to the Naga Jolokia, measuring over 1,000,000 SHU. Pure capsaicin, which is a hydrophobic, colorless, odorless, and crystalline to waxy solid at room temperature, measures 16,000,000 SHU.

Uses

The chili has a long association with Mexican cuisine as later adapted into Tex-Mex cuisine. Although unknown in Asia until Europeans introduced it there, chili has also become a part of the Korean, Nepal, Indian, Indonesian, Sri Lankan Szechuan, Thai and other cooking traditions.

The fruit is eaten raw or cooked for its fiery hot flavour, concentrated along the top of the pod. The stem end of the pod has most of the glands that produce the capsaicin. The white flesh surrounding the seeds contains the highest concentration of capsaicin. Removing the inner membranes is thus effective at reducing the heat of a pod.

Chili is sold worldwide fresh, dried and powdered. In the United States, it is often made from the Mexican *chile ancho* variety, but with small amounts of cayenne added for heat. In the Southwest United States, dried ground chili peppers, cumin, garlic and oregano is often known as chili powder. Chipotles are dry, smoked red (ripe) jalapeños.

Chili peppers are used around the world to make a variety of sauces, known as *hot sauce, chili sauce,* or *pepper sauce.* There are countless recipes.

Indian cooking has multiple uses for chilis, from snacks like bhaji where the chilis are dipped in batter and fried, to vindaloo. Chilis are dried, roasted and salted as a side dish for rice varieties such as daddojanam or Thayir sadam (curd rice) or Daal Rice (rice with lentils). The soaked and dried chillies are a seasoning ingredient in recipes such as kootu. It is called "mirapa") in telugu.

In Turkish or Ottoman cuisine, chilis are widely used where it is known as *Kirmizi Biber* (Red Pepper) or *Aci Biber* (Hot Pepper). Sambal is dipping sauce made from chili peppers with other ingredients such as garlic, onion, shallots, salt, vinegar and sugar, which is popular in Indonesia and Malaysia.

Fig. 22.2

Chili powder is important in Persian cuisine and used in a variety of dishes. Chili pepper plant leaves, mildly bitter, are cooked as greens in Filipino cuisine, where they are called *dahon ng sili* (literally "chili leaves"). They are used in the chicken soup, "tinola. In Korean cuisine, the leaves may be used in kimchi. In Japanese cuisine, the leaves are cooked as greens, and also cooked in *tsukudani* style for preservation. In Italian cuisine crushed red pepper is a common ingredient on pizza among other things.

Decoration

Chili peppers can also be used decoratively. Some chili peppers are not grown for consumption, they are instead grown for decorative qualities: "ornamental peppers". Some are too hot for typical cooking, or are not palatable. Regardless, ornamental peppers have unusual shapes or colours. Examples include Thai Ornamental, Black Pearl, Marble, and Numex Twilight. The Medusa pepper is a green plant that produces fruit starting purple, then ripening to yellow, orange, and red. Black Pearl has black leaves and round black fruit that ripen to a bright red.

Superstition

In India, chili is used with lime to ward off evil spirits and is seen in vehicles and in homes for that purpose. It is used to check the evil eye and remove its effects in Hinduism as people will also be asked to spit into a handful of chilies kept in that plate, which are thrown into fire. If the chilis make a noise - as they should - then there is no case of "drishti" (evil eye); if on the other hand they do not, then the spell of the evil eye is removed in the fire. Red chilis contain high amounts of vitamin C and carotene ("provitamin A"). Yellow and especially green chilis (which are essentially unripe fruit) contain a considerably lower amount of both substances.

In addition, peppers are a good source of most B vitamins, and vitamin B6 in particular. They are very high in potassium and high in magnesium and iron. Their high vitamin C content can also substantially increase the uptake of non-heme iron from other ingredients in a meal, such as beans and grains. They are rich in vitamin C. Psychologist Paul Rozin suggests that eating chilis is an example of a "constrained risk" like riding a roller coaster, in which extreme sensations like pain and fear can be enjoyed because individuals know that these sensations are not actually harmful.

This method lets people experience extreme feelings without any risk of bodily harm.

Evolutionary Advantages

Birds do not have the same sensitivity to capsaicin as mammals because capsaicin acts on a specific nerve receptor in mammals. Chili peppers are eaten by birds living in the chili peppers' natural range. The seeds of the peppers are distributed by the birds that drop the seeds while eating the pods, and the seeds pass through the digestive tract unharmed. This relationship may have promoted the evolution of the protective capsaicin. Products based on this substance have been sold to treat the seeds in bird feeders to deter squirrels and other mammalian vermin without also deterring birds. Capsaicin is also a defense mechanism against microbial fungi that invades through punctures made in the outer skin by various insects.

Spelling and Usage

The three primary spellings are *chili, chile* and *chilli,* all of which are recognized by dictionaries.

- *Chili* is widely used, although in much of South America the plant and its fruit are better known as *ají, locoto, chile,* or *rocoto.* However, this spelling is discouraged by some in the United States of America, since it also commonly refers to a popular Southwestern-American dish (also known as chili con carne (literally chili with meat); the official state dish of Texas as well as to the mixture of cumin and other spices (chili powder) used to flavor it. Chili powder and chile powder, on the other hand, can both refer to dried, ground chili peppers.
- *Chile* is an alternate usage, the most common Spanish spelling in Mexico as well as some parts of the United States of America and Canada, which refers specifically to this plant and its fruit. In the American southwest (particularly northern New Mexico), *chile* also denotes a thick, spicy, un-vinegared sauce, which is available in red and green varieties and which is often served over most New Mexican cuisine.
- *Chilli* was the original Romanization of the Náhuatl language word for the fruit (*chilli*) and is the preferred British spelling according to the *Oxford English Dictionary,* although it also lists *chile* and *chili* as variants. This spelling is discouraged by some, since it would be pronounced differently in Spanish, into which it was first Romanized.

The name of the plant bears no relation to Chile, the country, which is named after the Quechua *chin* ("cold"), *tchili* ("snow"), or *chilli* ("where the land ends"). Chile is one of the Spanish-speaking countries where chilis are known as *ají*, a word of Taíno origin.

There is also some disagreement about whether it is proper to use the word *pepper* when discussing chili peppers because *pepper* originally referred to the genus Piper, not Capsicum. Despite this dispute, a sense of *pepper* referring to Capsicum is supported by English dictionaries, including the Oxford English Dictionary (sense 2b of *pepper*) and Merriam-Webster. Furthermore, the word *pepper* is commonly used in the botanical and culinary fields in the names of different types of chili peppers.

Medicinal Use

Capsaicin is a safe and effective analgesic agent in the management of arthritis pain, herpes zoster-related pain, diabetic neuropathy, and postmastectomy pain.

Possible Health Benefits

All hot chili peppers contain phytochemicals known collectively as capsaicinoids.

- Capsaicin was shown, in laboratory settings, to cause cancer cell death in rats.
- Capsaicin in chilies has been found to inhibit chemically induced carcinogenesis and mutagenesis in various animal models and cell culture systems.
- Recent research in mice shows that chili (capsaicin in particular) may offer some hope of weight loss for people suffering from obesity.
- Researchers used capsaicin from chillies to kill nerve cells in the pancreases of mice with type 1 diabetes, thus allowing the insulin producing cells to start producing

insulin again. Research in humans found that "after adding chili to the diet, the LDL, or bad cholesterol, actually resisted oxidation for a longer period of time, (delaying) the development of a major risk for cardiovascular disease". Researchers found that the amount of insulin required to lower blood sugar after a meal is reduced if the meal contains chili pepper.

- Chilli peppers are being probed as a treatment for alleviating chronic pain. Spices, including chilli, are theorized to control the microbial contamination levels of food in countries with minimal or no refrigeration. Hot peppers are claimed to provide symptomatic relief from rhinitis, but a review study found no effect.
- Several studies found that capsaicin could have an anti-ulcer protective effect on stomachs infected with *H. pylori* by affecting the chemicals the stomach secretes in response to infection.

• By combining an anesthetic with capsaicin, researchers can block pain in rat paws without causing temporary paralysis. This anesthetic may one day allow patients to be conscious during surgery and may also lead to the development of more effective chronic pain treatments. Possible health risks and precautions.

A high consumption of chili is associated with ·stomach cancer.

Chili powders may sometimes be adulterated with Sudan I, II, III, IV, para-Red, and other illegal ·carcinogenic dyes.

Aflatoxins and N-nitroso compounds, which are carcinogenic, are frequently found in chili powder.

Chronic ingestion of chili products may induce gastroesophageal reflux (GER). Chili may increase the number of daily bowel movements and lower pain thresholds for people with rritable bowel syndrome.

Chilis should never be swallowed whole; there are cases where unchewed chilis have caused bowel obstruction and perforation.

Consumption of red chilis after anal fissure surgery should be forbidden to avoid postoperative symptoms.

Index

A

ABC Model of Flower development, 306

Aci biber (hot pepper), 320

Agriculture, 1-27

- agriculture and petroleum, 21-24
- agriculture safety and health, 26
- ancient origins, 6-7
- climate change, 20
- costs and benefits of GMOs, 16-17
- crop alteration and biotechnology, 13-14
- crop production systems, 9-10
- crop statistics, 10-12
- distortions in modern global agriculture, 20-21
- environmental impact, 18
- etymology, 2
- eutrophication, 19
- food safety and labeling, 17-18
- genetic engineering, 15
- herbicide-tolerant GMO crops, 15
- history, 5
- insect-resistant GMO crops, 15-16
- introduction, 1-2
- land transformation and degradation, 19
- livestock issues, 18-19
- middle ages, 7
- mitigation of effects of petroleum shortages, 24-26
- modern era, 7-9
- overview, 3-5
- pesticides, 19-20
- processing, distribution and marketing, 13
- production practices, 12-13
- Untied States, 26-27

Aktas Ngungut, 281

Alleppey Green Bold (AGB), 130

Alleppey Green Extra Bold (AGEB), 130

Alleppey Green Superior (AGS), 130

Amborella trichopoda, 310

American Civil War, 203, 239, 251

Amomum, 133, 136

Androecium, 303

Api, 113

Arabidopsis thaliana, 305

Archaefructus, 310

Archives of Internal Medicine, 222

Areca catechu, 104

Arecanut, 94-115

arecanut curing, 106-107, 108-109
arecanut processing, 104-106
chewing betel nut alone has been linked to oral submuicous fibrosis, 101
curing of arecanut in Meghalaya, 108, 110-111
dried ripe nuts, 113
economics, 112
effects on health, 99-100
Kalipak, 113
method of consumption and curing in NE region, 107-108, 109-110
method, 111-112
modern day consumption, 102-104
preservation of fruits, 112
scented supari, 114
sources attribute the increase to the spread of arecanut cultivation to non-traditional areas, 106
term betel nut and the colonial legacy, 95-97
tradition, 97-99
uses of arecanut constituents and byproducts, 114-115
alkaloids, 114
areca husk, 115
areca stem and leaf sheath, 115
fat, 114
tannins, 114
vernacular names, 101
Artichokes, 7
ASEAN-Canada Forest Tree Seed Centre (ACFTSC in 1986), 282
Aseer asab, 199
Asimina triloba, 307
Aubergines, 7
Ayurvedic and Traditional Chinese medicines, 95

B

Bacillus thuringiensis (Bt), 15, 242
Banana, 172-188
allergic reactions, 185
Australia, 184
blue fluorescence, a recent discovery, 188
cultivation, 181-182
early cultivation, 179-180
east Africa, 184-185
fibre, 186
major diseases, 182-184
paper, 186
peels, 187
pests, diseases and natural disasters, 182
plantation cultivation, 180-181
properties, 174-177
storage and transport, 186-187
symbols, 188
trade, 177-179
Beedi, 262
Ben Tree Province, 285
Betel nut (paan supari, paan masala or sada paan), 123
Betel, 116-128
Bangladesh, 125
Cambodia, 128

chewing, 119-122
compounds, 119
cultivation, 117-119
culture, 124-125
culture, 124-125
effects on health, 123-124
India, 125-126
medicinal properties, 122
Myanmar, 126-127
paan, 122-123
Pakistan, 127-128
Philippines, 126
varieties, 123
vernacular names, 116
Vietnam, 128
Betelnut, 69
BioSafety Protocol, 17
Black pepper, 141-152
ancient times, 146-147
China, 149-150
flavour, 151-152
ground black pepper and pepper shaker, 143-145
history, 145-146
medicine, 150-151
postclassical Europe, 147-149
world trade, 152
Bodhidharma, 294
Boll Weevil Eradication Program (BWEP), 244
Bourbon, 163
British Empire in 1882, 239
Brontispa longissima, 278

C

C. canephora, 204
C. sinensis assamica, 291
Cachar, 104
Camellia sinensis, 289, 290
Capsaicinoids, 318
Capsicum frutescens, 317
Cardamom, 69, 129-140
attributed medicinal properties, 132
black cardamom, 136
culinary uses, 131
etymology, 138
green cardamom, 129-130
names in different languages, 137
other names, 132-133
plant description and cultivation, 132
spice description, 130-131
traditional medicine, 136-137
used part, 137
uses, 134-136, 138-140
varieties, 133-134
Cash crop, 69-83
bamboo, 80
flowers, 75
getting help, 83
herbs, 75-77
landscaping plants, 79
marketing techniques, 81-83
nut crops, 79
seeds, 80-81
small fruits, 73-74
speciality crops, 79
sprouts, 81
vegetables, 77-79
Cavendish, 184

Central Arecanut and Cocoa Marketing and Processing Cooperative Limited (CAMPCO), 105
Central Plantation Crop Research Institute, 279
CFTRI, 115
CGIAR, 185
Cha Jing, 294
Chewing tobacco, 262
Chicago, 61
Chikani, 108, 110
Chilli pepper, 316-325
- decoration, 320-321
- evolutionary advantages, 321-322
- intensity, 318-319
- medicinal use, 323
- possible health benefits, 323-325
- spelling and usage, 322-323
- superstition, 321
- uses, 319-320

Chocolate Habanero, 318
Christian era, 235
Christians, 148
Christopher Columbus, 228, 317
Cigarettes, 263
Cigars, 263
Citrus aurantium, 227
Citrus maxima, 226
Citrus reticulate, 226
Citrus sinensis, 227
Cocoa, 216-225
- child labour in the cocoa production industry, 224
- chocolate, 220-221
- chocolate production, 220
- cocoa trading, 225
- environmental impact, 225
- harvesting, 218-219
- health benefits of cocoa consumption, 221-222
- non-human animal consumption, 222-223
- organizations that directly support sustainable cocoa, 224
- processing, 219
- roundtable for a sustainable cocoa economy, 223
- sustainable cocoa, 223

Coconut, 274-288
- coconut production in the middle east, 279-280
- culinary, 283-285
- cultivation, 278
- fruit, 280-282
- growing in the united states, 279
- harvesting, 280
- husk, 282
- inflorescence, 283
- natural habitat, 276-277
- non-culinary, 285-288
- origins, 275-276
- pests and diseases, 278-279
- production, 280
- roots, 282
- uses, 283

Cocos nucifera, 274
Coffea arabica, 204
Coffea esliaca, 205
Coffee, 200-215

biology, 204
caffeine content, 215
coffee as a commodity, 207
cultivation, 204-205
economics, 206-207
etymology, 201-202
health and pharmacology, 213-215
history, 202-204
preparation, 209-211
presentation, 211-212
processing, 207
production, 205-206
roasting, 207-209
social aspects, 212-213
storage, 209
types of popular coffee beverages, 212
Common Agricultural Policy (CAP) in 205, 204
Cornell University, 222
Corolla, 303
Costa Rica, 178
Cotton, 234-250
competition from synthetic fibres, 245-246
critical temperatures, 250
cultivation, 241-242
fair trade, 249-250
genetically modified cotton, 242-243
international cotton trade, 248
leading cotton-producing countries, 248-249
mechanized harvesting, 245
organic cotton, 243-244
pests and weeds, 244-245
tanguis cotton, 240-241
uses, 246-248
CPCRI, 115
Cratopus retuse, 161
Creamy snuff, 263
Cultivation of Areca, 128
Cultivation, 2, 21
Cunningham, 312

D

Darjelling tea, 298
Deois flavopicta, 194
Desi Mahoba, 123
Dhiyaa hakuru, 284
Diatraea saccharalis, 194
Dipping tobacco, 263
Directorate of Economics and Statistics, 106
DNA, 15
Dominican Republic, 191
Dorsett-Morse Oriental Agricultural Exploration Expedition to China, 8
Dutch East India Company, 297

E

East India Company, 235
Elakkai, 138
Electronic cigarette, 263
Elettaria, 133
Epitrix cucumeris, 260
Eriophyes guerreronis, 278
Eschirichia coli, 60
Ethipian Orthodox Christians, 213
European Union, 173

Eutrophication, 19

F

FAO, 11, 177

Fertile Crescent of the Middle East, 6

FIFA World Cup, 229

Flower, 300-315

attraction methods, 307

development, 304

evolution, 309-312

fertilization and dispersal, 309

floriculture, 315

flower-pollinator relationships, 309

flower specialization and pollination, 301-302

flowering transition, 304-305

morphology, 302-304

organ development, 305-306

pollination, 306-307

pollination mechanism, 308-309

symbolism, 312-313

Food and Drug Administration (FDA), 254

Food and Nutrition Board of the National Research Council, 64

Framework Convention on Tobacco Control, 254

Fusarium vasinfectum, 240

G

Gaia hypothesis, 56

Genetic engineering, 15

Genetically Modified Organisms (GMO), 10, 15-17

Gossypium barbadense, 236, 238

Gossypium hirsutum, 236, 238

Grape, 266-273

anthocyanins and other phenolics, 271-272

concord grape juice, 273

description, 267

distribution and production, 268

grapevines, 267-268

health claims, 269

raisins, currants, and sultanas, 269

resveratrol, 270-271

seed constituents, 272

seedless grapes, 268-269

Green Revolution, 4, 21

Gregor Mendel, 14

Guarab, 199

Guiana method, 168

Gutka, 264

Gynoecium, 303

H

Habanero Negra, 318

Haraam, 212

Harvard Medical School, 221

Hindu mythology, 313

Hookah, 264

Howly, 104

Husori, 99

I

ILO (International Labor Organization), 224

Importance of climate, 84-93

air mass, 87-88

climate change, 91-92

climate classification, 86-87
climate models, 92-93
koppen, 88-90
paleoclimatology, 91
thornthwaite, 90-91
Indus Valley Civilization, 235
Intergovernmental Panel on Climate Change (IPCC), 85
International Agency for Research on Cancer (IARC), 99, 100, 123
International Cocoa Organization (ICCO), 218, 223
International Institute of Tropical Agriculture, 185
International Monetary Fund, 9
International Service for the Acquisition of Agri-biotech Applications (ISAAA), 242

J

JAMA/Archives journals, 222
Jamnagar, 113
Jinni, 113

K

Kabsah, 138
Kalipak, 113
Kalpa vriksha, 283
Kattha, 120
Kerala Agricultural University, 279
Kirmizi Biber (Red Pepper), 320
Kreteks, 264
Kuk Swamp, 179
Kuna Indians, 222

L

Land of Coconut, 285

M

Macapuno, 283
Maglalatik, 287
Mahboos, 138
Mangalore Agriculturists Sahakari Sangha (MASS), 105
Masala chai, 136
Max Havelaar Foundation, 206
Medline Plus, 101
Meetha paan, 123
Mesopotamia, 60
Migdolus fryanus, 194
Milky Way, 53
Ming Dynasty, 295
Moti Elaichi, 136
Moti, 113
Musa acuminate, 175
Mushrooms, 80
Muslim, 7
Muslim Arabs, 180

N

Nagavalli, 116
NARO, 185
Natural resources, 28-34
classification of natural forms, 29
natural capital, 30-32
non-renewable resources, 30
renewable or non-renewable, 32-34
renewable resources, 29
New York Board of Trade, 231
New York Mercantile Exchange (NYMEX), 207
Newport Beach, 279

Nga-nga, 126
NGOs, 223
Nicotiana rustica, 258
Nicotiana tabacum, 256, 257
Nicotiana, 251, 255
Nile Canal, 146

O

OECD, 12
Old World to the New, 7
Orange, 226-233
  acidity, 230
  blood orange, 230
  etymology, 230-231
  fruit, 227
  juice and other products, 231
  navel orange, 228-229
  Persian orange, 227-228
  production, 230
  products made form oranges include, 231-233
  Valencia orange, 229
Oxford English Dictionary, 322
Oyster Mushrooms, 80

P

P. sarmentosum, 122
Paan daani, 126
Paan, 117
Pacific Coast Highway, 279
Paleoclimatology, 84
Pandaung, 127
Pan-tamul, 99
Periplus of the Erythraean Sea, 146
Peruvian process, 168
Phytophthora, 160
Pipe smoking, 264
Piper betle, 116, 122
Piper caninum, 145
Piper longum, 145
Piper nigrum, 141
Piper nigrum, 143
Pleasure Club of New Orleans, 286
Port Silt Loam in Oklahoma, 41
Puga, 101
Pugaphala, 101

Q

Qahwa al-arabiya, 138

R

Rafflesia, 307
Red sea, 146
River Yangtze, 50
Rivers Historical Society Museum at Browntown, 196
Roll-your-own, 264
Rubiaceae, 204
Rupahi, 104

S

Saffron, 7
Saula ferruginea, 161
Schinus molle, 143
Shanghai, 61
Shimoga District in Karnataka, 102
Shrivardhani, 106
Shupari, 101
Snuff, 264
Snus, 265
Soil and water, 35-68
  agriculture, 62
  aquatic life forms, 60

biological factors, 39-40
characteristics, 41-43
chemical uses, 67
climate, 38
and organics, 46-47
degradation, 49-51
dissolving agent or solvent, 65-66
effects on human civilization, 60-61
effects on life, 59-60
extinguishing fires, 66
fresh water storage, 58
health and pollution, 61-62
humus, 45-46
nature, 47-48
organic matter, 45
parent material, 37-38
recreation, 67-68
scientific standard, 63-65
soil classification, 43-44
soil forming factors, 35-37
soil horizons, 43
soil orders, 44-45
soil solutions, 47
tides, 58-59
time, 40-41
topography, 38-39
types of water, 53
uses, 48-49
water, 51-53
water and habitable zone, 55-56
water cycle, 57-58
water in the universe, 53-55
water on earth, 56-57

Spatial Synoptic Classification System (SSC), 87
Spatial Synoptic Classification, 84
Species Development, 105
Sri Lanka, 285
Srivardhan, 113
Staphylococcus, 114
Sugarcane, 189-199
Sugarcane: cane ethanol, 197-198
cultivation, 192-193
and uses, 189-190
history of sugarcane, 190-192
milling, 194
nitrogen fixation, 199
pests, 194
processing, 194
refining, 196-197
ribbon cane syrup, 197
sugar crystals, 194-196
sugarcane as food, 198-199
Supari, 101, 114

T

Taambuul, 116
Tamalapaku, 116
Tambaku paan (tobacco), 123
Tamboolam, 94
Tang Meng, 149
Tea, 289-299
blending and additives, 292
china, 295-297
content, 292-293
cultivation, 290-291
economics of tea, 299
India, 297-298

origin and history, 293
origin myths, 293-294
potential effects of tea on health, 298-299
processing and classification, 291-292
production, 299
tea and the tang dynasty, 294-295
tea spreads to the world, 297
Tea classics, 296
Tempak sirih, 126
TERI, 105
Tesco supermarkets, 104
Tobacco, 251-265
consumption, 262-265
contemporary, 254-255
demographic, 259
early developments, 253
economic, 260
etymology, 253
health, 259
impact, 258-259
nicotiana, 255-256
popularization, 254
production, 260-262
types, 256-258
Tobacco Master Settlement Agreement (MSA), 254
Topical tobacco paste, 265
Transport, 22
Trento (olarno paan), 123
Tsaoko, 137

U

UN-FAO, 19
Union Ministry of Agriculture in 2007, 105
United Fruit Company, 178
United Nations Framework Convention on Climate Change (UNFCCC), 92
United States National Research Council, 64
United States, 8, 173, 233
Unites States Liquid, 212
Untied States Geological Survey, 29
UNU Ghana-based Institute for Natural Resources in Africa, 5
US Customs, 104
US Department of Agriculture, 83, 244
US Government Printing Office in Washington, 74
US National Association of Attorneys General (NAAG), 260
USA, 9, 14, 170, 181

V

V. planifloia, 153
V. pompano, 153
V. tahitensis, 168
Vandana Shiva, 16
Vanilla, 153-171
bourbon curing method, 166-168
curing of Tahiti vanilla, 168-169
harvesting and curing, 161
market for vanilla, 170
Mexican curing methods, 163-166
mulching, 156-161
planting, 155-156
quality requirements, 161-162

traditional curing methods, 162-163
yield, 169
Veeleya/vilya, 116
Vetrilai, 116
Vishnu, 313
Vitis amurensis, 268
Vitis labrusca, 267
Vitis riparia, 268
Vitis rotundifolia, 268

W

Western Highlands Province of Papua New Guinea, 179
WHO, 254
World Cocoa foundation, 224
World Food, 104
World Health Organization (WHO), 20, 243, 253
World Meteorological Organization (WMO), 85

Y

Yellow River in China, 41

Z

Zulu Social Aid, 286